IMAGES
of America

SUSSEX AND WANTAGE

ON THE COVER: An outing at Locust Grove is pictured here. This farm was located off today's Route 23 behind where the "old totem pole" stood. Around 1905, M.C. House owned this farm. He provided boarding, and the farmstead was located along the Clove Brook as it wound its way down the lush valley below High Point Mountain toward Sussex Borough. (Courtesy of Space Farms.)

IMAGES
of America

SUSSEX AND WANTAGE

William R. Truran

ARCADIA
PUBLISHING

ISBN 978-0-7385-9139-1

Published by Arcadia Publishing
Charleston, South Carolina

Printed in the United States of America

Library of Congress Control Number: 2011938597

For all general information, please contact Arcadia Publishing:
Telephone 843-853-2070
Fax 843-853-0044
E-mail sales@arcadiapublishing.com
For customer service and orders:
Toll-Free 1-888-313-2665

Visit us on the Internet at www.arcadiapublishing.com

This book is dedicated to my family, whose support has been incomparable. This assistance has taken the shape of supplying knowledge of the area where we have lived through the family's length of time here in America, stretching back to the 1700s. This knowledge of places and people has been passed on in the form of family stories, photographs, and letters. My family has provided time and space for me to contemplate, compile, and compose manuscripts to make explicit the tacit history, as shown in this volume. My family has also encouraged me by their comfort—the warmth of familial love that has embraced and energized me to strive for and complete large projects like this book. Thank you.

Contents

ACKNOWLEDGMENTS

As Sir Isaac Newton said, we are able to see farther because we stand on the shoulders of giants. I must acknowledge the great debt that I owe to those who came before me, alive and dead; to those wonderful people, it has been a pleasure to speak with and share your wealth of knowledge, gifts of images, and the mutual respect and love for Sussex County, New Jersey. The following people are some of those who had an impact on this book: Howard Case, Sussex Borough historian; Jennie Sweetman, expert historian for Sussex County and the surrounding area, who had a great impact on this book; Stella Truran, my mom; and Sydney Hall, my grampop, a photographer and the forerunner for me in recording history.

I'd also like to thank the following: Olga Bazylevich Stefkowich and the family of Mike the Jeweler; Mary Case; A.J. Bloom and his glass-plate photography from the 1890s and Art Jordan who has recovered this treasure; Mary Eleanor Eppler, a Sparta historian; Frank Decker, superintendent of schools; Amelia Stickney Decker; Hal Wirths; Parker and Jill Space; Butch and Bonnie Osborne; Jeff Parrott and Mayor Chris Parrott and the hospitable workers at the Sussex Inn; Jane L. Gilman; and Margaret Checkur Gilman and family.

The following authors and publications were also helpful: Peter Lott, Unionville farmer and poet; Charles E. Stickney (1841–1930), the 1895 author of *A History of Deckertown*; James P. Snell and his article "History of Sussex and Warren Counties 1881;" *Our Wantage Heritage*; *1895 History of Sussex*; *New Jersey Herald*; *Sussex Independent*; and *Wantage Recorder*.

Thanks also go to the following: Ashley Touw Ziccardi; Rev. Peter Kanouse and his historical sermon "Memorial to the Inhabitants of Wantage, Sussex County, New Jersey," preached on January 7, 1844; John W. Barber and Henry Howe; Harvey Barlow; John Kolic; Irene Elizabeth Reaves-VanDunk (née Rose, January 31, 1931, to November 25, 2005), who provided a spirit for the town of Sussex and the Methodist church; Jane Sandford Lockwood; Lois Harden Wright; the Chinkchewunska Chapter of the Daughters of the American Revolution; Hal Wirths, local enthusiast and civic leader; and Lori and Fred Space, with a special tribute to Space Farms, its noted presence in Beemerville, and its contribution of photographs, historical information, and its resident superb knowledge of our area of Wantage and Sussex County, New Jersey. Most of the images have been supplied courtesy of Space Farms Zoo and Museum of Beemerville, New Jersey, and the people associated with Space Farms, who have been most helpful. Unless otherwise noted, all images are courtesy of Space Farms.

INTRODUCTION

The Sussex Borough and Wantage Township part of Sussex County, New Jersey, are snapshots of the rural farming community of yesteryear.

Along the rolling hills and Blue Ridge Mountains are fields of wheat, corn, and alfalfa that wave in the breezy highlands of New Jersey. Along back roads, one can find life lived in a slower fashion, with cows in the pasture and farmers harvesting their crops.

The beautiful setting that makes up Wantage Township has not changed much since it was first inhabited about 300 years or so ago. The first settlers came down along the Wallkill River from Esopus on the Hudson River or over New Jersey's tallest mountain from the Port Jervis area—where frightening accounts were written about the Indian raids from across the Delaware River. First, it was the Dutch, followed by the English, who settled here. Today, many of the farms still remain in the families of those original settlers. Revolutionary War veterans are buried alongside Civil War veterans in local cemeteries, with scenic views that still defy the onset of modern times. The sight of pumpkins and deer and the smell of livestock and tilled soil still retain the essence of times past. In views from years ago and from more recent years, similar sights and experiences will be presented and encountered in this book.

Sussex Borough is in the center of Wantage and represents the "town-country" of northwestern New Jersey in a microcosm. Sussex Borough has been the center where farmers would bring their produce to market or gather around a potbelly stove on a cold winter's day. In Sussex Borough, there was a creamery for the dairy products that would then be taken by train to New York City, making this a prime hub for dairy production for the metropolitan area many years ago. After 100 years, much remains the same in Sussex Borough. The same bank building stands, and the pharmacy and stores still occupy the brick buildings along Main Street, just as when Main Street was a dirt road and was traversed by horse-drawn wagons. The Deckertown Plow was built here and it helped to manage the furrows in the times of horse-drawn farming equipment. We can still see vestiges of the past, from the footpaths of colonial times to the stagecoaches and other horse-powered journeys of the early 1800s to the railroads of about 1870, which hastened travel to the city and beyond.

Our visual journey through Sussex Borough and Wantage Township will help enlighten us to the great wonder of the area. From this book, we will gain an understanding of how the beauty of the land has been retained and how long-standing families are still able to make a living in this rural location, which is only 50 miles or so from New York City. Come with us on this illustrated passage to a simpler time when life was less busy and the pastoral setting gave us bucolic rest on shady lanes.

The book is laid out in the following format: there is the introduction to the history of the area, followed by a more in-depth look at the several hamlets and localities that dot the beautiful rolling hills. We then look at Sussex Borough, which was once called Deckertown, followed by a view of the people themselves—bringing milk to market in town, or at pastimes such as parades or concerts. There are several chapters that feature a sequence of events, covering such things as a very important horse race, milk production from 100 years ago, the arrival of the train, and the use of horse and carriage to bring passengers to town. I hope you like the layout and the book!

—Bill Truran
December 4, 2011

One

Wantage in History

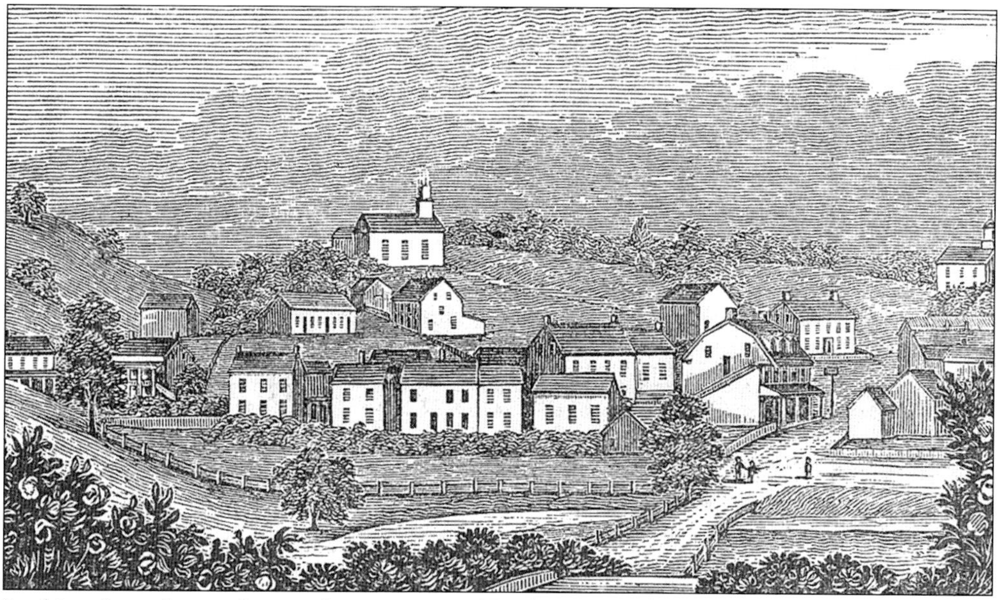

Looking from the southwest, this is a view of Deckertown. The largest locality in Wantage, it is known today as Sussex Borough, or "the Boro." John W. Barber and Henry Howe made this woodcut image during their visit to the area in 1844.

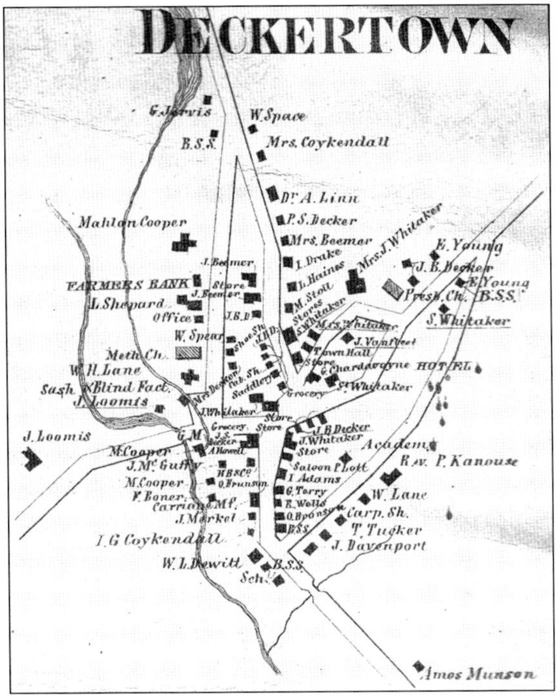

A map of Deckertown from 1860 is show here. This is a part of the Hopkins map of 1860, which was produced in Philadelphia. Hopkins created a number of Sussex County maps, meant to be rolled up as a scroll and hung on the wall. The Sussex County map measures 52 inches wide and 56 inches tall. These maps have been found in the homes of several old families who have lived in the area for generations; to this day, some of the maps have surprisingly remained on the walls. They are very valuable and sell at a high price at auction. (Author's collection.)

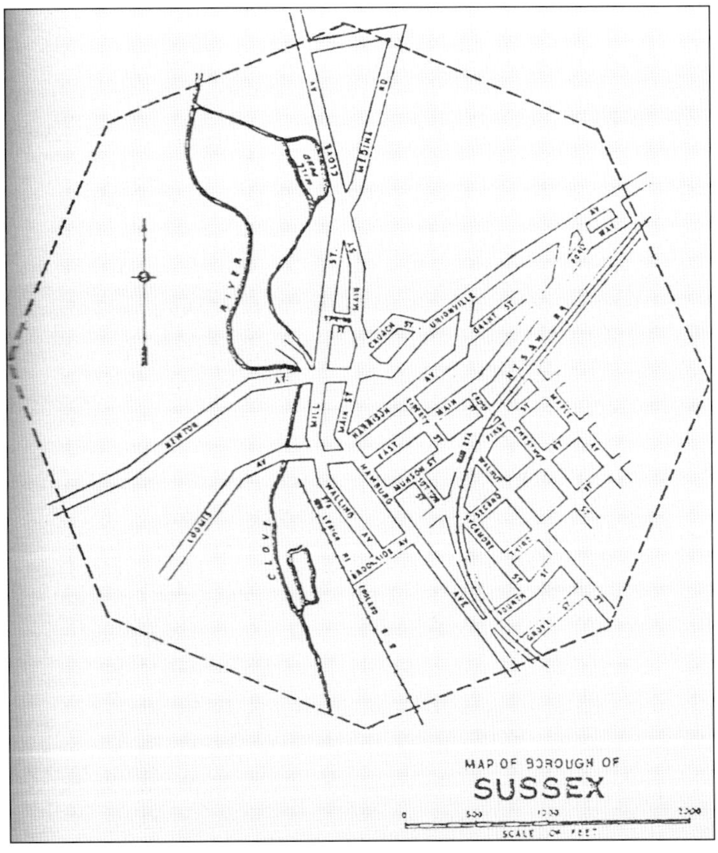

Shown here is a map of Sussex Borough from the year 1900. This simplified map shows how the street patterns had changed since 1860. In the year 1902, the name changed from Deckertown to Sussex Borough. Note the geometric symmetry of the town boundary. (Author's collection.)

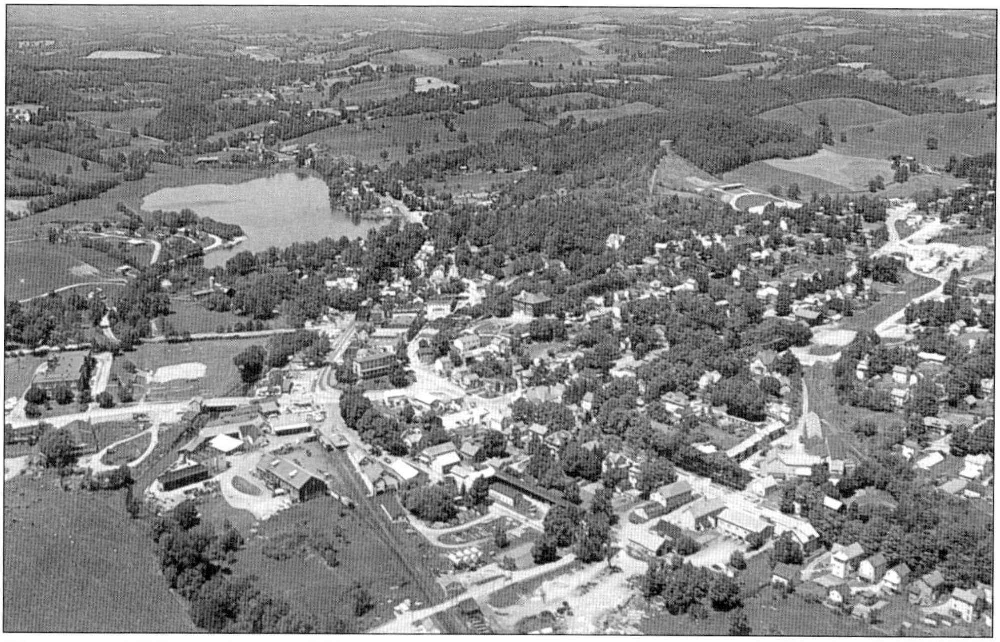

This is a c. 1973 aerial view of Sussex. The photograph was taken looking from south to north. One can see the beautiful Kittatinny Ridge Mountains in the distance, which is where the High Point Monument is located. High Point is the highest point in New Jersey at 1,808 feet above sea level. (Author's collection.)

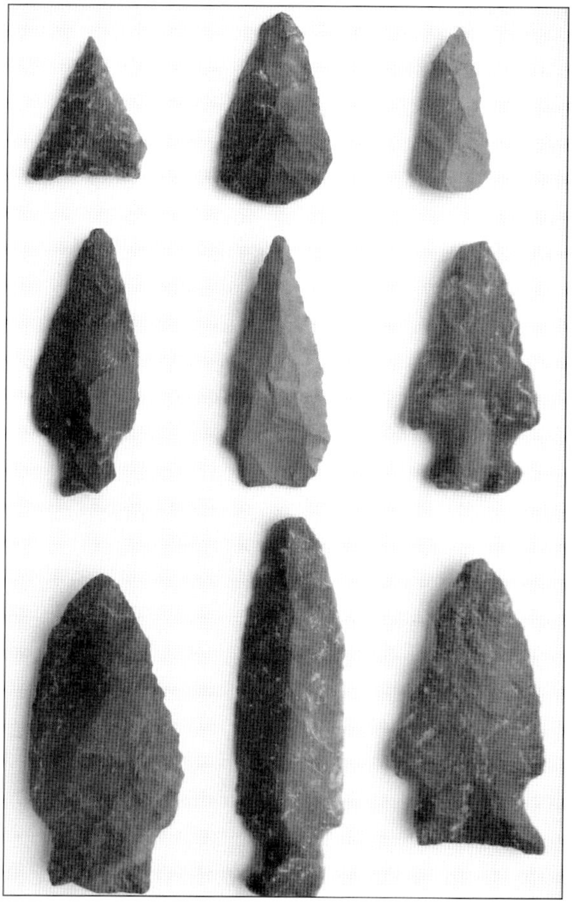

Sussex and Wantage have a long history, much of which has been lost to time. The Native Americans, who called this their home for tens of thousands of years, left little trace of their existence, but occasionally found in the soil throughout the county are stone implements that the Indians used to sustain their rudimentary life. Since the area was a rich hunting ground, the most commonly unearthed artifacts are arrowheads. (Author's collection.)

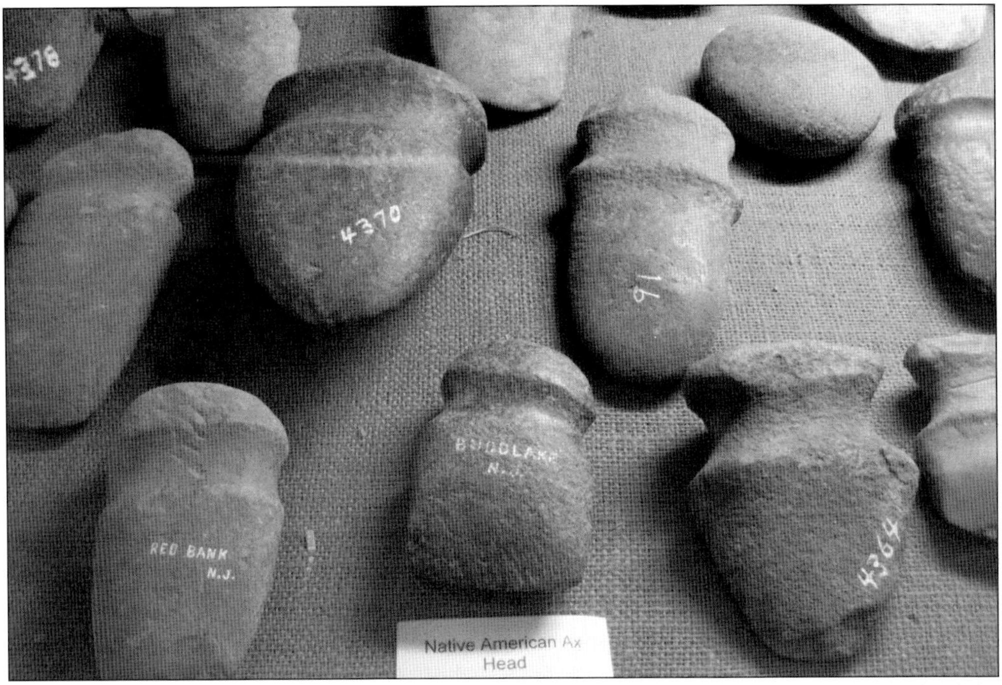

The Minsi ("Wolf") tribe of the Lenni Lenape ("Original Tribe"), who were in turn a branch of the Delaware, used stone-grooved ax heads. They wore wolf skins on their heads during ceremonies. The Lenape, according to the Italian navigator Giovanni da Verrazzano, were of fine physique and well groomed. They were calm and pleasant and had sparkling black eyes and long black hair that was sometimes braided.

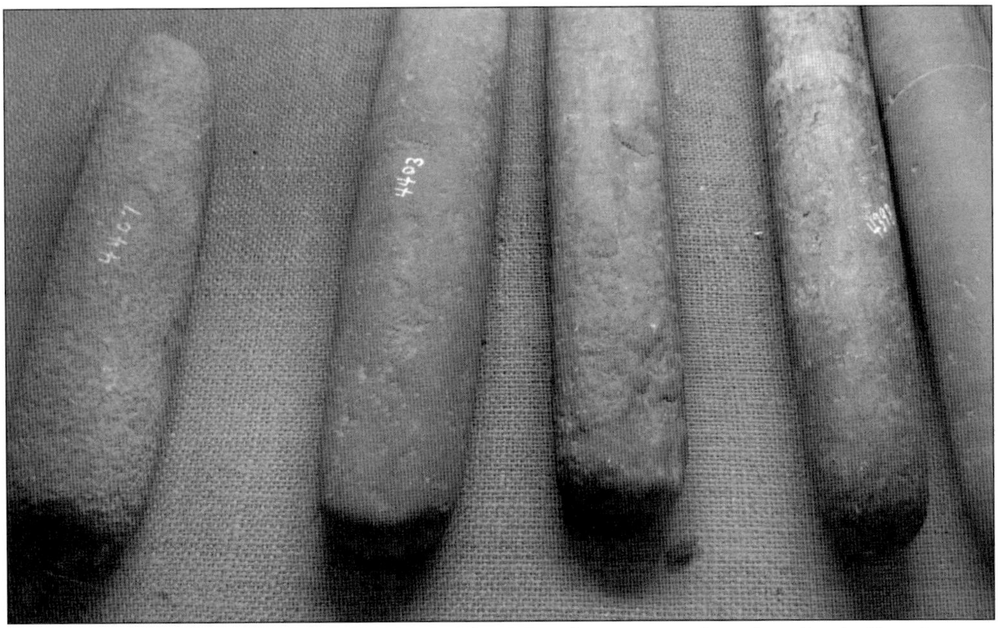

These implements, possibly stone pestles used to pound corn, were found in the shallow furrows of a planted field in the Sussex-Wantage area. The Indians would grow maize and then use a pestle with a flat rock to mill the corn into meal.

Two

Wantage Township

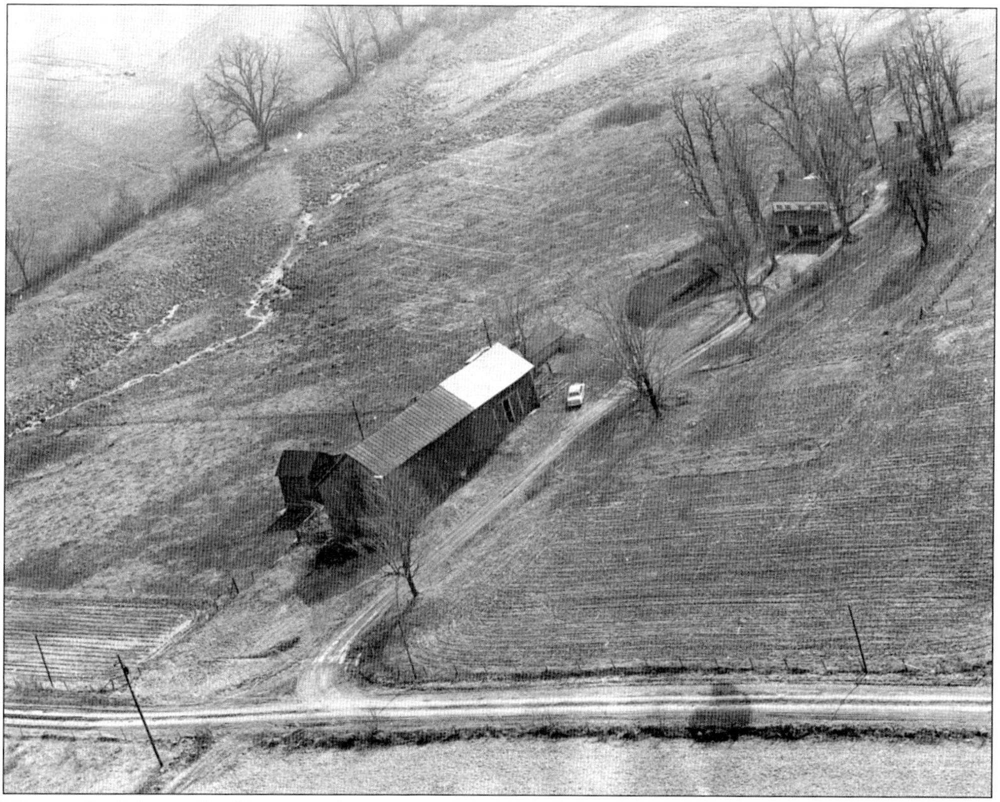

This is the Merritt L. Haggerty farm around 1955, a time when there were still "more cows than people" in Sussex County. Note the dirt roads. The largest locality in the township is Sussex Borough, formerly known as Deckertown. It was set off from Wantage Township on October 14, 1891, with its name changing to Sussex Borough on March 2, 1902. Wantage includes the following localities: Beemerville, Colesville, Lake Neepaulin, Lewisburg, Libertyville, Martins, Mount Salem, Plumbsock, Sussex Borough, Woodbourne, Wolf Pit, Rockport, and Wantage (just north of Sussex Borough).

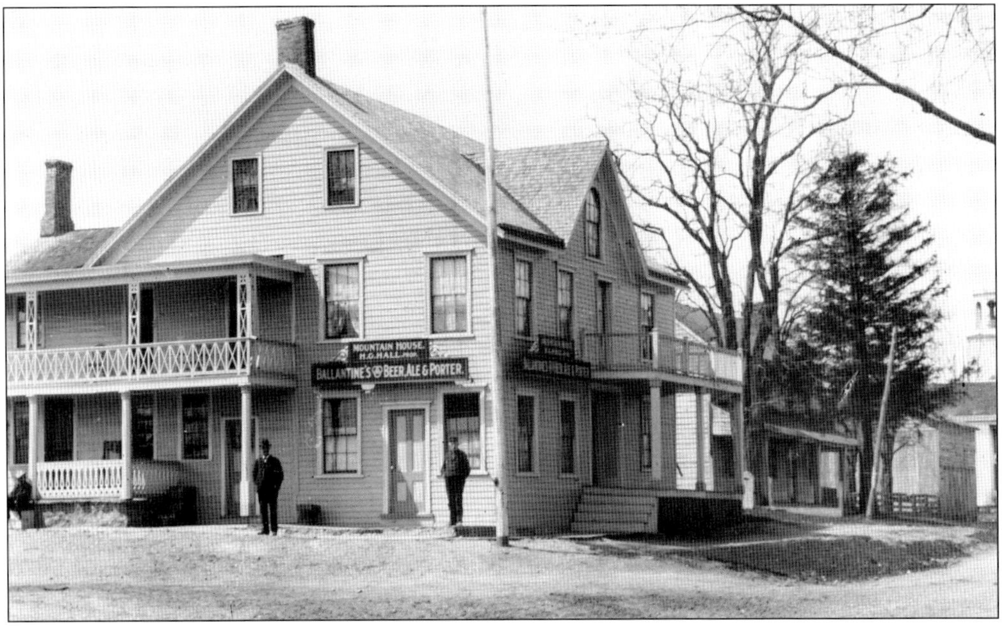

This early-1900 image is of the Mountain House, one of the main dwellings in Beemerville. Beemerville was a significant hamlet about 100 years or so ago. Today, Beemerville has a rustic rural flavor to it. The Mountain House testifies to the location at a crossroads, with the Kittatinny Ridge looming above at a short distance away to the west, just out of view. H.G. Hall was the owner of the building, and liquor could be had here. The Mountain House is now gone.

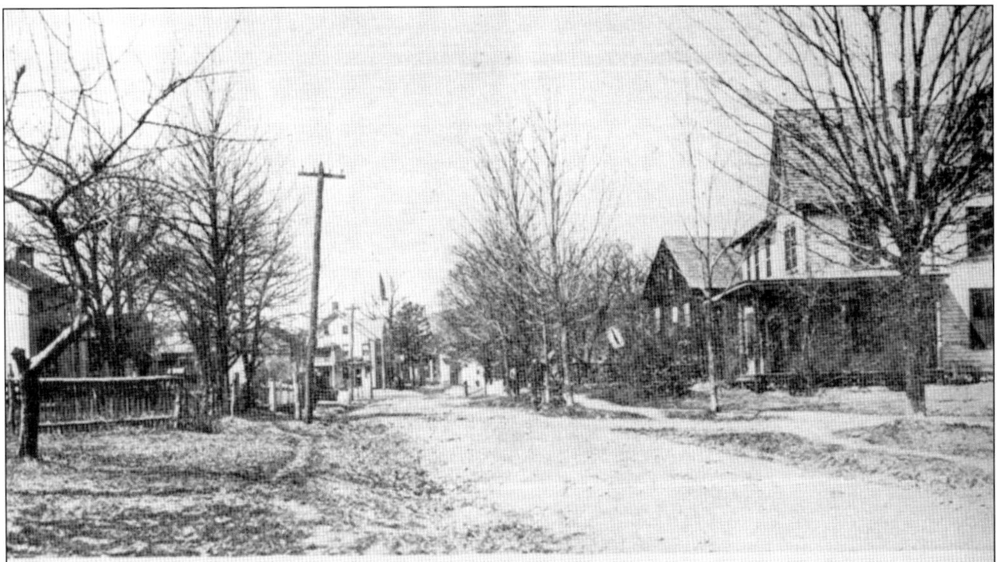

BROADWAY, BEEMERVILLE, N. J.

This is a look down Broadway in Beemerville. This photograph shows the main thoroughfare in the hamlet of Beemerville around 1905. The Mountain House can be seen in the distance, with the American flag on a flagpole at the intersection. There are mountains beyond this view in the background where today's Sunrise Mountain and the state park are. Many people have gone to Sunrise Mountain to view the beginning of the day in the east, perhaps after camping out the night before in one of the shelters along the Appalachian Trail.

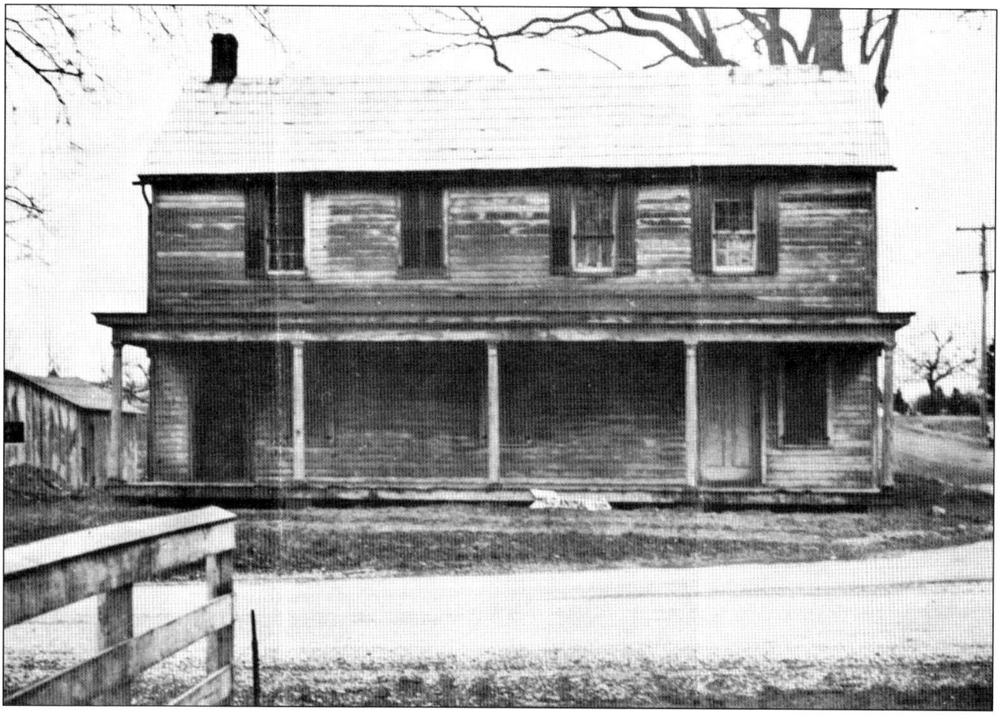

This was known as the Beemer house. It is mostly likely the original home of the Beemer family, the namesake of Beemerville. Located on the southeast slope of the Blue Mountains at the foot of Sunrise Mountain, Beemerville had at one time been called Broadway.

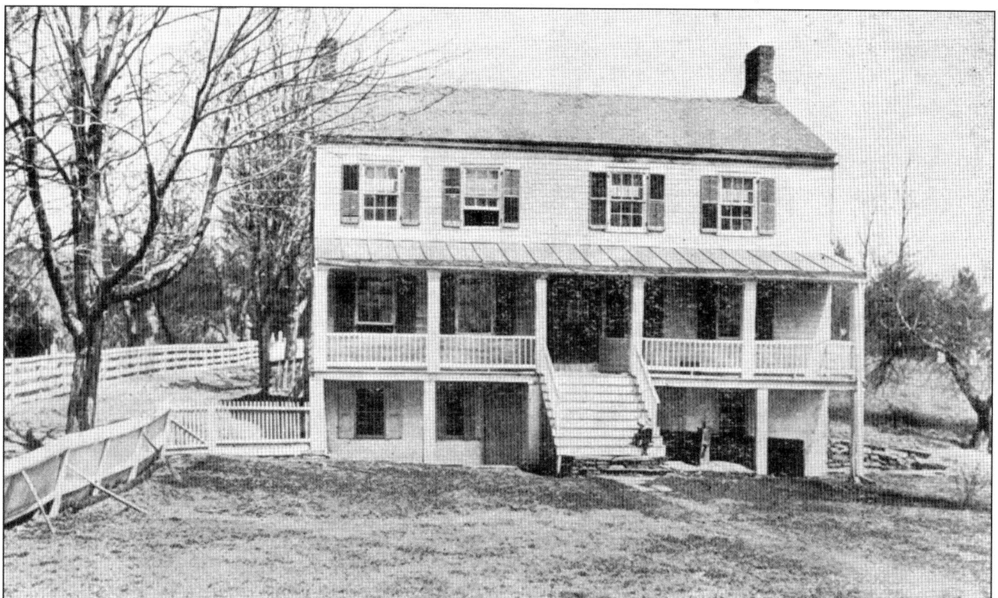

PRESBYTERIAN PARSONAGE, BEEMERVILLE, N. J.

This home was known as the Presbyterian Parsonage for Beemerville in the early 1900s. The home is located in town along the main road, which at one point was called Broadway. This is where the pastor for the church resided.

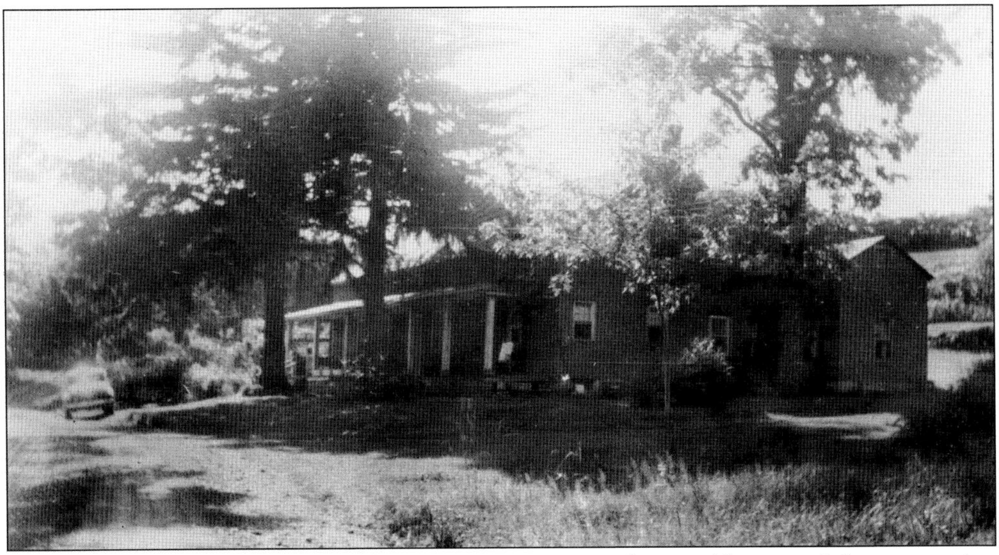

The author's great-aunt, Mary Coddington Garrity, grew up here and has stated that it served as a meetinghouse before the church was built for religious services. This structure is located across from the small pond at the foot of Card Road. This early-1900s photograph was taken when dirt roads were still very prevalent in Beemerville and Wantage. The dwelling was built in 1787.

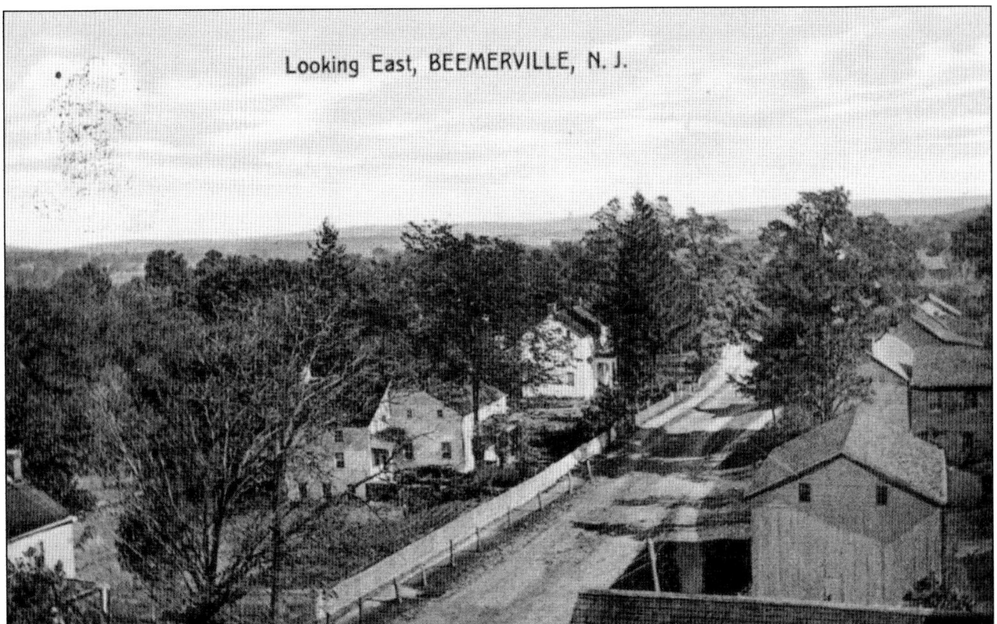

This postcard is a bird's-eye view of Beemerville. Probably taken from the roof of the Mountain House, the photograph looks to the east from the heart of the hamlet of Wantage of Beemerville. As postcards came to popularity around 1900, a bird's-eye view of a village was frequently found.

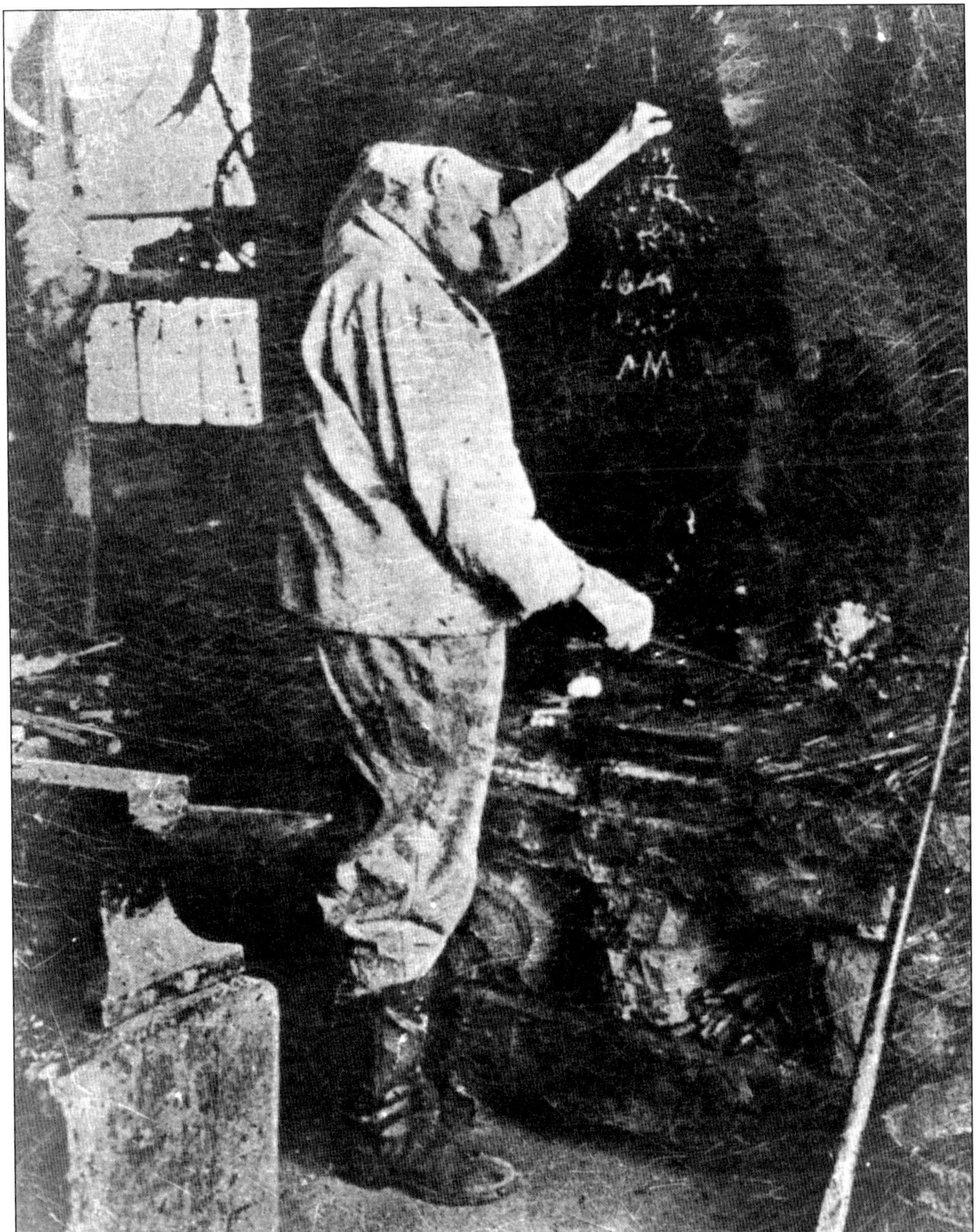

Over 100 years ago, the blacksmith was an important and integral part of a community. He made the iron utensils for home and hearth, farm implements, horseshoes, and carriage wheel rims. Andrew Adrion was the local blacksmith, with a business in the middle of Beemerville. Though it was a dirty job, the artisans were seldom kept away from their daily tasks by illness. Adrion worked until near his death since there was no one else to carry on the trade. Shown here making a horseshoe, Adrion is pounding away with a hammer on the anvil. This shoe has caulkins or studs, which help a horse, most likely a draft or working horse, to have traction.

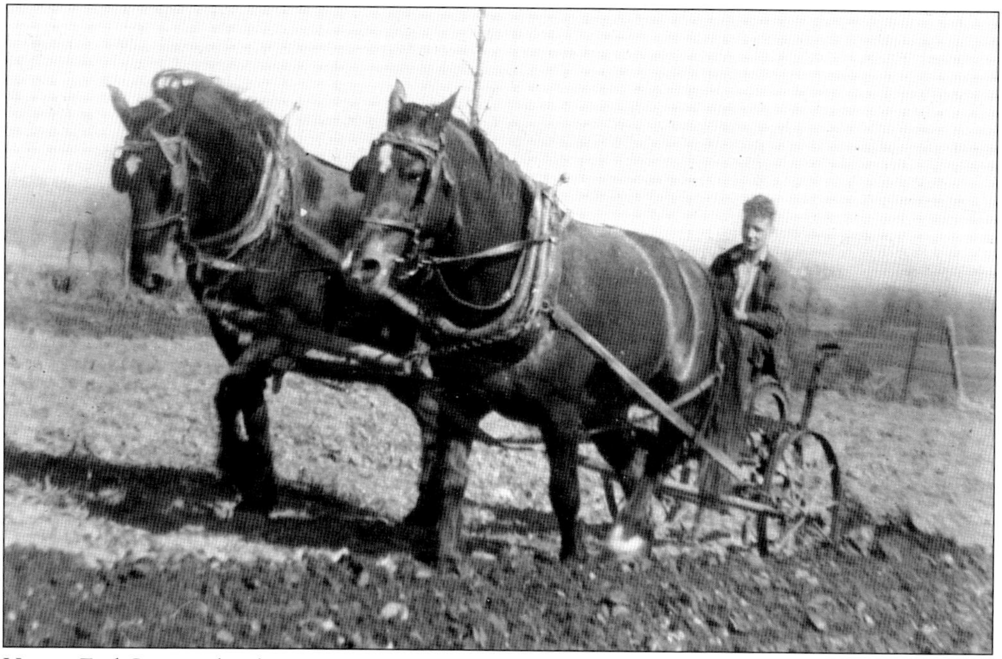

Here is Earl Courtright plowing a field with two draft horses in the Beemerville area of Wantage. Earl is probably preparing a field for planting seeds for corn. Beemerville is representative of the rolling hills of Sussex County, with many fields of corn, pastureland for Holstein cows, and tranquil ponds and streams. Earl is related to the author's aunt. The photograph is from about 1940.

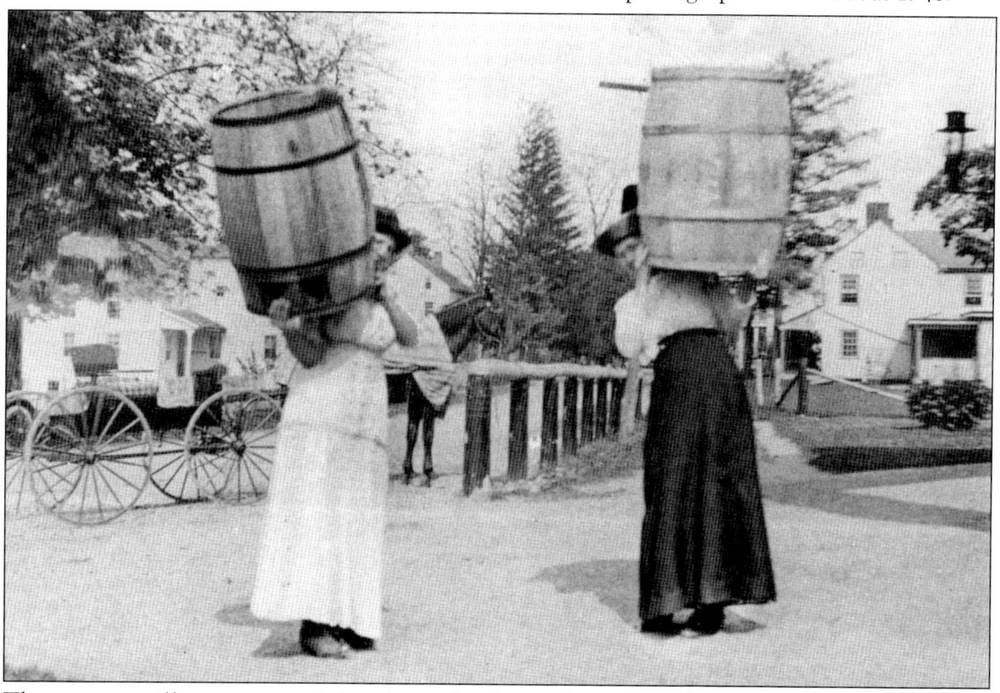

These women illustrate one of the physically demanding jobs of bygone years. These are new barrels, which probably used iron hoops made at the Adrion blacksmith shop. This scene is on the main street in Beemerville.

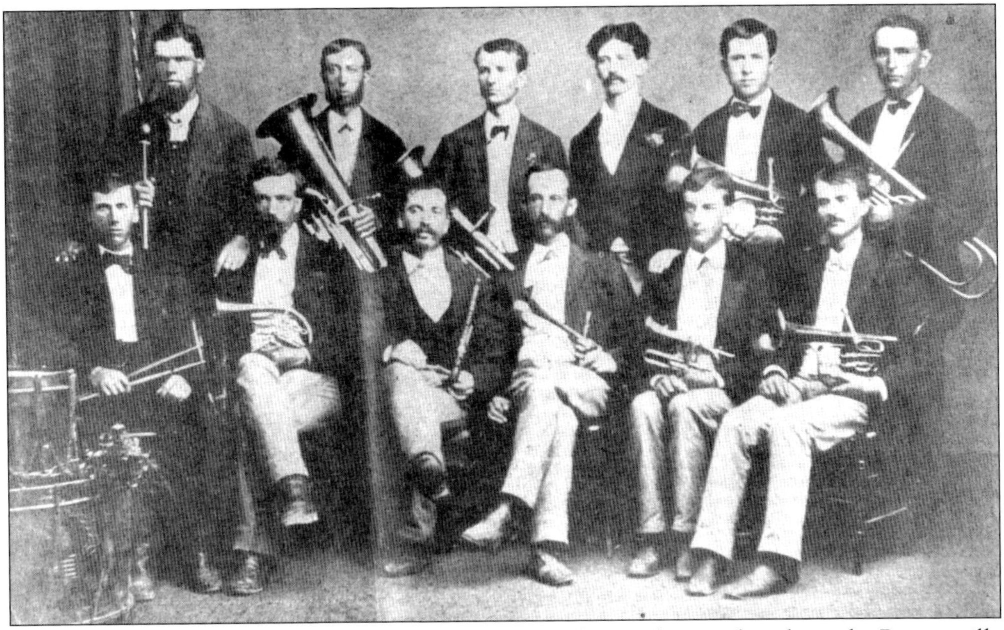

One of the earliest of the prominent bands that Sussex County has produced was the Beemerville Cornet Band, shown in 1872. From left to right are, (first row) Bross Davey, Britton Cosner (leader), Mr. Katz, Dr. Mortimer Lampson, Amzi N. Cosner (son of the leader), and Charles Dolson; (second row) Janson Bross, Charles Cosner, Charles Simmons, Louis Proudfoot, Ed Coddington, and Manley Hough. Amzi used his training with the Beemerville band to become a leader of the Newton Cornet Band around 1880.

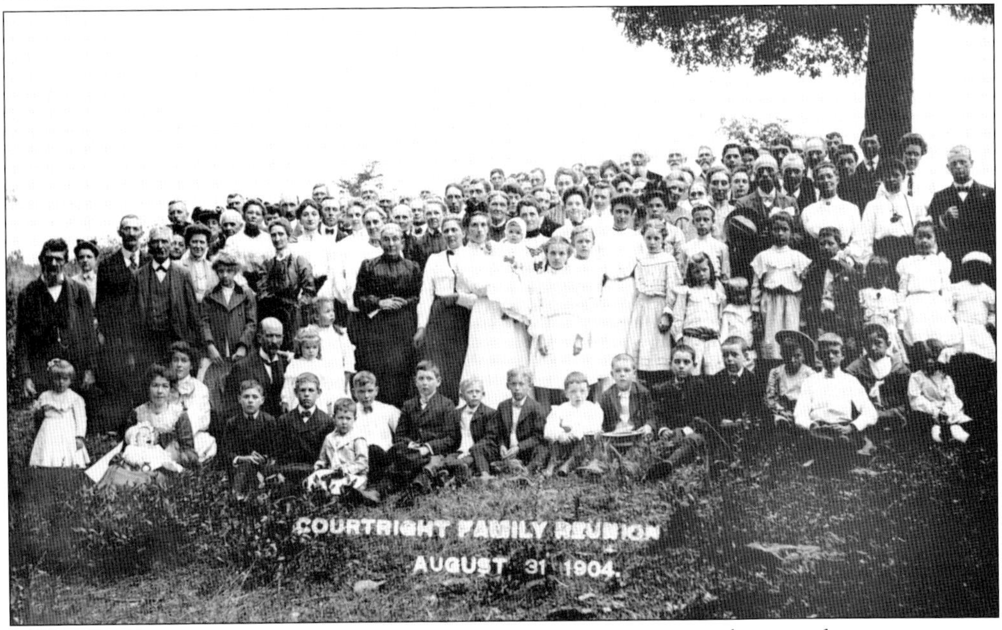

The extended Courtright family is shown in this happy summer gathering of many years ago. Some local photographers, whose images on glass-plate negatives, postcards, portraits, and other reminders of another time in American history aid historians, were A.J. Bloom of Hamburg, Harold N. Corielle of Newton, A.C. Tomely of Newton, and Frank S. Allyn.

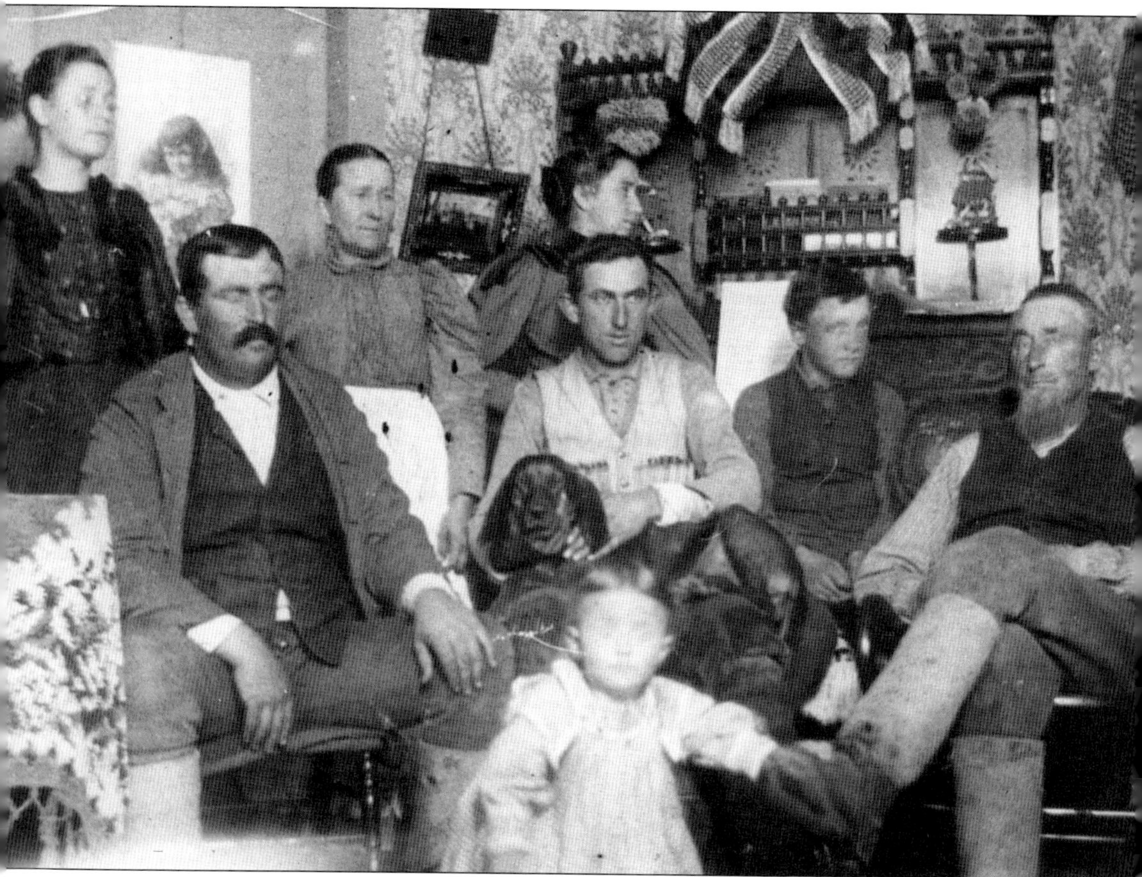

The Space family has played a significant role in the development of Beemerville and the rest of Wantage. They are owners of the world-famous Space Farms located in the town of Beemerville and have served the township and county in various capacities. Pictured are, from left to right, (first row) Edna Space, born 1897; (second row) Fred Space Sr., George Space, Van Auken, and William B. Space; (third row) Mary Space Ayers, Belle Space, and Kate Ackerman Space. Another old family of Beemerville, whose log cabin was located off Beemerville-Branchville Road, was the Wallen Simonson family. Wallen lived with his wife, Jane, and Wallen's sister Lavina Simonson Courtright, the wife of Denmark Courtright. A reflection of the times, it is recorded that they had a well, a barrel for hot water, and tools on the front of the cabin, including chains and a grindstone to keep a keen edge on the ax. They also slaughtered hogs that were hung on the walnut tree to drain and then be dressed (cleaned) for eating. The grandsons of the Courtrights were Frank and Emmett Courtright of Sussex.

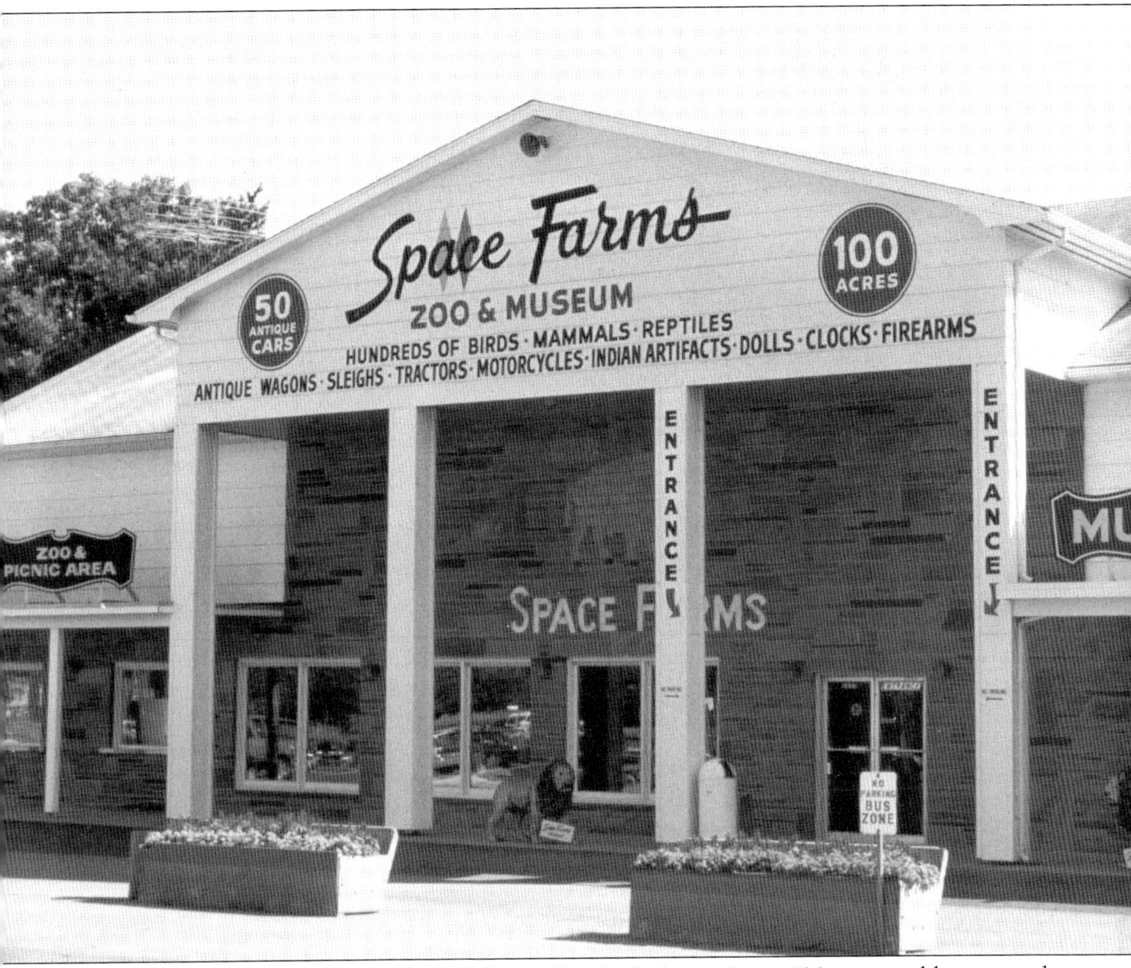

Space Farms was founded in 1927 by Ralph and Elizabeth Space. It is a 100-acre world-renowned zoological park of over 100 species in natural settings. Ralph also founded a wonderful Americana Museum, home to antique cars, motorcycles, antique firearms, tractors, household items, dolls, toys, and Louis Larsen paintings. The Space Farms Zoo and Museum complex is a unique visitor attraction in Sussex County.

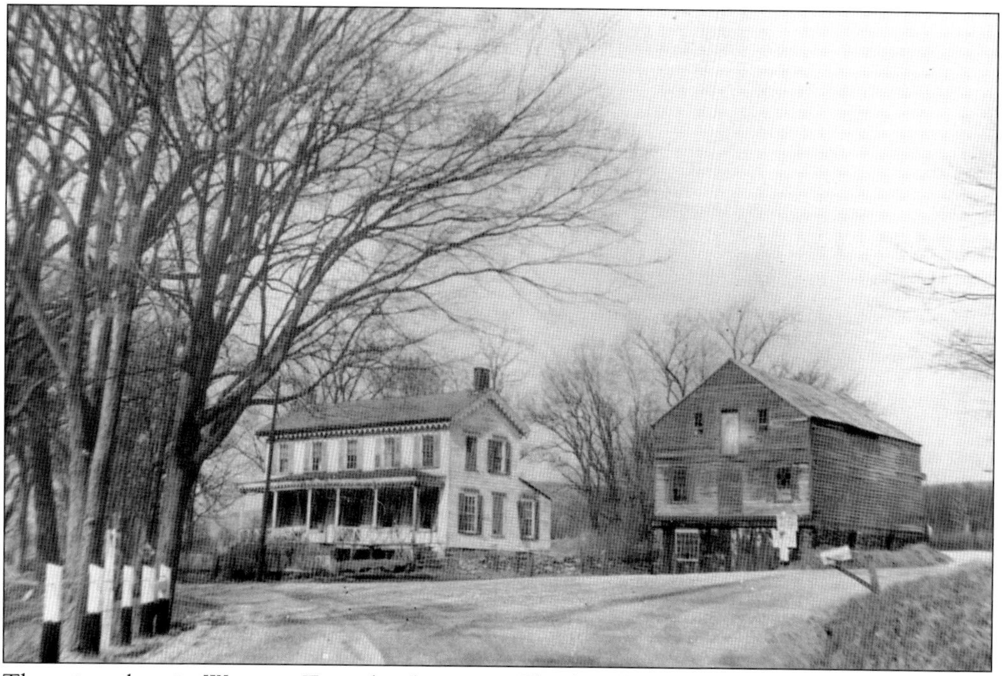

There is a place in Wantage Township known as Plumbsock, and located in Plumbsock at this intersection of roads were the Westfall house and G.L. Dunning Store and Post Office, according to the 1860 map. This was obviously a gristmill at one point in time; there were several mills and a sawmill along this part of the Papakating River. Plumbsock was known as Lower Broadway at one time. (Courtesy of Nelle Skellenger.)

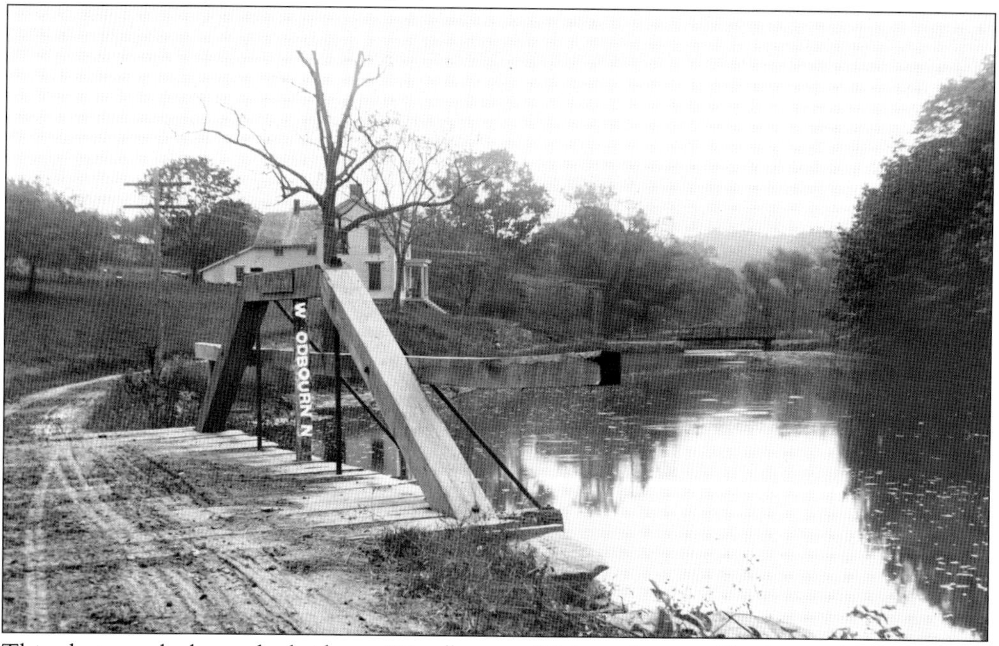

This photograph shows the bridge at Woodbourne. This roadway and bridge washed out in the big rains and wind of Hurricane Irene during the summer of 2011. There were several dams along the steep series of natural waterfalls, and the waterpower created was used by several mills.

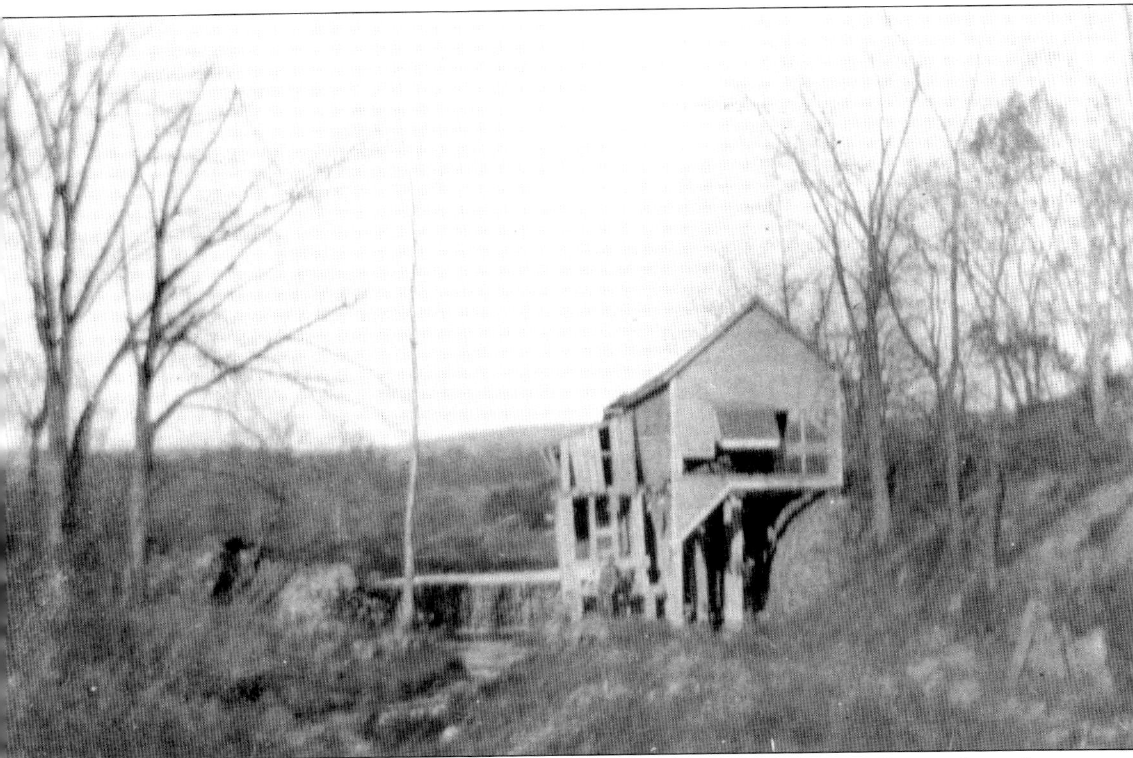

This is a view of the gristmill at Woodbourne Pond. Having been in operation from at least the 1870s, it is shown here in poor condition in the early 1900s. The Woodbourne area of Wantage was where the Papakating River flowed down the mountain to the valley below and cascaded naturally over the rocks. Several dams were located on the river here and provided waterpower before coal arrived in the area on the railroads. Gristmills, sawmills, and electric power were manifestations of the energy harvested from the water downstream.

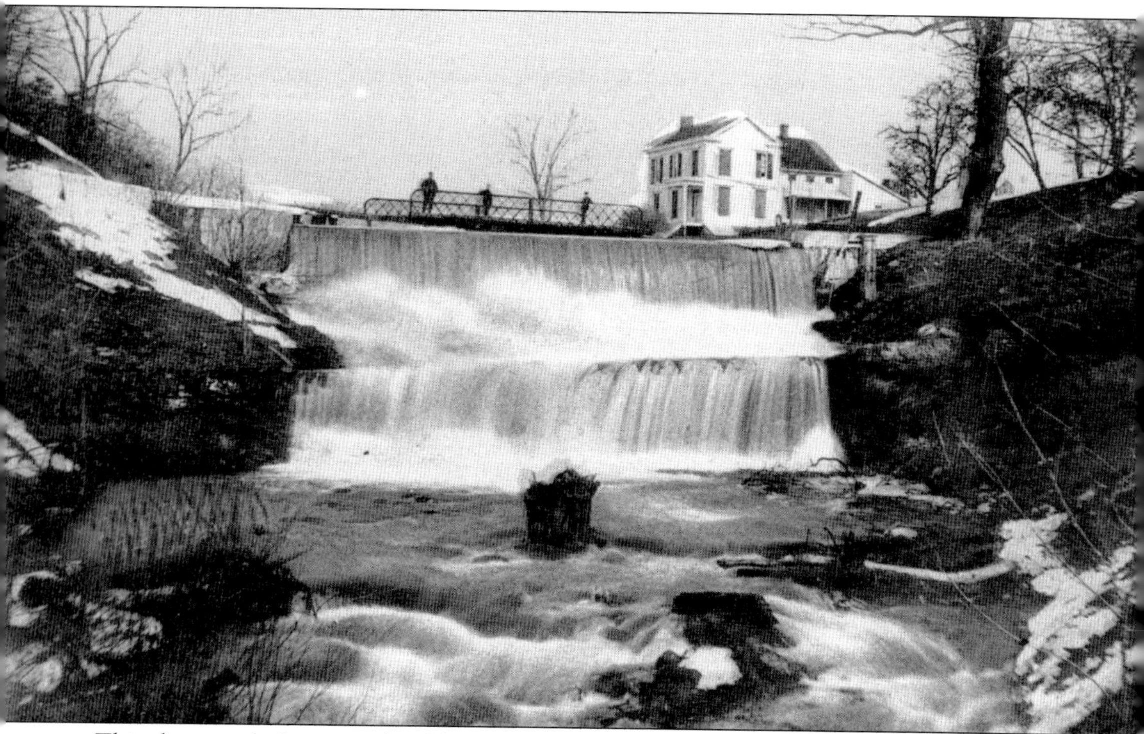

This photograph shows another fall located below the mill at Woodbourne Pond. Gristmills were an essential part of early America, and Wantage Township was no exception. This one is located just north of today's High Point High School. This beautiful scene has been depicted on glass-plate negatives, postcards, and paintings, such as by local painter Louis Larsen.

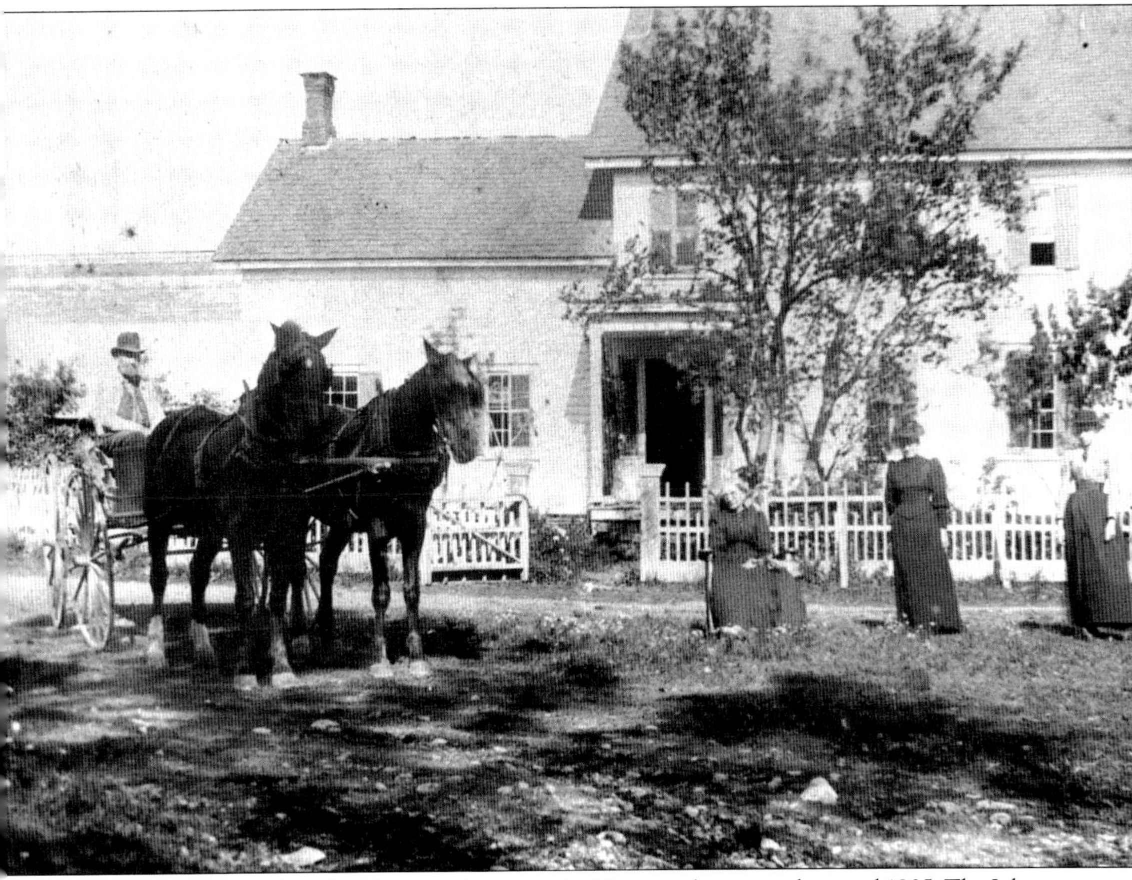

Seen in this photograph is the Haggerty family at the Haggerty homestead around 1905. The John Vander Groat farm is another name associated with this land. Five of the six sons of W.D. Haggerty were born here. The Haggerty family is well known, with many descendants. Other families who have been residents of the Wantage area for many generations, with many descendants, are the Coddingtons, Courtrights, and Deckers.

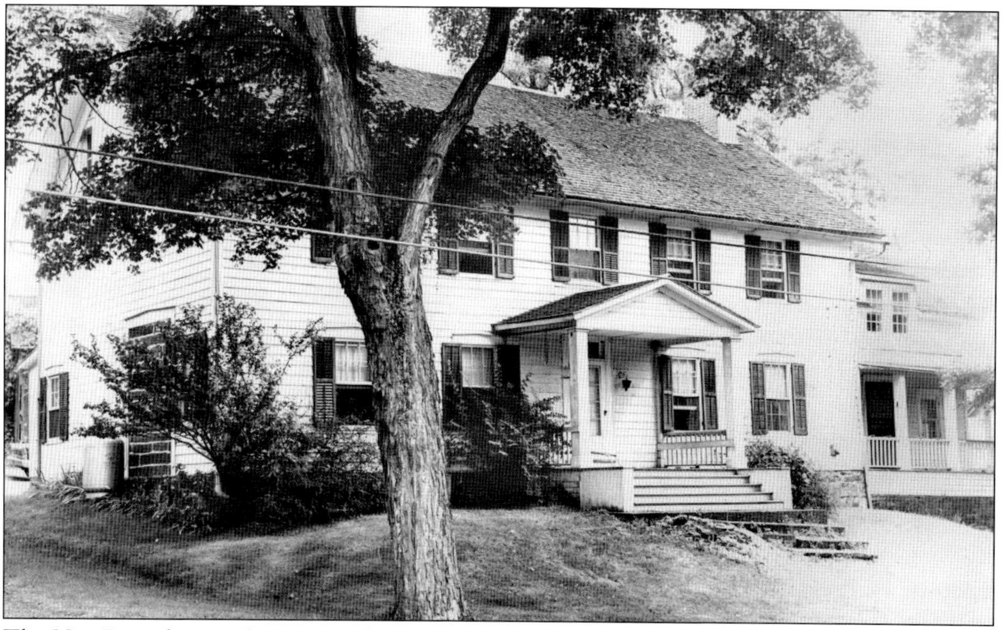

The Van Bunschooten house is today the home of the Chinkchewunska Chapter of Daughters of the American Revolution. It was built in 1787 for the Reverend Elias Van Bunschooten, a Dutch Reformed minister and a farmer, mill operator, and large landowner. The farm was part of a 1,000-acre plantation. The house and outbuildings were listed in the National Register of Historic Places in 1974.

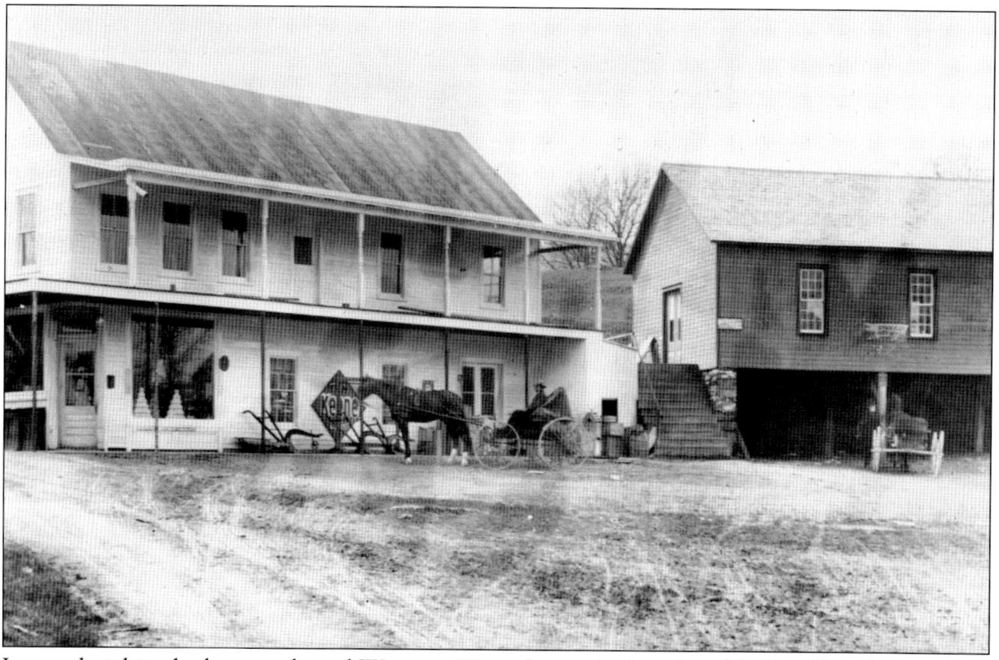

Located within the large and rural Wantage Township is the hamlet of Colesville. This area had been settled early on by the Dutch who came from along the Hudson River and up the Wallkill River to this rich farmland. The general store seen here was located on the northwestern side of the main road, now State Route 23. The new store was built about 1905.

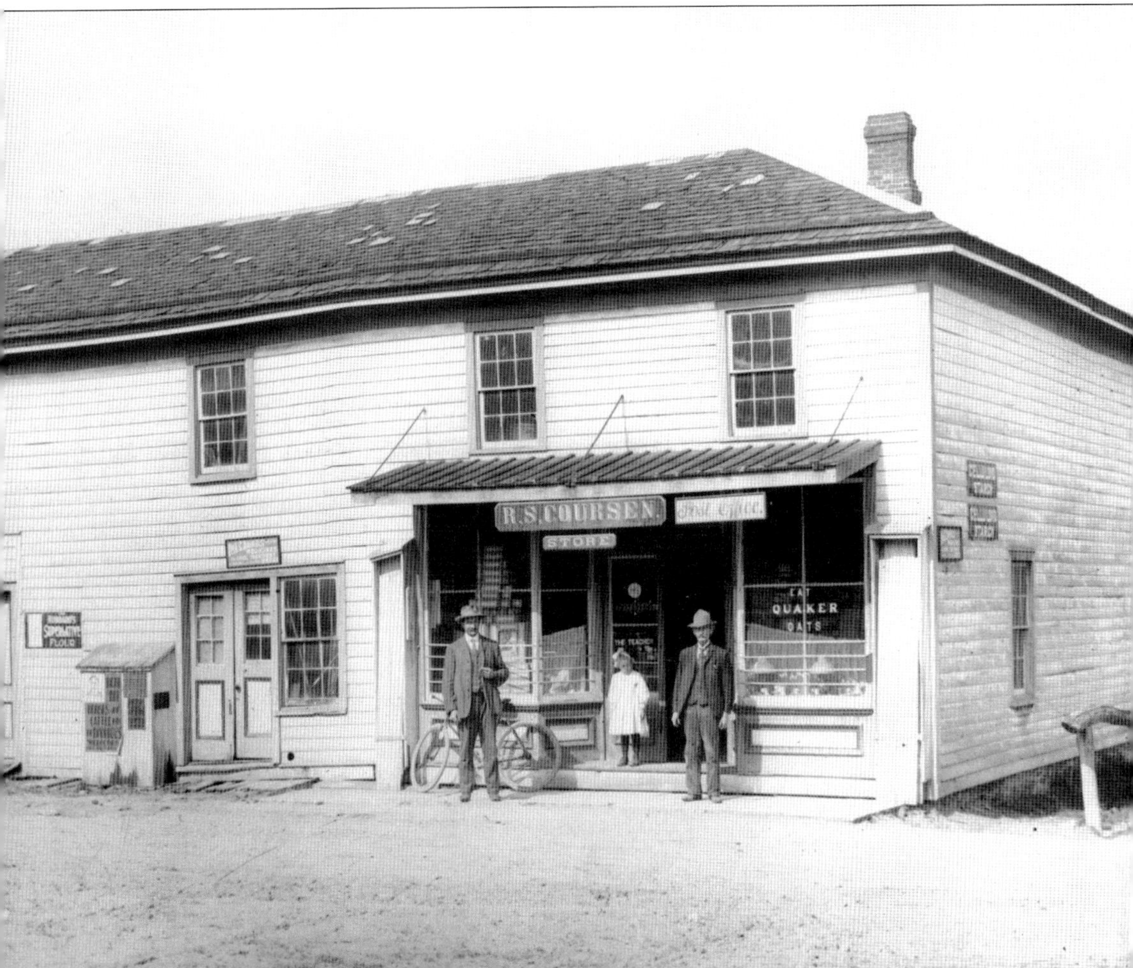

This is the old store. It was across the road from the present one. It burned about 1905, so this photograph was certainly taken before then. Shown are, from left to right, Raymond Coursen, an unidentified young girl, and George Davenport. Smoking cigars was common. Note the ads for flour, which is no longer made in the local gristmills. There is a horse tied up at the hitching rail to the far right. (Courtesy of LMH.)

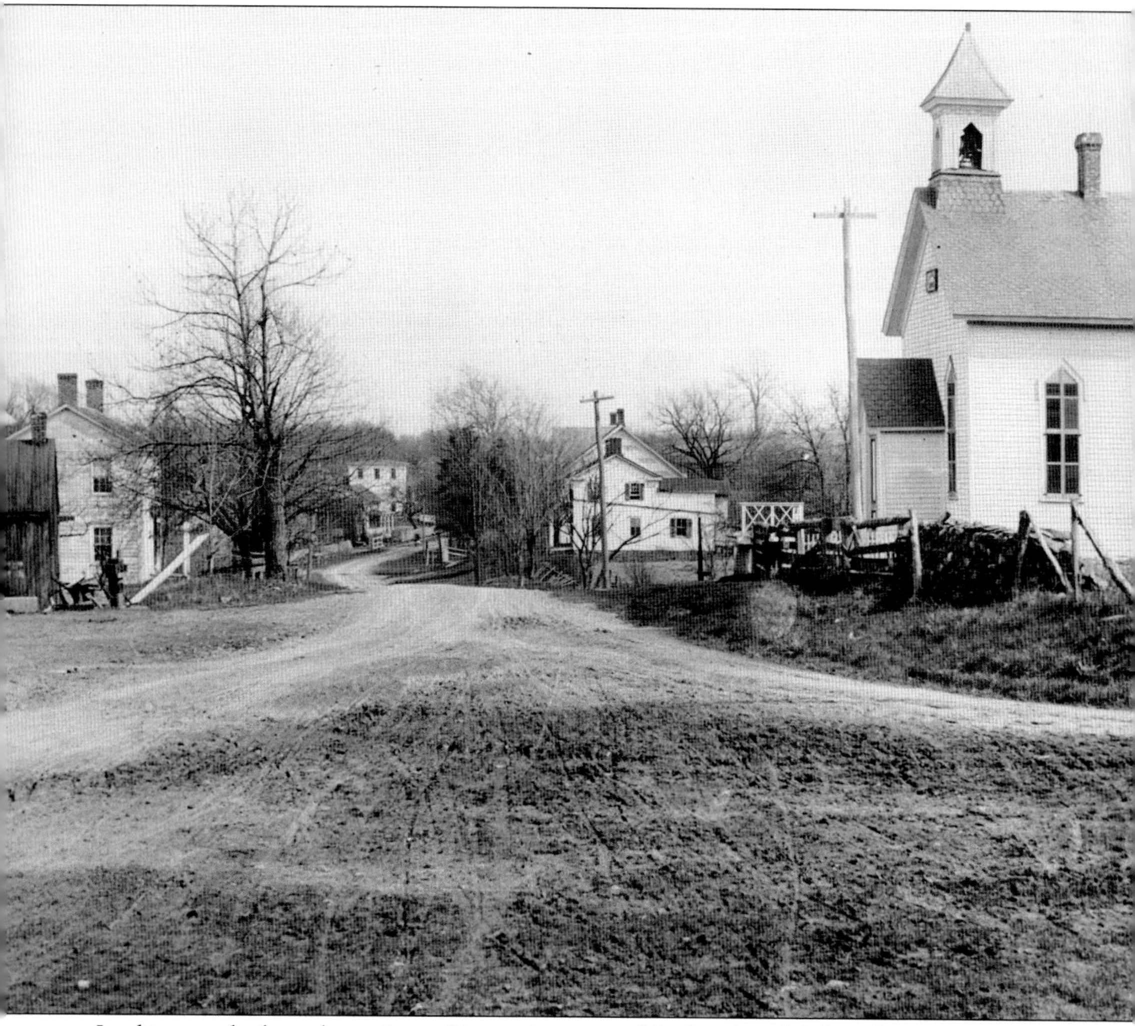

Looking south along the main road is another view of the hamlet of Colesville around 1900. The hamlet is named for early settler Elias Cole. Another of the author's ancestors was the Roloson (or Roleson) family. They had a store here and a business in Beemerville. The Rolesons were noted as early settlers in Kanouse's historic sermon of 1844. They and many other pioneers came to the area in the late 1790s. A known blacksmith in Colesville was "Uncle" Jim Post, who opened a shop in Colesville on May 26, 1870, and shod horses and built and repaired wagons. He moved to Unionville on June 26, 1923. Perhaps the earliest blacksmiths in the area were in Deckertown and joined Major Meeker as he passed though on his way to the Battle of the Minisink, which took place on July 22, 1779, during the Revolutionary War, and in which two local men were killed.

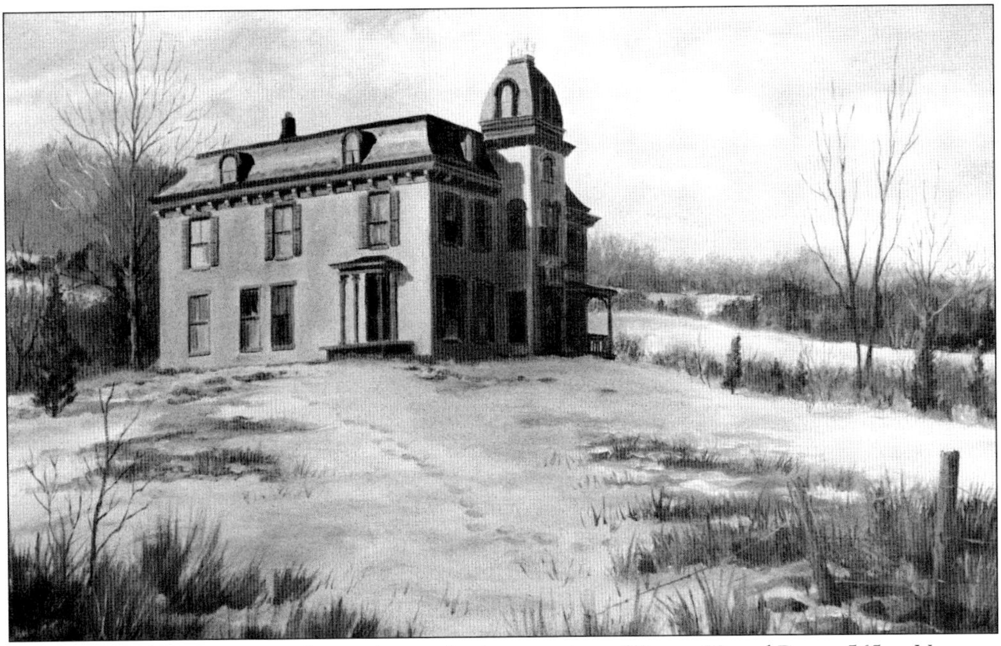

Another locality is Martins, located near the intersection of Route 23 and Route 565 to Vernon. This was an original dairy farm of the Martin family for over seven generations. At this same intersection had been the Cardinal Coat factory, which is now a car dealership. This home on the hill was removed, and a gas station/convenience store has taken its place. A generation or so referred to it as "the haunted house," as it was unoccupied and bore a resemblance to a home in a Hitchcock thriller. (Courtesy of Richard Martin and family.)

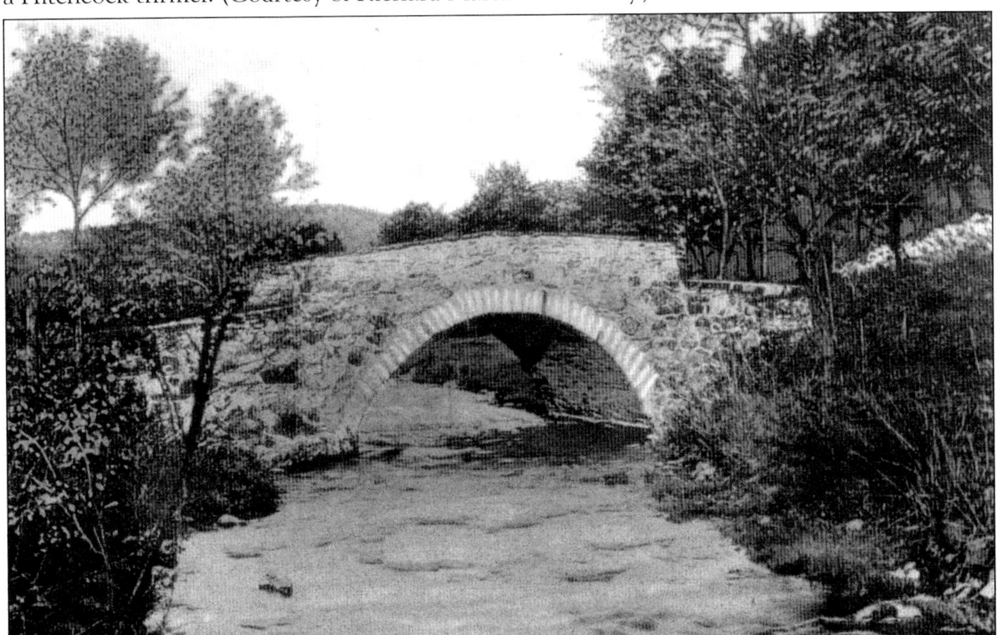

This is a typical view of the stone arch bridge that was built in the 1800s to serve the public along the Sussex County roads. Some are still in existence, and some may be found beneath the pavement and I-beams of today's roadways.

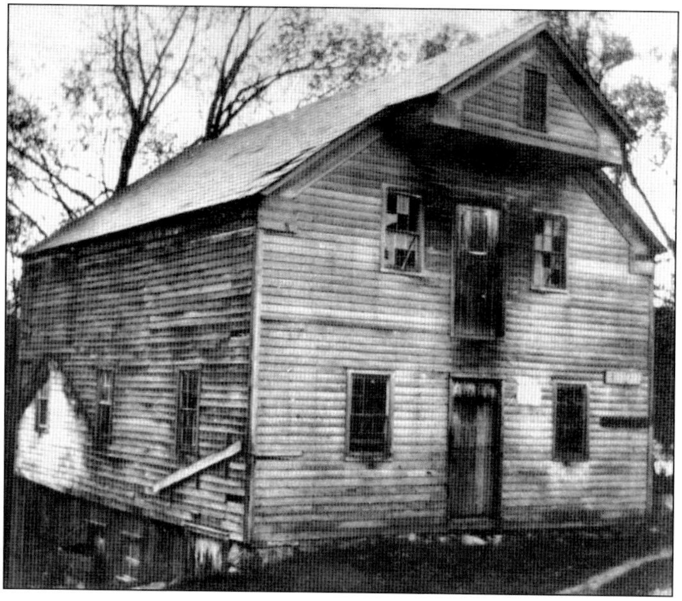

A gristmill from the past, this was known as Coxe's Mill. Note that the mill had several stories. The farmer brought grain in his wagon, and it was then raised to the top floor. Different grains were sent to different floors to begin the process; which floor depended not only on the type of grain but also the size desired. While the farmer usually took some of the product home, he also paid some of the flour to the miller for his services and sold some locally to the general store for others to buy as a staple food.

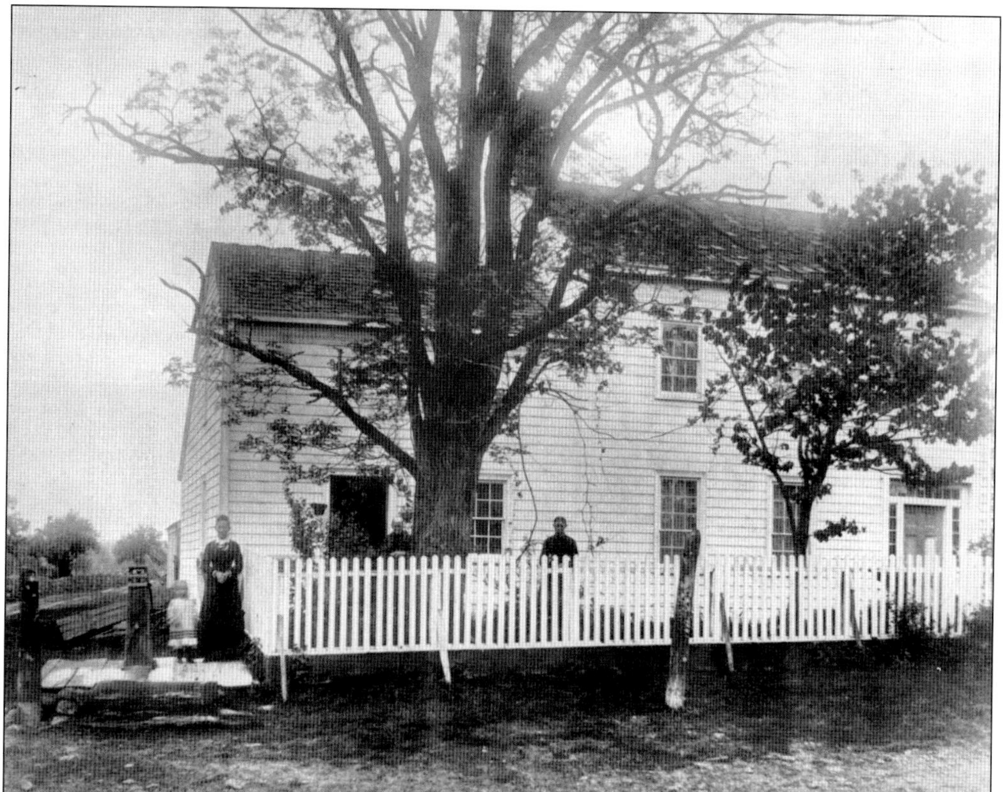

This is an old glass-plate negative image of the Decker house. The foundation was laid on the corner opposite Ed Decker's home around the year 1900. Shown are, from left to right, Hattie Diliston, the child standing by the water pump; Mary Decker, a sister of Isaac Decker and married to Rev. Baker Smith; Mrs. Eben Decker, near the tree; and Sarah Decker, a sister of Isaac Decker.

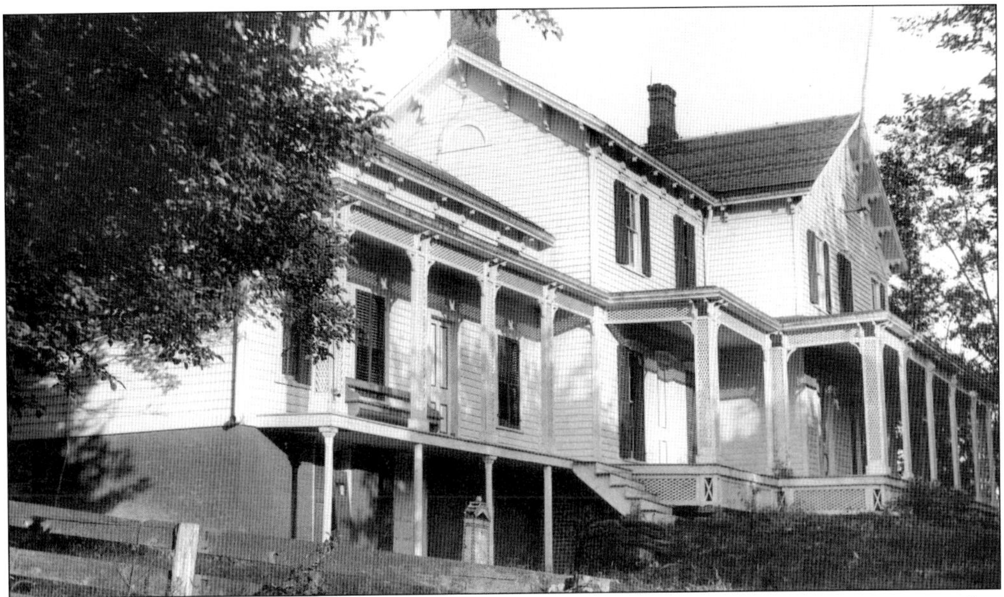

This is the homestead of local celebrity Gen. Judson Kilpatrick (January 14, 1836, to December 4, 1881). He came from a local family, was schooled at the nearby Mount Retirement School, graduated from West Point in 1861, served for the Union during the Civil War, and was the US minister to Chile. His rise to prominence occurred due to his leadership of Union cavalry troops in many battles and during Sherman's March to the Sea. Among his descendants are socialite Gloria Vanderbilt and present-day news personality Anderson Cooper.

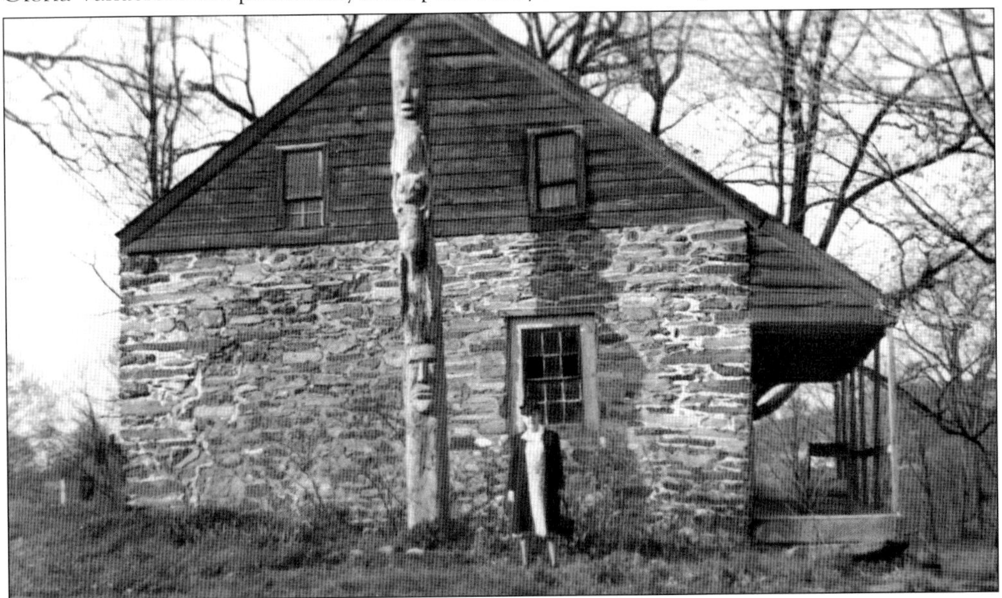

Seen here at the Clove is the locally famous totem pole. Many Sussex County residents remember the old totem pole that was among the trees along Route 23. This area, near Clove Church, has been known as the Clove from the early 1800s. The Clove Brook runs nearby. This stone dwelling dates back to the 1750s and was reputedly a fort during the French and Indian War. A road ran in front of the stone dwelling and to the other buildings that are shown on the following pages and on the front cover.

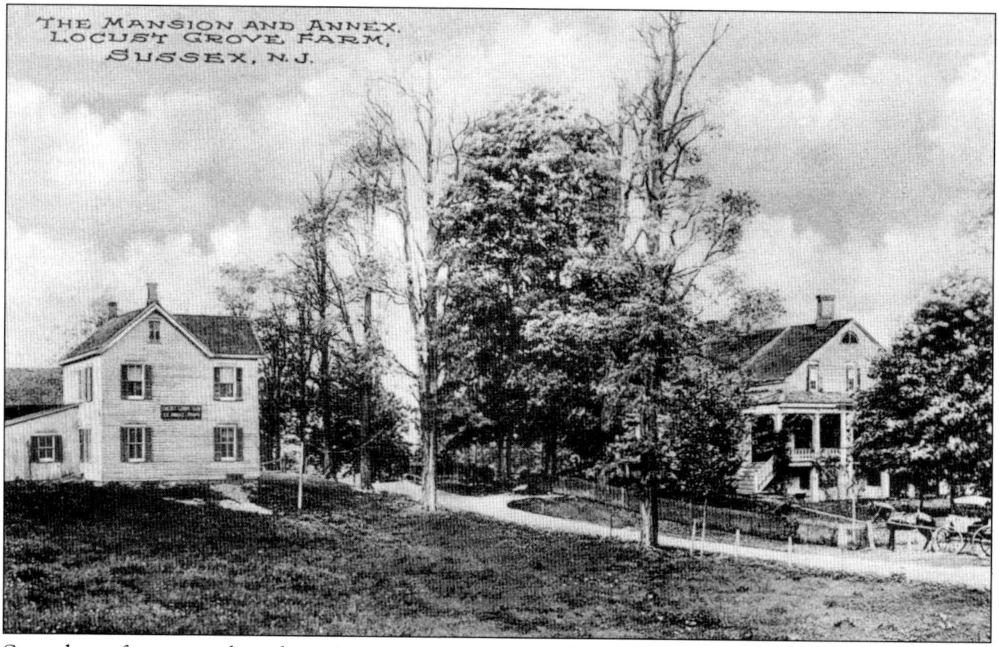

Seen here from another direction is a more comprehensive view of the Clove and Locust Grove. The roadway went along the front of the stone dwelling and to this cluster of buildings. (Author's collection.)

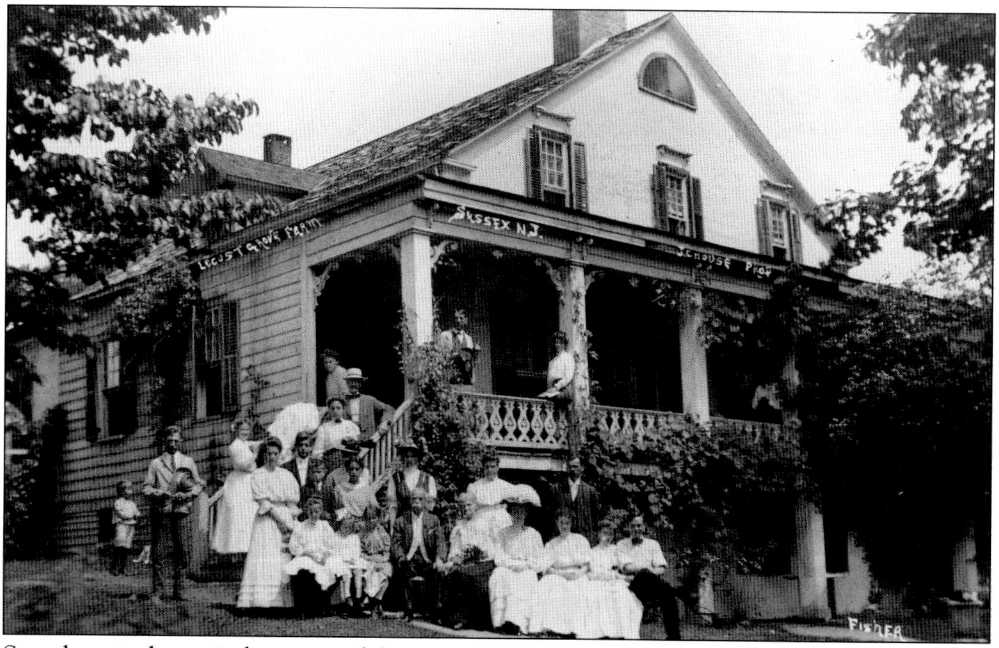

Seen here is the main house, used for guests and known by the owner's name of J.C. House. Located in the immediate area (known as Locust Grove) were the main house, a guest house, the stone dwelling that also served as a trading post along Route 23, and the Clove Brook. The area served as a farm and hotel in this rich farmland of Wantage Township. Today, cattle graze, corn is raised, horses are run, and Christmas trees are grown along the rich bottomlands of Clove Brook as it winds southward toward the Papakating and Wallkill Rivers.

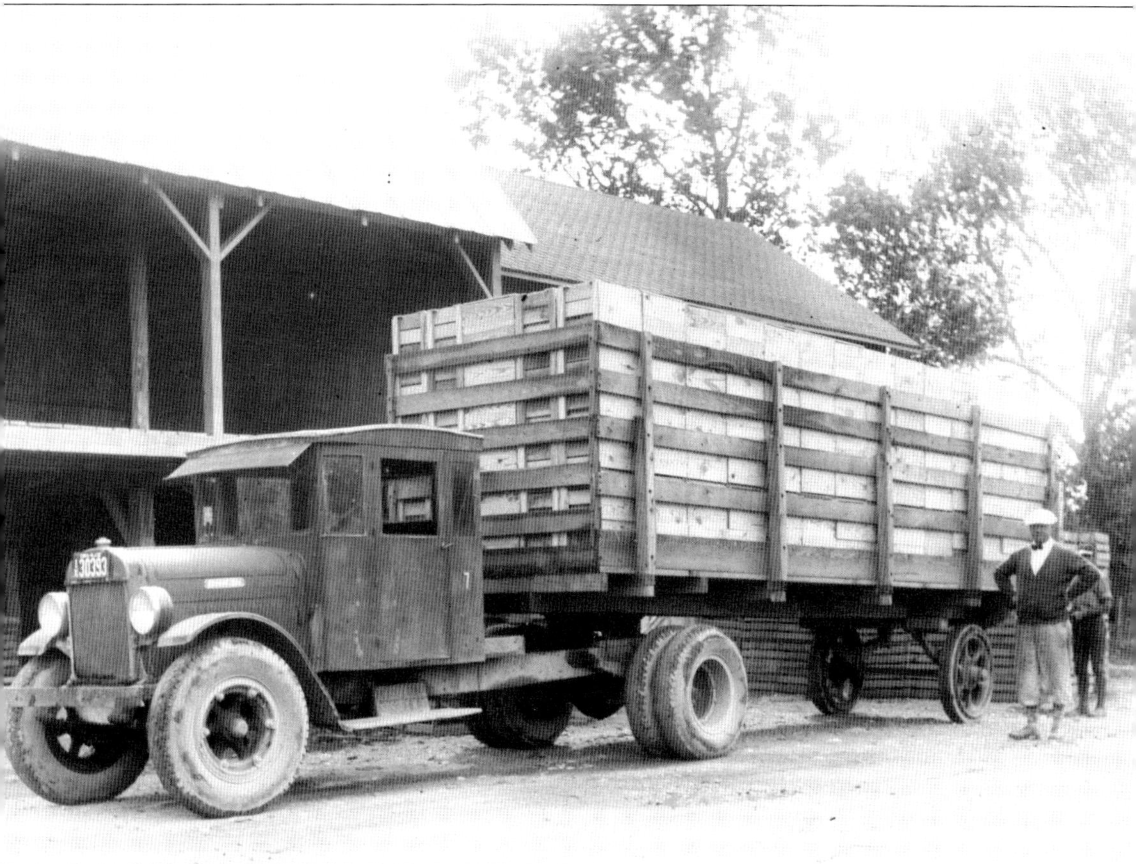

While the horse and wagon served to take produce to market in the 1800s and railroads did as well in the late 1800s, trucking became popular as the roads and the vehicles improved. Shown here at the lumberyard is "Doc" Brownell in Sussex.

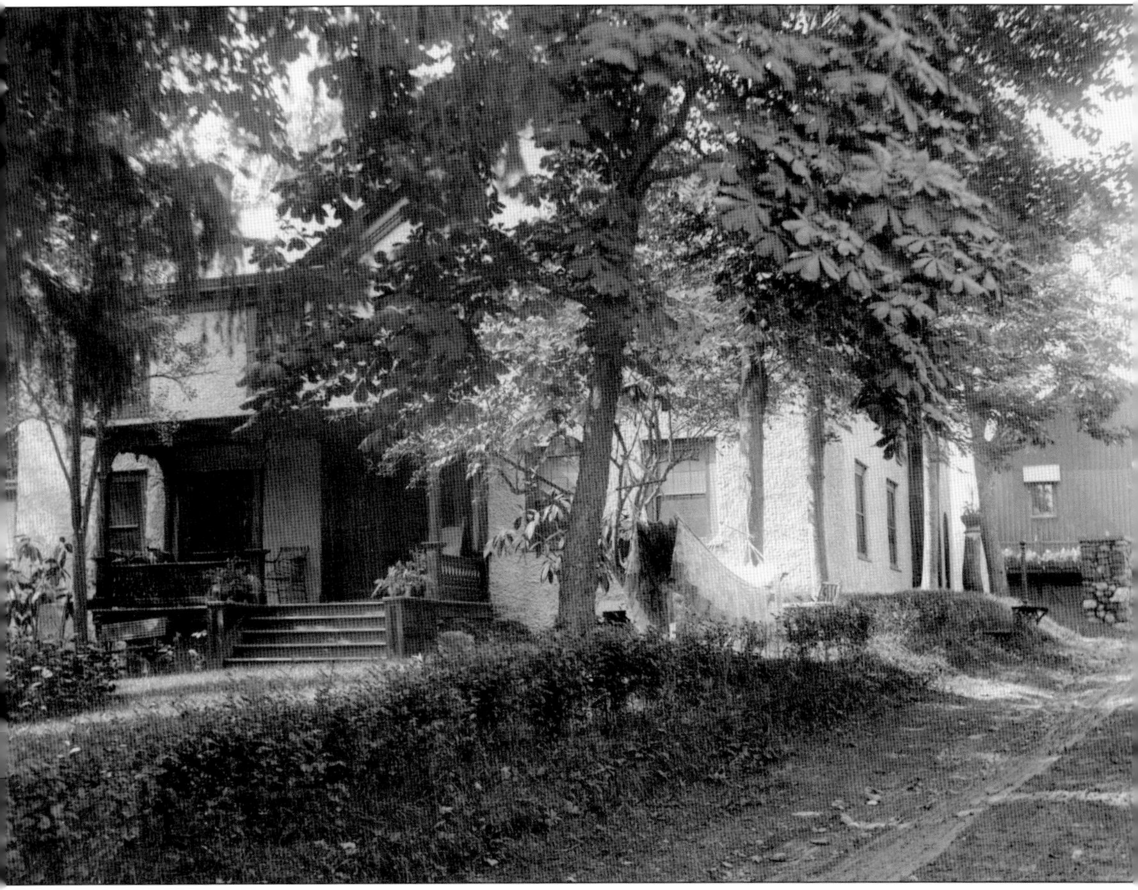

Here is a nice easy summer day out in the hammock, with tulip flowers below the windows in the barn. In the driveway, there looks to be a custom metal hitching post for visitors with horses, with steps for the ladies to get into the carriage. At the time of this c. 1905 photograph, this was the residence of Clarence E. Brown. This farm was, and still is, known as Brookcroft.

Three

DECKERTOWN SUSSEX BOROUGH

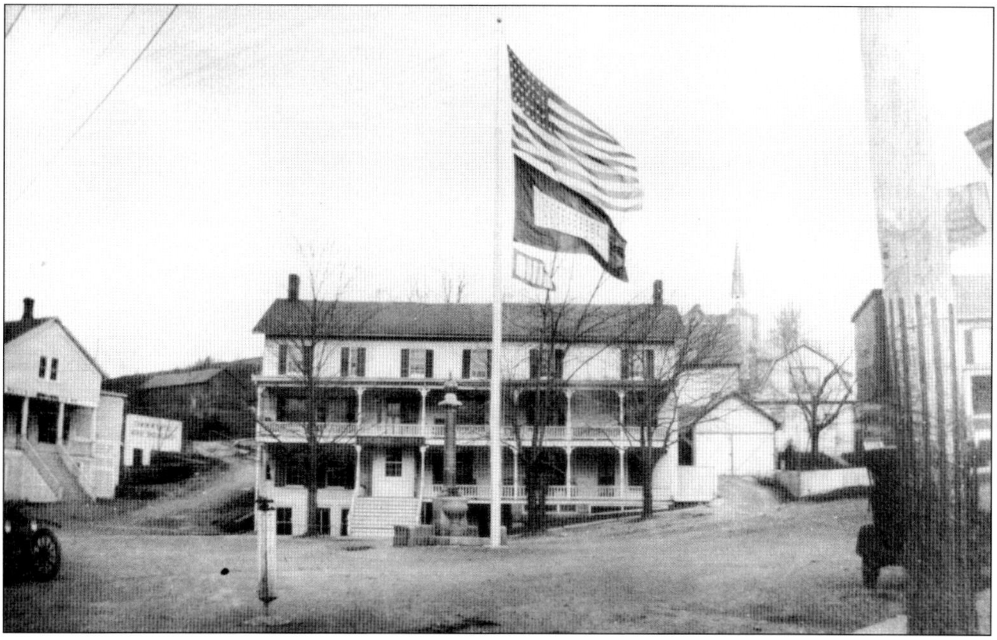

This building was built in 1823 as the De Camp Hotel. It has also been known as the Chardavoyne's, Chrisman House, Goble Inn, and the Fountain Square Inn. This view is from about 1919, as determined by the flags. Beneath the American flag is the Blue Star Service Banner from World War I. There is a blue star for every serviceman in the war from the area. This is similar to the Gold Star Banner shown for a service member killed during the conflicts of World War I, World War II, and more recent actions.

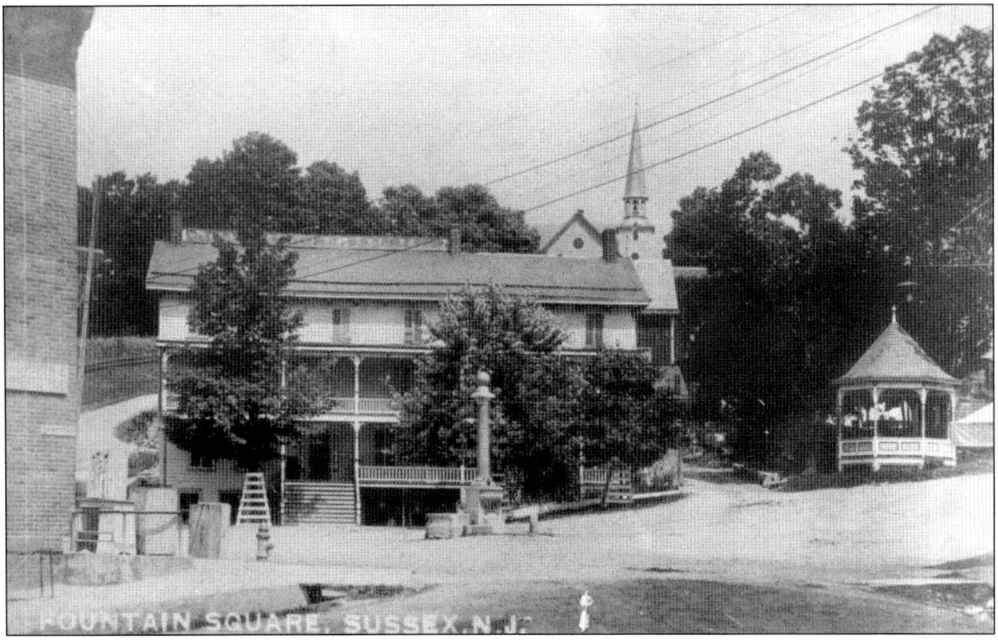

Seen to the right of the Goble Inn, now the Fountain Inn, is the gazebo that graced the middle of Sussex. In the late 1800s, a popular form of entertainment in small towns like Sussex was cornet bands such as the Union Band or the Beemerville Cornet Band, whose images can be seen elsewhere in this book. The gazebo was gone by the end of World War I.

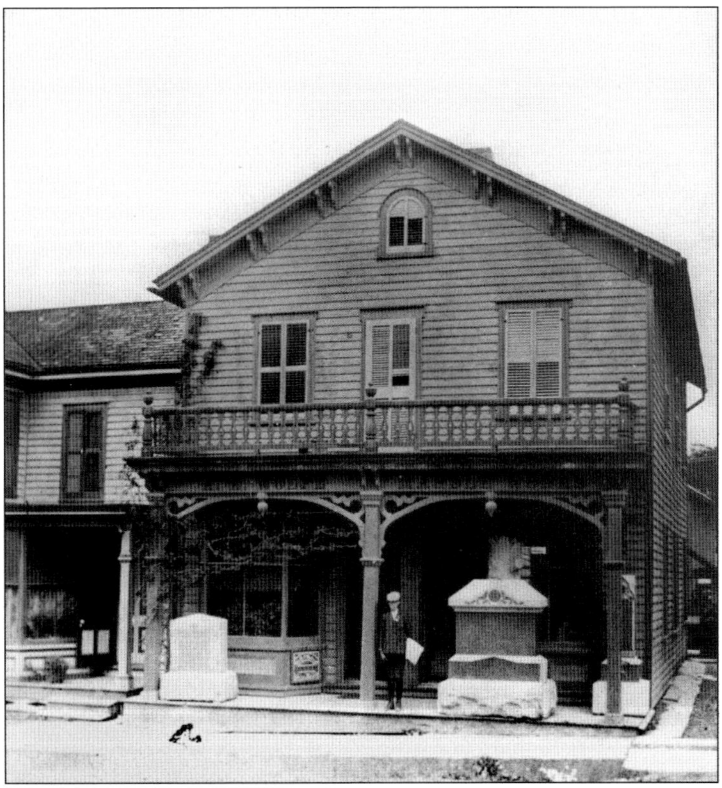

One of the oldest and longest surviving businesses in town is the A.E. Wolfe Marble works. In 1872, they advertised as "manufacturers of marble monuments, tombstones, etc. Orders solicited and work executed artistically and promptly. Deckertown Marble Work, at the corner of Main St and Newton Avenue." Today the business is known as Wolfe Granite Works, Monuments and Markers, and is located nearby on Main Street.

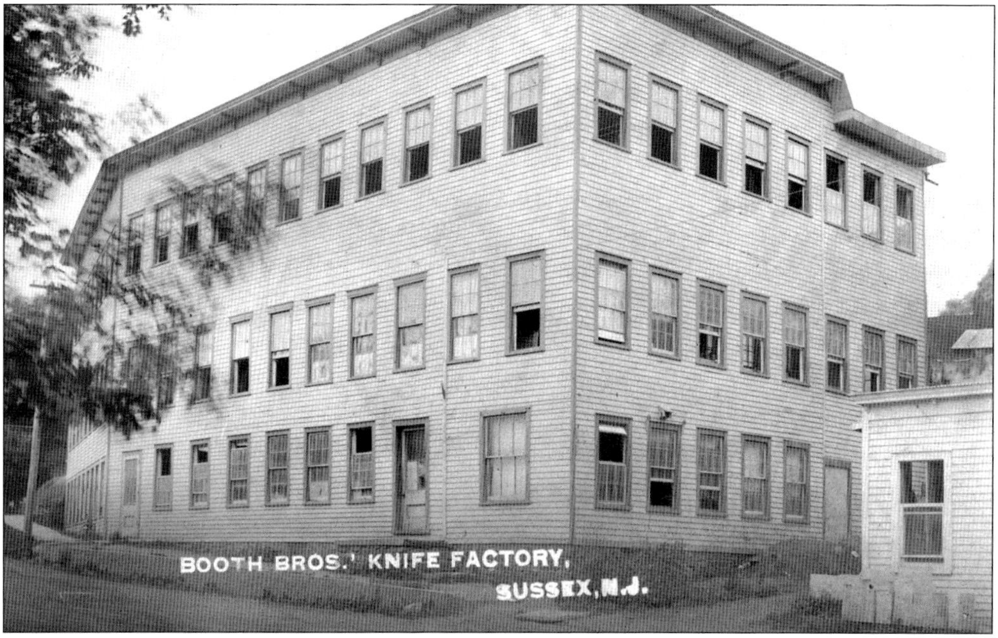

Booth Brothers Knife factory was started in Newark, New Jersey, in about 1864 and moved to Boonton around 1879, to Stockholm along the Hamburg Turnpike, and to Sussex. Booth Brothers then sold the equipment to a concern in Pennsylvania. The structure was later occupied by the Ewald Brothers Shoe Factory from Newton, then the McBee Bindery, and the Radio Kimmell factory in the 1930s, which was when the factory burned down in one of the greatest fires of Sussex.

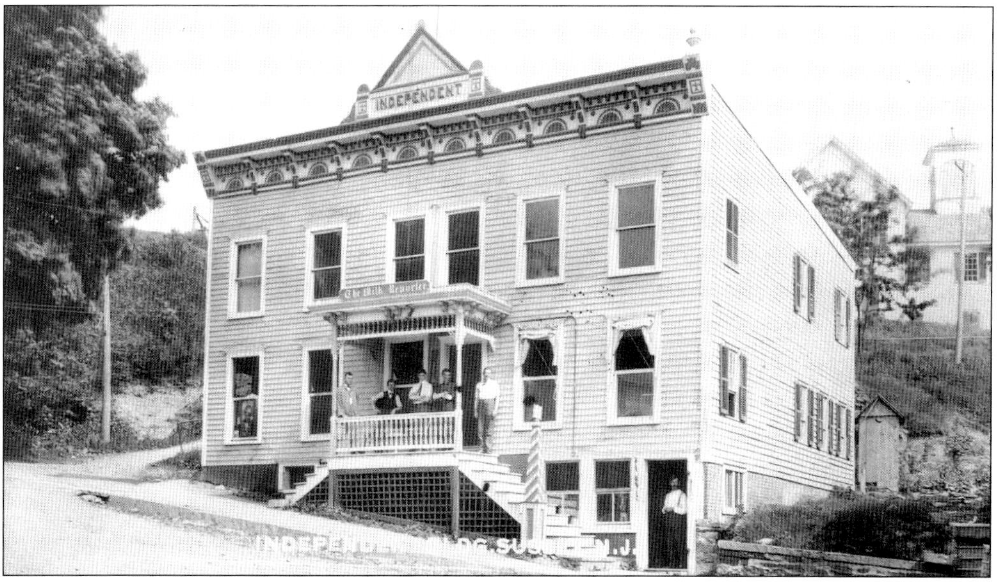

Several newspapers have been in the area over the last 200 years. The *Sussex Register* ran from 1813 in Deckertown, then Lewisburg, then Newton, finally merging with the *New Jersey Herald* in 1943. The *Sussex Independent* (shown here) ran from 1870 until its 1952 merger with the *New Jersey Herald*. The *Wantage Recorder* ran from 1894 to 1943, merging with the *New Jersey Herald*. The *Wantage Press* was about a quarter mile west of the *Independent*. A more recent publication is the *Advertiser-News* (North and South). (Courtesy of Olga Bazylevich Stefkowich and family of Mike the Jeweler.)

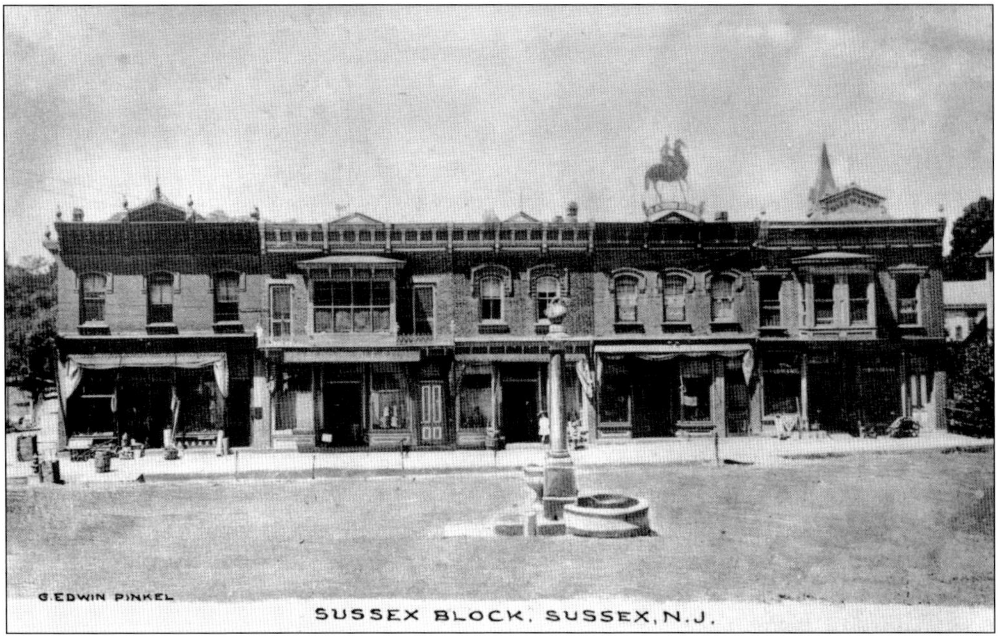

This group of buildings was known as the Sussex Block and also Fountain Square. The square itself had been known as De Camp Square and Fountain. Note the sign depicting a rider on a horse; this is typical of the work of local artist Louis Larsen. Also, compare the metal hitching posts in front of the Sussex Block to the ones in front of the Hornbeck Block on page 39.

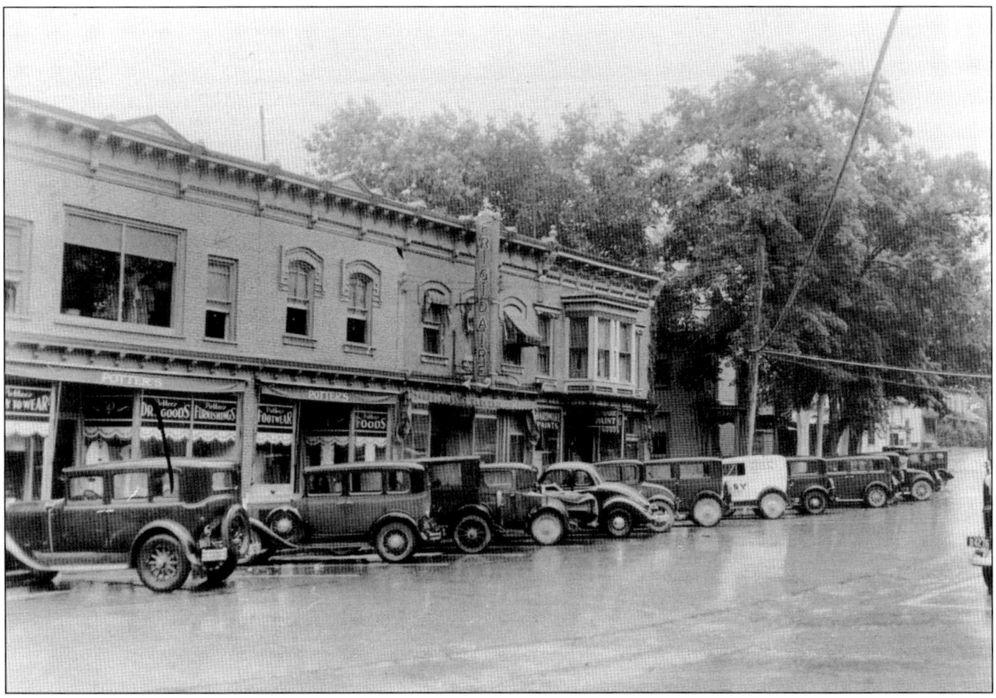

Across from the Goble Inn stood a block of buildings that housed commercial establishments. This was known as the Sussex Block. Note that the square was paved by the mid-1930s and the horse-drawn wagons were gone, replaced by automobiles.

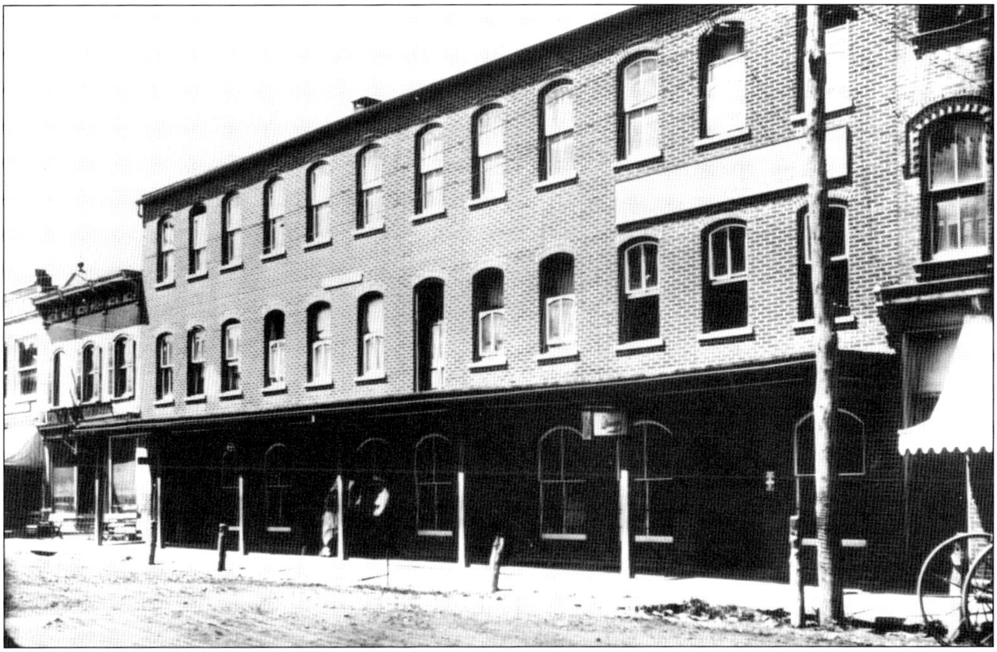

Hornbeck Block was built of brick in the late 1800s. During the 1870s, J.E. Hornbeck owned the Deckertown flour mill, used for wheat, rye, and buckwheat flour and corn meal feed. Hornbeck Hall had many functions, including the reunion of the local Civil War veterans of the 15th Regiment of New Jersey Volunteers on September 18, 1902.

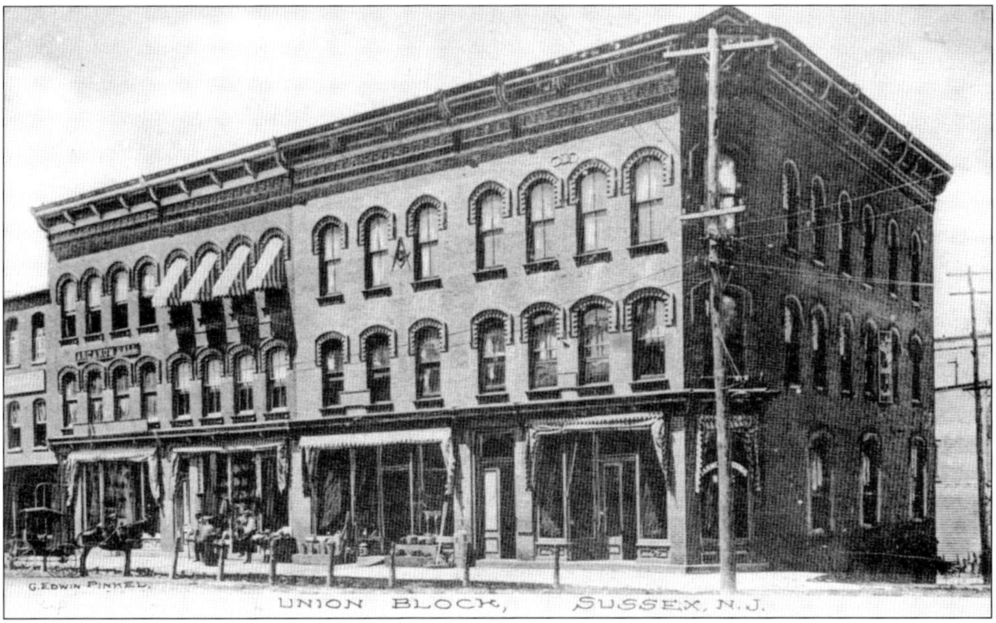

The Union Block is a row of brick buildings in Sussex. It can be compared to the Hornbeck Block next door, Cannon Block across the street, and Sussex Block. Note that this cluster has the Arcanum Hall and the Masonic square and compass. Meetings for the Masons, Odd Fellows, and other groups were held here almost every day of the week. The Farmers Bank was in the right-hand corner of the building; presently, that location is home to another bank.

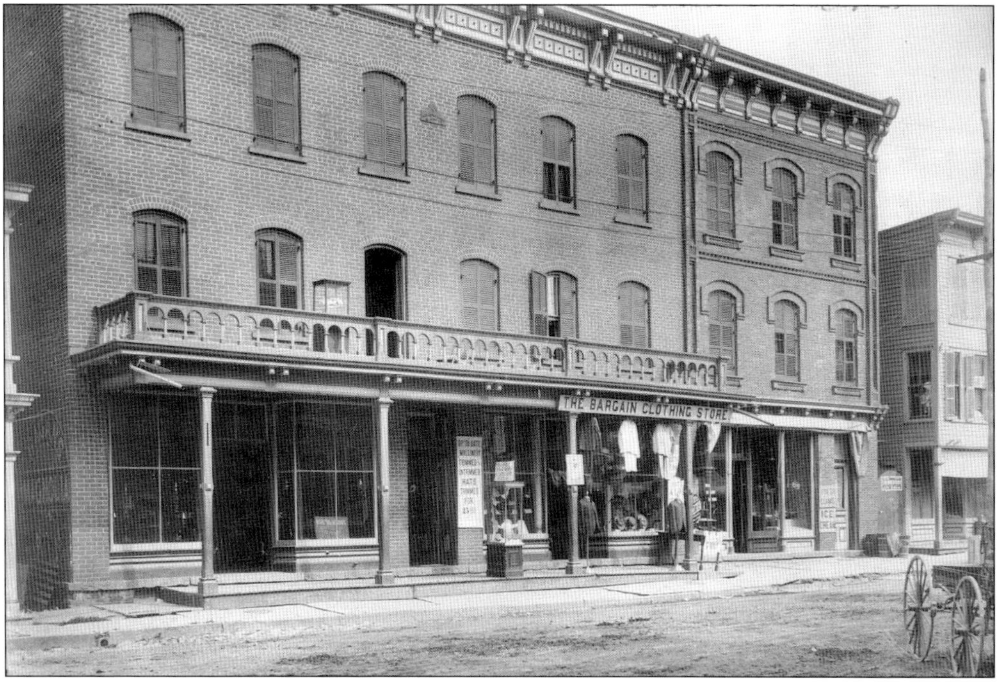

Cannon Block is another group of brick buildings constructed in the town of Sussex. This is on the eastern side of Main Street across from the Hornbeck Block, which is very similar in appearance. Note the "modern" sidewalk and the raised wooden platform along the storefronts. Keeping out of the muddy streets was an important consideration in city planning.

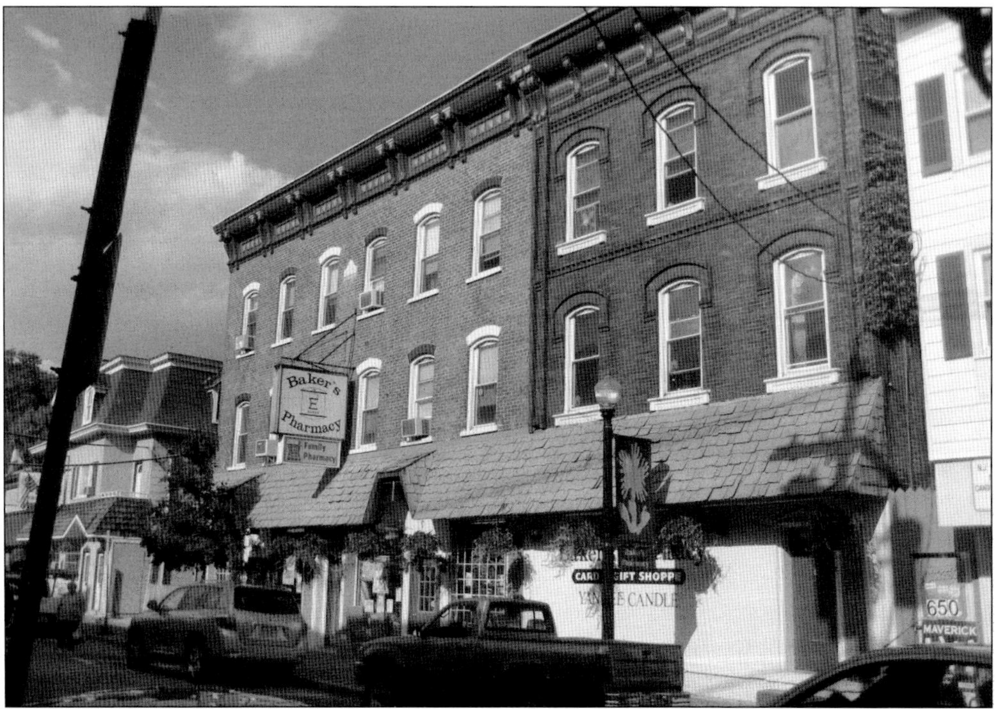

Here is a view of the Cannon Block today. Business still thrives along Main Street in Sussex.

Here is a view of Church Street in Sussex from Main Street after some snow. Stables for horses were located behind the Goble Inn. There were also stables behind the Union Inn (now known as the Sussex Inn). Visitors either came to town for trips or were passing through on the stagecoach or train. If they were here on their own transportation, the horses, as well as the passengers, needed lodging and food!

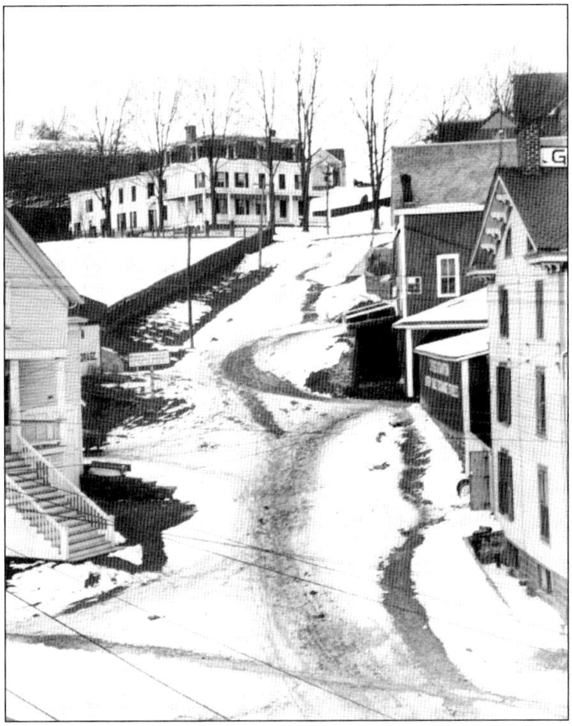

Here is Main Street after a snowstorm in Sussex. This is a tranquil scene before any of the horse-and-buggy traffic got back on the streets. Note the swept and well-kept sidewalks in front of the stores.

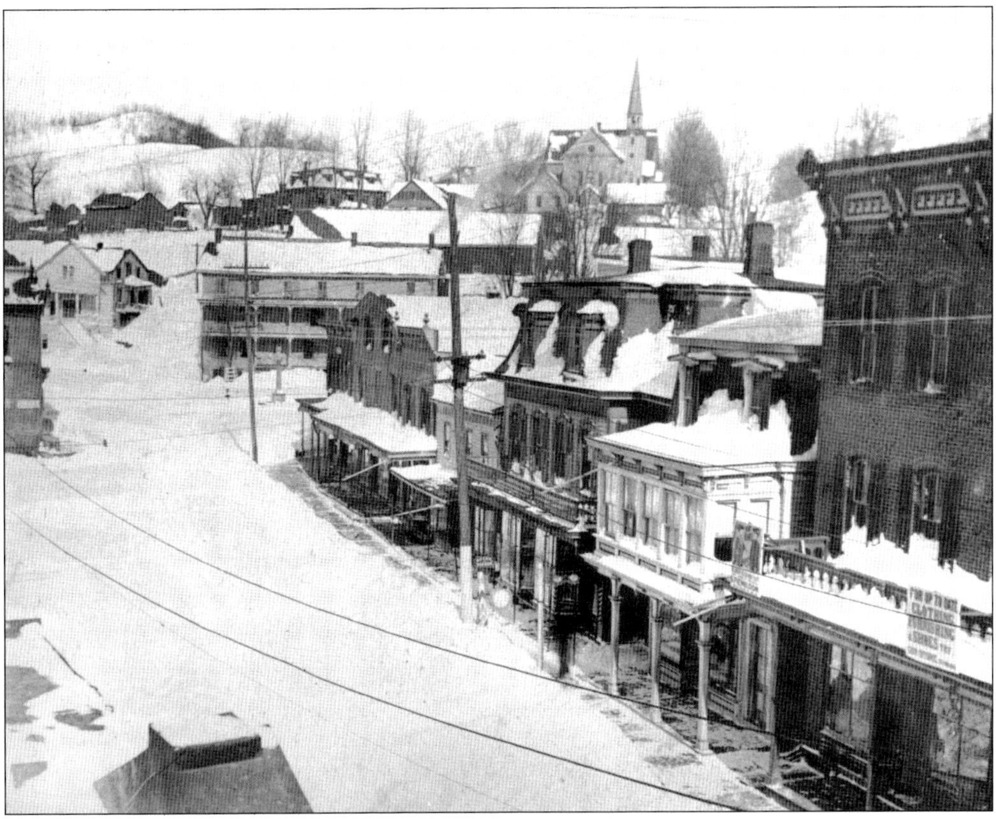

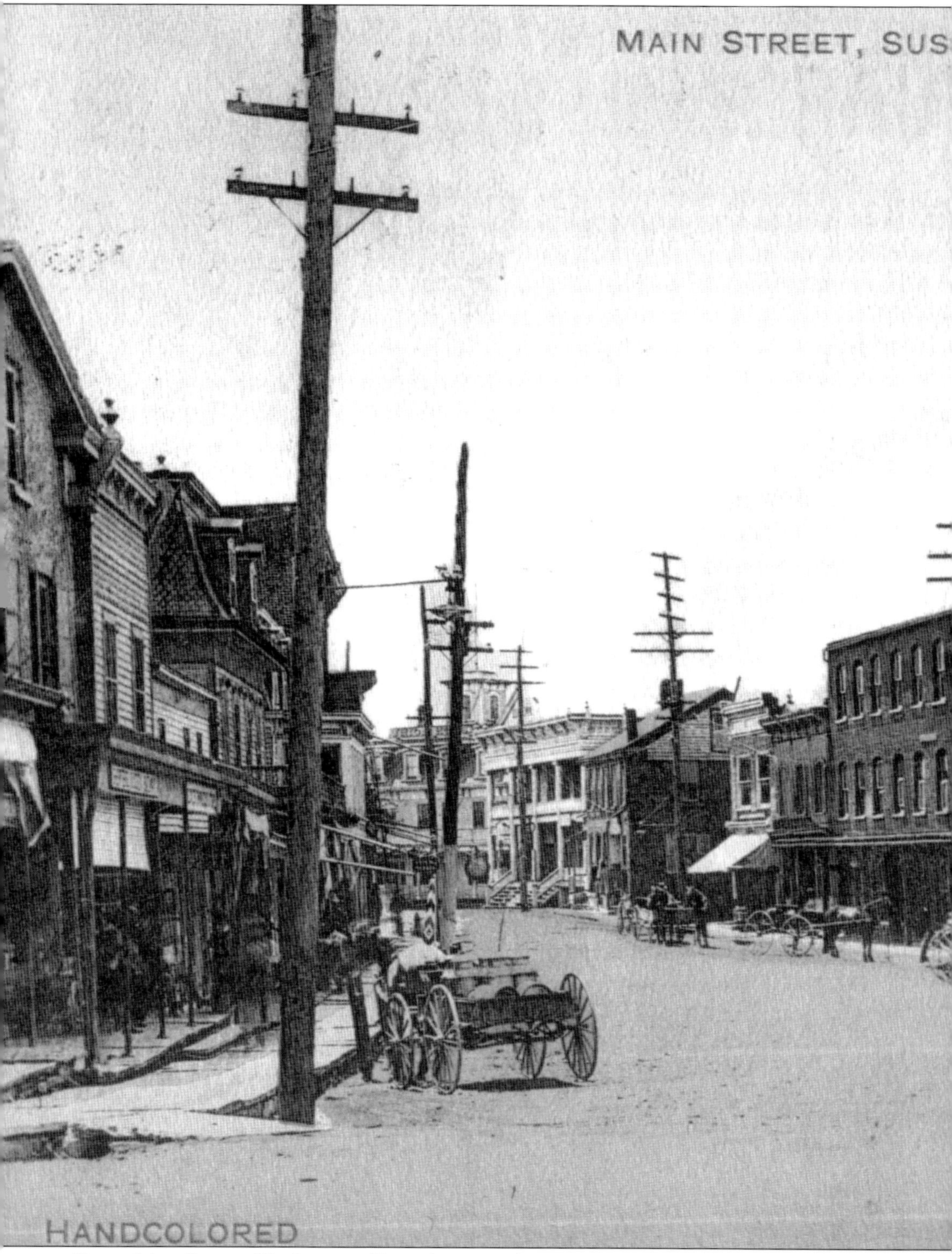

Here is Main Street of Deckertown (Sussex) in an earlier time, a quintessential representation of the rural nature of this farming community. In 1910, Woodrow Wilson spoke here when campaigning

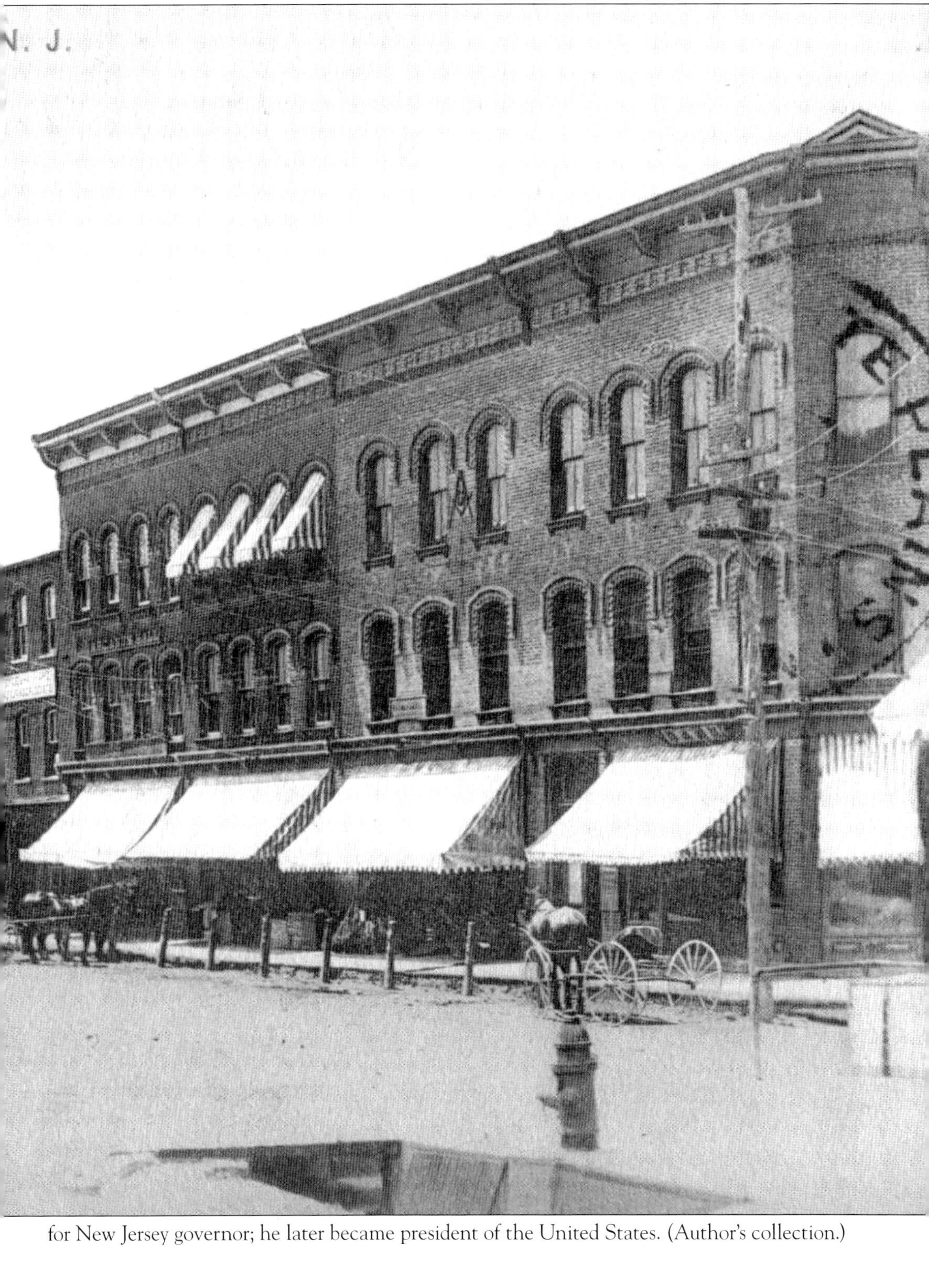

for New Jersey governor; he later became president of the United States. (Author's collection.)

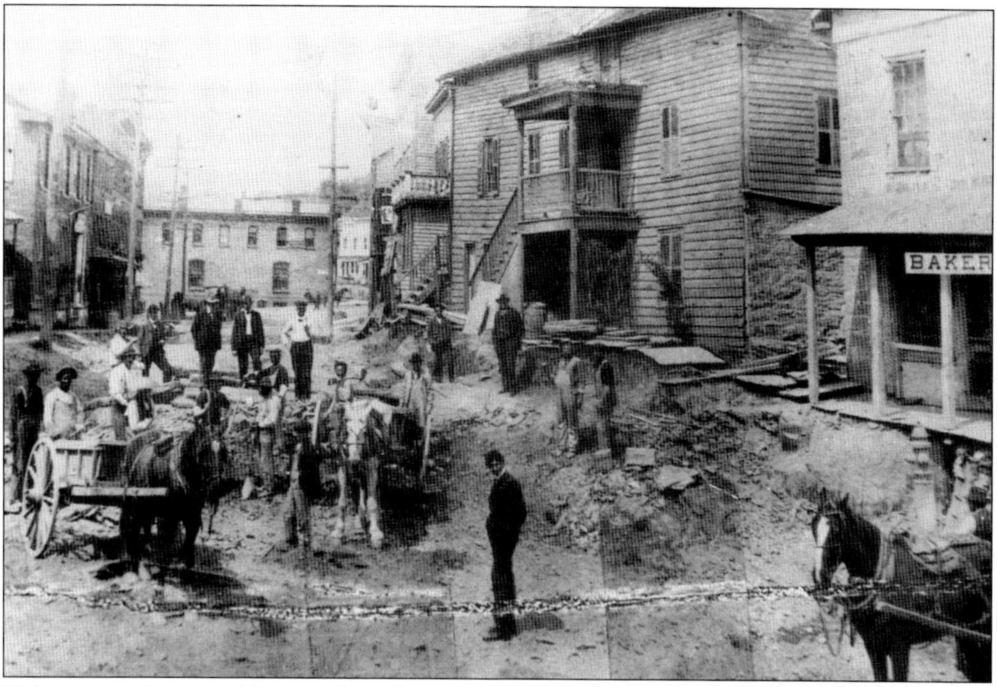

This is an early view of Sussex when the southeast end of Main Street was being lowered. Note the heavy reliance on hand labor and carts. Stores on the southeast end of Main Street afterward had to rely on steps to get customers inside.

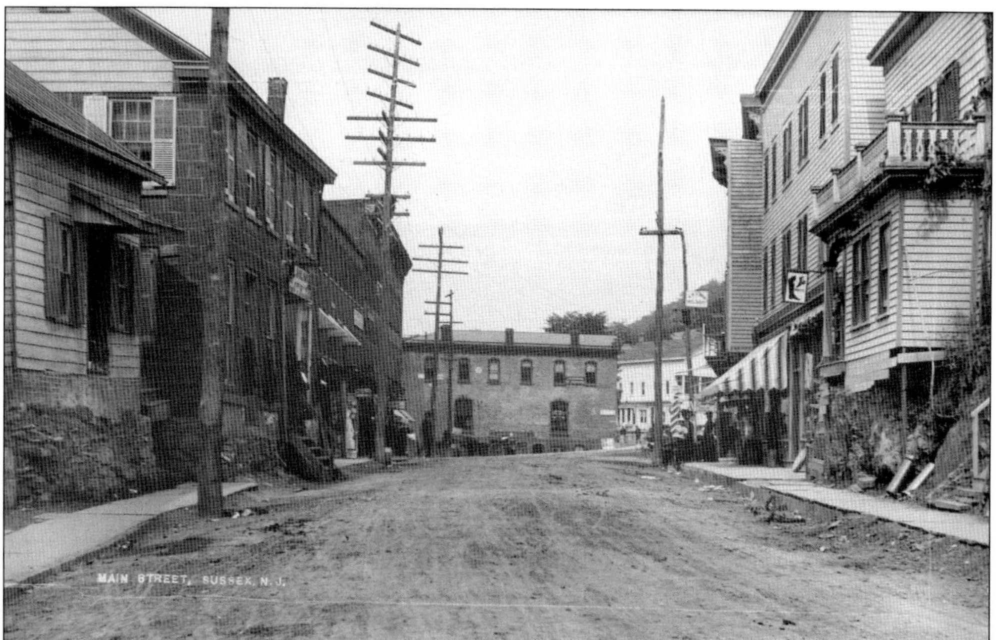

This photograph shows the change in the elevation of Main Street. This is one of three photographs showing the transformation of Main Street in Sussex during this last century. As the book progresses sequentially, it also has traveled to the eastern end of Main Street, having already covered the northwestern end near Fountain Square.

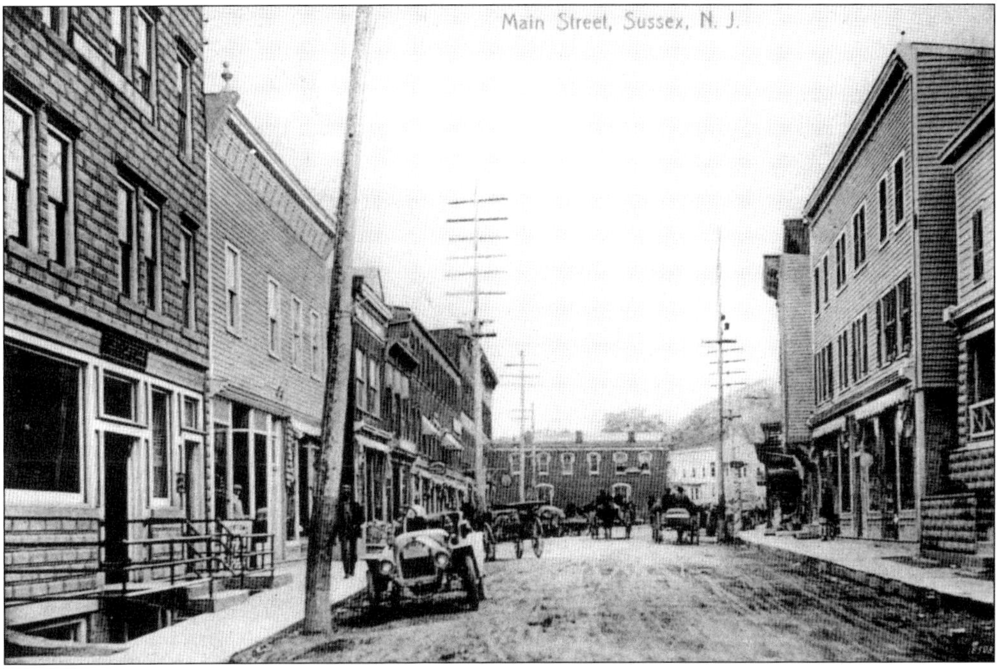

This view of Main Street, Sussex, is looking northward and depicts the dirt road that had been in existence from the earliest days of the town. This c. 1915 view shows how the automobile was becoming a part of the community, though the horse and carriage still remained.

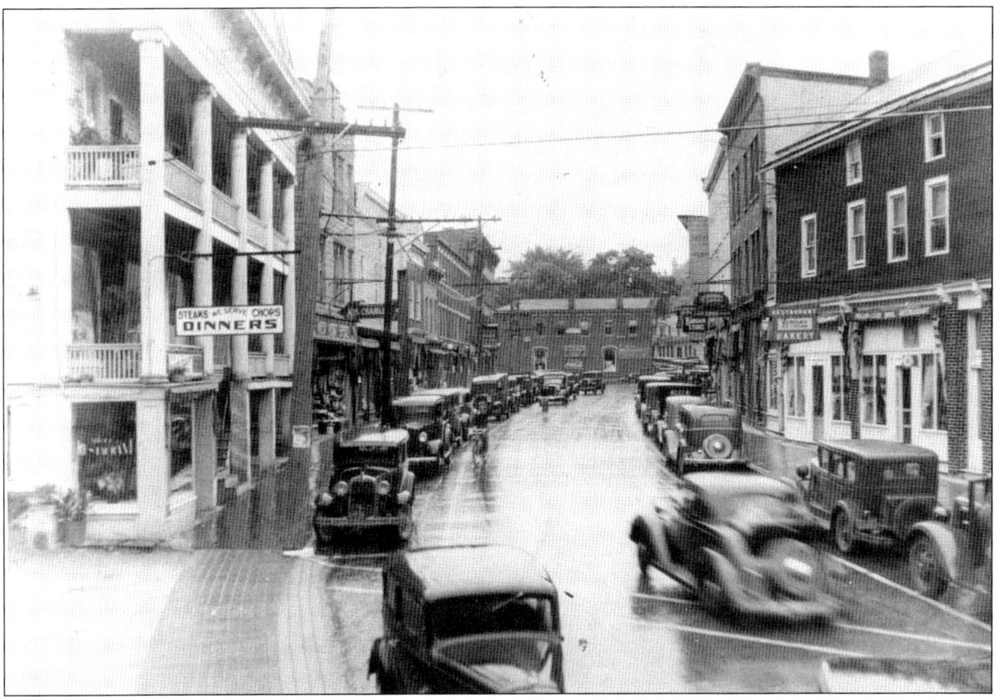

This view of Main Street looking north is from the 1930s and shows the great change in society and technology. From dirt to a paved road, the mode of transportation on the street now consists entirely of automobiles.

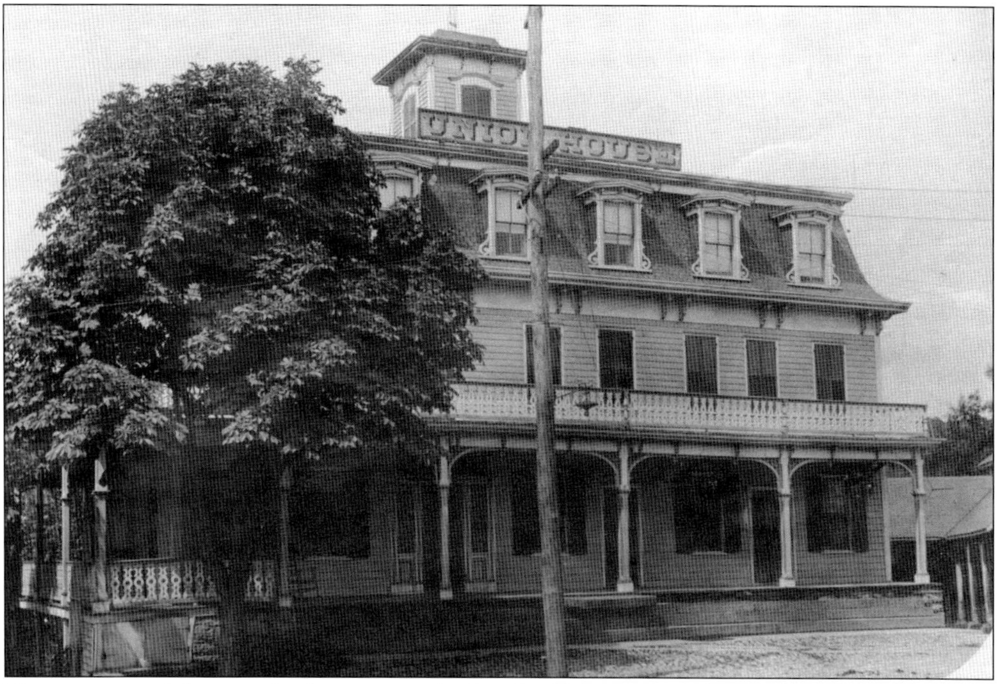

This sequence of photographs shows a main landmark of Sussex Borough, the Union House or Sussex Inn, over a period of time. This early view shows it before the lower level was revealed through the lowering of Main Street. This image may have come originally from a glass stereoscope pair. The stereoscope image gives a good impression of depth. This view was probably from the 1880s.

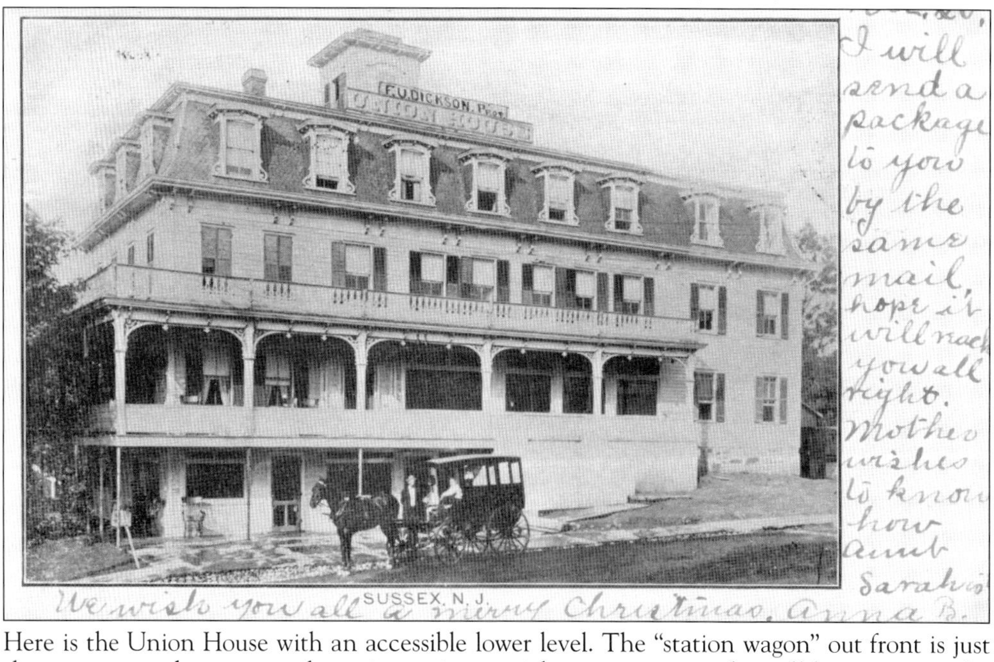

Here is the Union House with an accessible lower level. The "station wagon" out front is just that—a wagon that goes to the train station to pick up passengers who will be staying at the hotel. Later in this book there is a sequence of photographs that depict the journey of a traveler into town in the early 1900s.

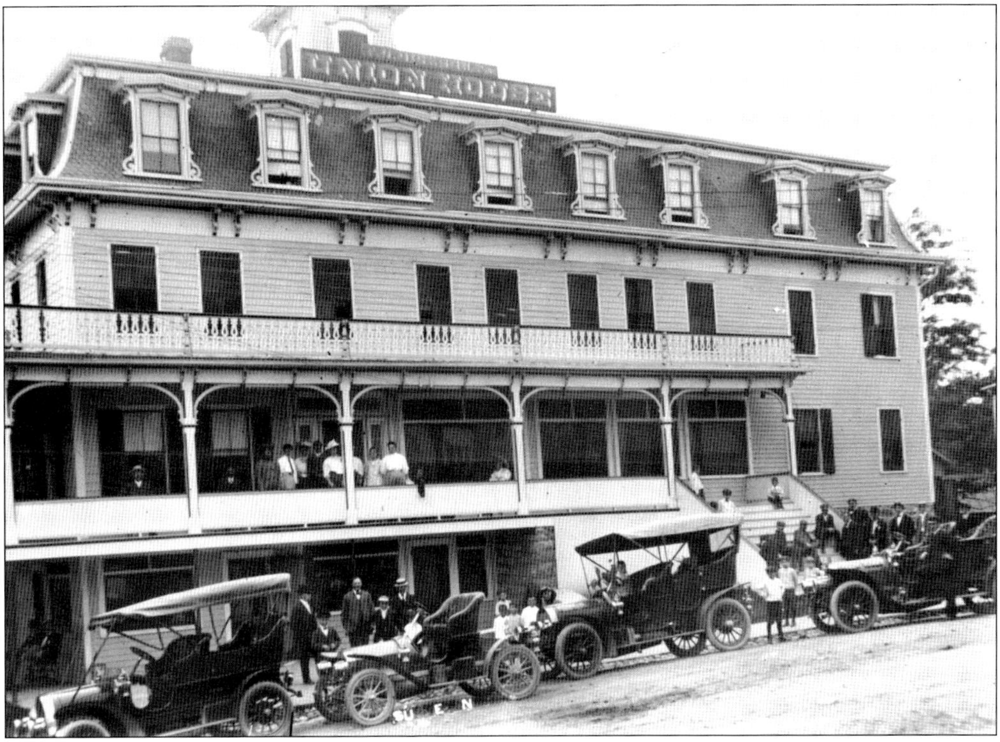

This is another view of the Union House when F.U. Dickson was still the proprietor. Note the change in transportation to automobiles, which is how it remains today.

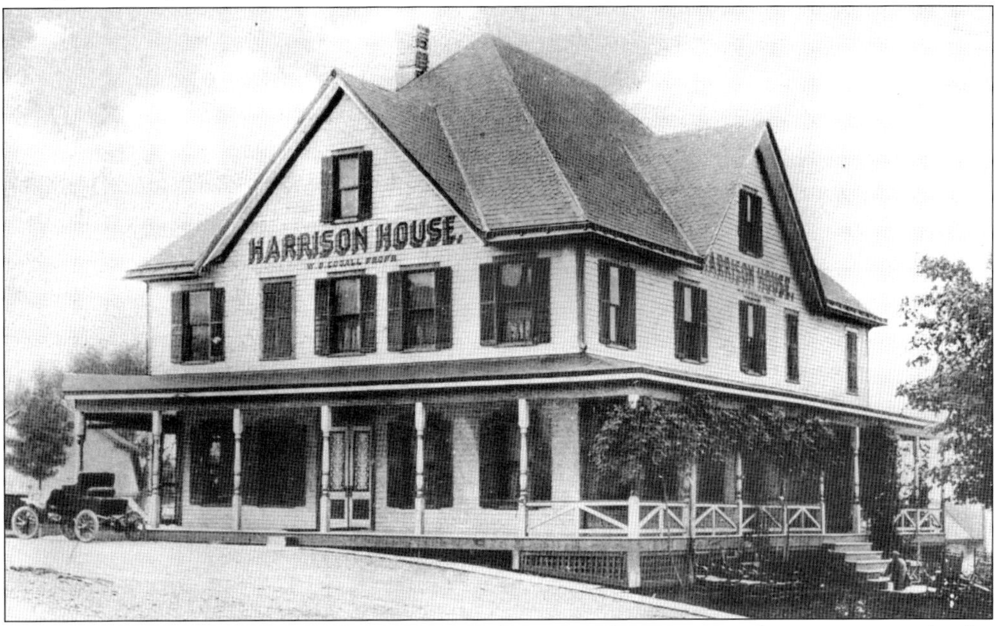

The Harrison House was a hotel at the top of the town of Sussex near the train station for the Midland Railroad, later known as the New York, Susquehanna & Western Railway. This was also near to the racetrack on the way north toward Unionville, New York. There will be much more about racing in a later chapter.

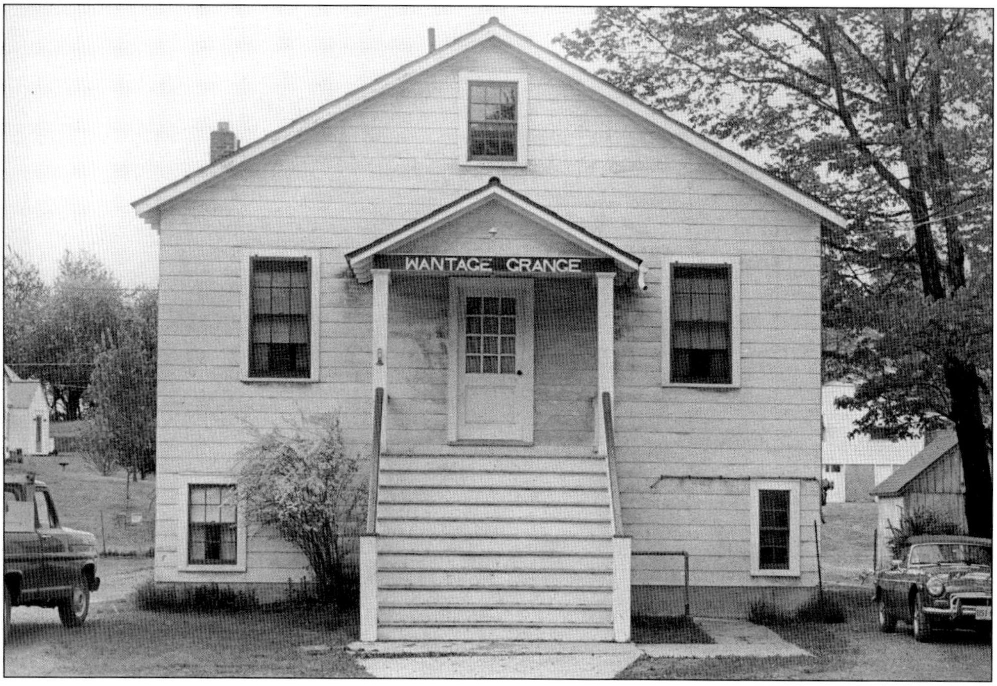

This is the Wantage Grange Hall. The name is short for the National Grange of the Order of Patrons of Husbandry. The Grange is a fraternal organization for American farmers that encourages farm families to band together for their common economic and political well-being. The organization was formed nationally in 1867. This is one of the several organizations that thrived in town in the late 1800s and early 1900s.

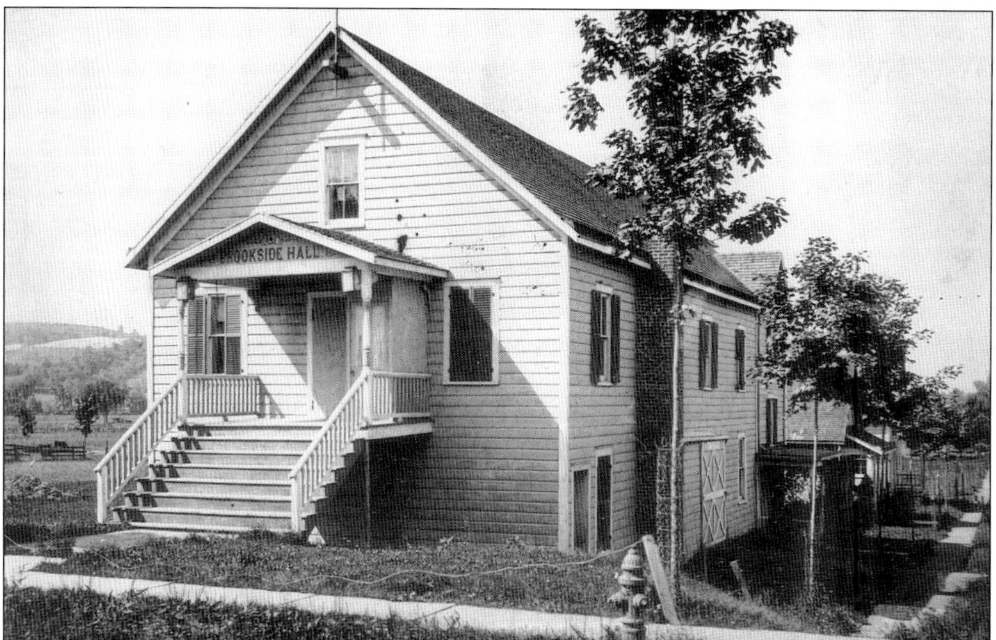

Brookside Hall was located off today's Route 23 on Brookside Avenue. It was a place for meetings or other public events. (Courtesy of Olga Bazylevich Stefkowich and family of Mike the Jeweler.)

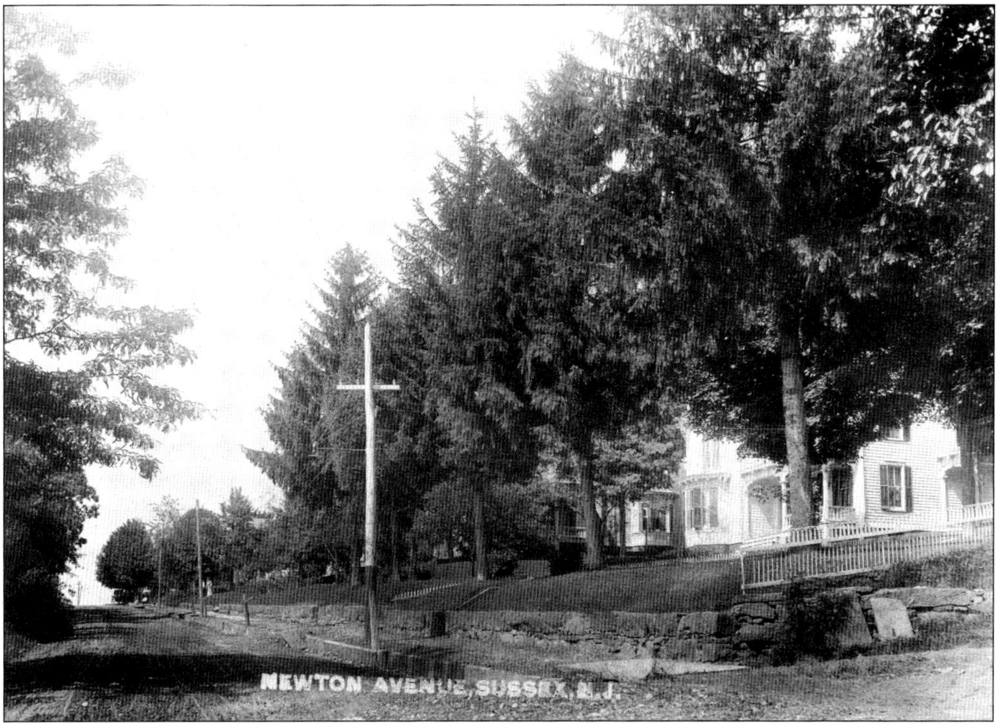

This is a view of Newton Avenue in Sussex. The road went to Newton, the county seat, on a bridge out of town over the Clove Brook. There were many homes constructed of wood here, with rather large and ornate designs.

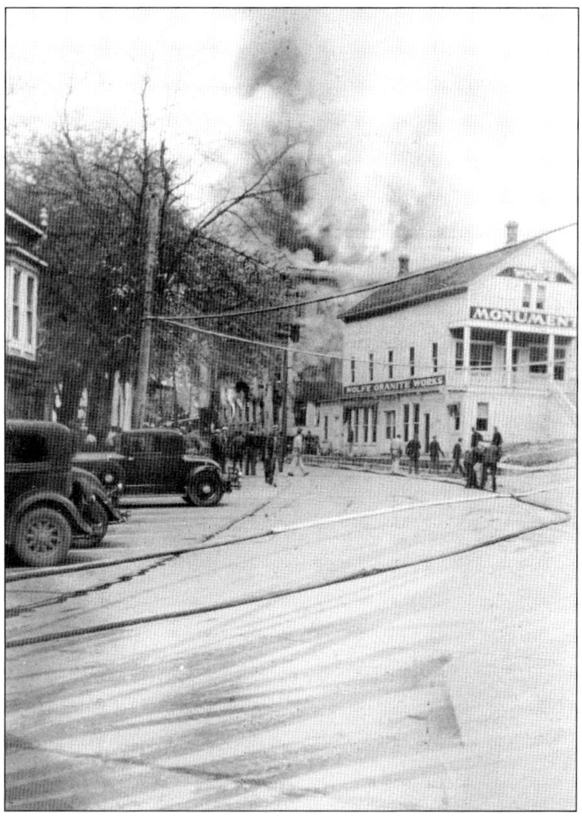

Here is a view of the day of the largest fire in Sussex. On October 22, 1937, the Radio Kimmel Building (the old Booth Brothers' wooden structure on Main Street) burned down. Other fire departments responded, including from Franklin and Vernon.

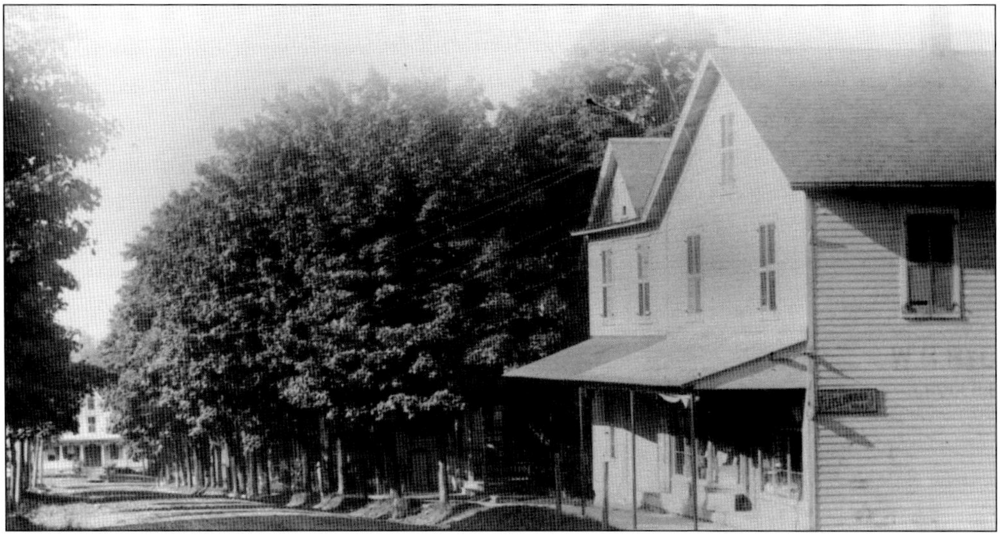

This view is looking downhill toward today's Route 23 from Munson Street. A grocery store is to the right. Amos Munson, who subdivided a large area for homes in the late 1800s, owned this large plot of land. Town historian Howard Case's grandfather John Jensen had a general store at Liberty and Munson Streets near the Harrison House. Jensen was from Scandinavia and spent time with town painter and artist Louie Larsen since they were from the same area of Europe.

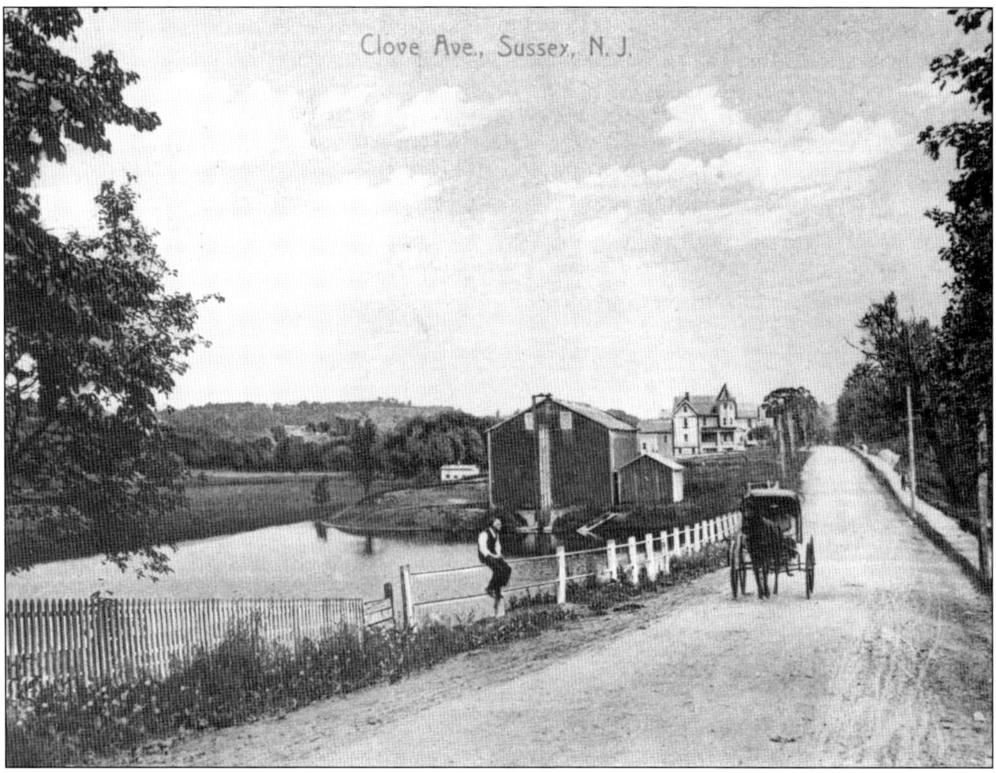

This street view is looking north as one heads out of town on what was known then as Clove Avenue. The Clove Pond is seen to the left above the dam. In the distance is an icehouse to store the ice harvested off the lake in the winter.

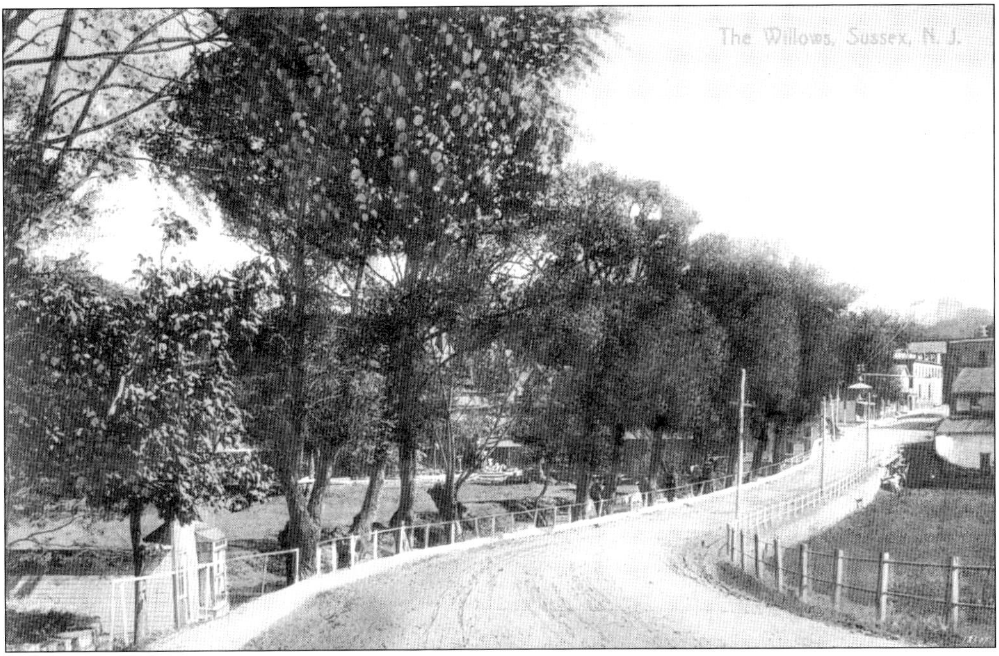

On the west side of town is Loomis Avenue, known today as Sussex County Road 639. There was a lovely copse of willow trees along the wetlands beside the Clove Brook as the brook skirted the low side of town. The street is named after John Loomis (born 1817), who had the following businesses nearby in town: a woolen factory, a gristmill, and a fulling, carding, and clover mill. (Courtesy of Mary Eleanor Eppler.)

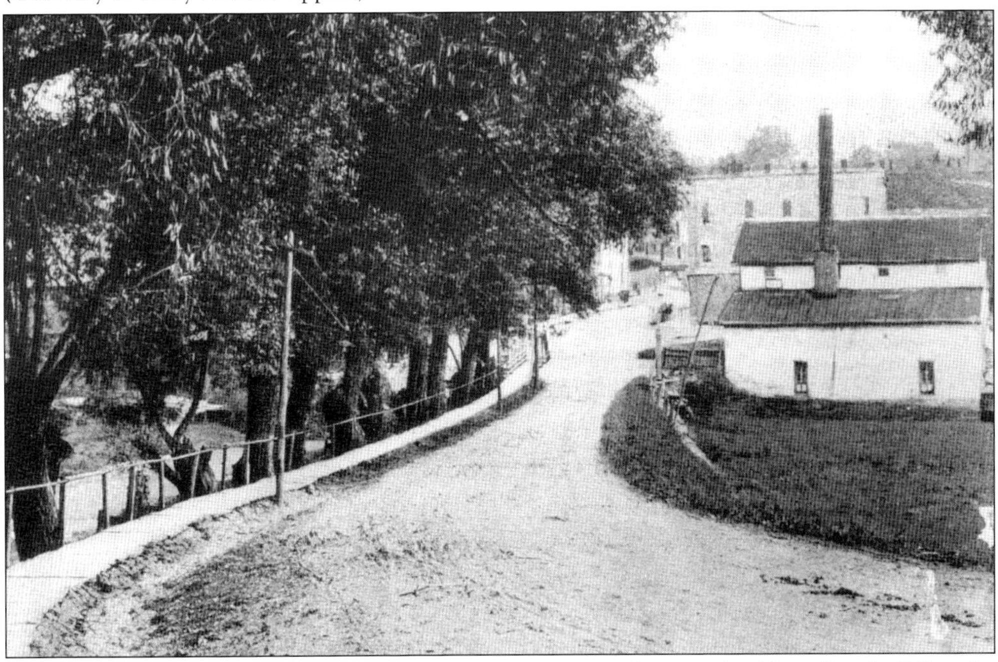

When moving toward town along Loomis Avenue, one gets closer to the Clove Brook. Off to the right is a representative of industry in town. It utilized the waterpower of the Clove Brook, and at the time of this c. 1900 photograph, coal or wood for steam power.

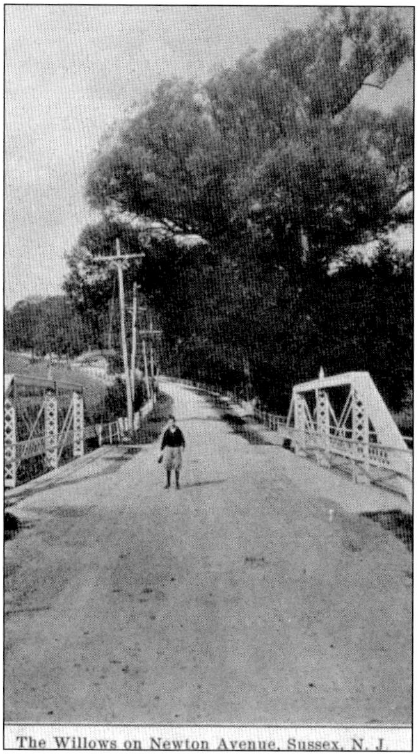

Bridges like the one shown here were typical in Sussex County and had been put in place by the late 1800s. This one is along Loomis Avenue over the Clove Brook. Today's Sussex Borough grammar school is located just to the right of this photograph. (Courtesy of Mary Eleanor Eppler.)

People would come from cities to the east—New York, Newark, Paterson, and the like—to the countryside of Sussex County for fresh air and rest from the sooty and hectic life. One such place to vacation was Vaughan's Sanitarium. A common belief in the late 1800s (before the time of antibiotics) was that rest and good nutrition helped people to ward off sickness or to recover from illnesses such as tuberculosis. (Courtesy of Olga Bazylevich Stefkowich and family of Mike the Jeweler.)

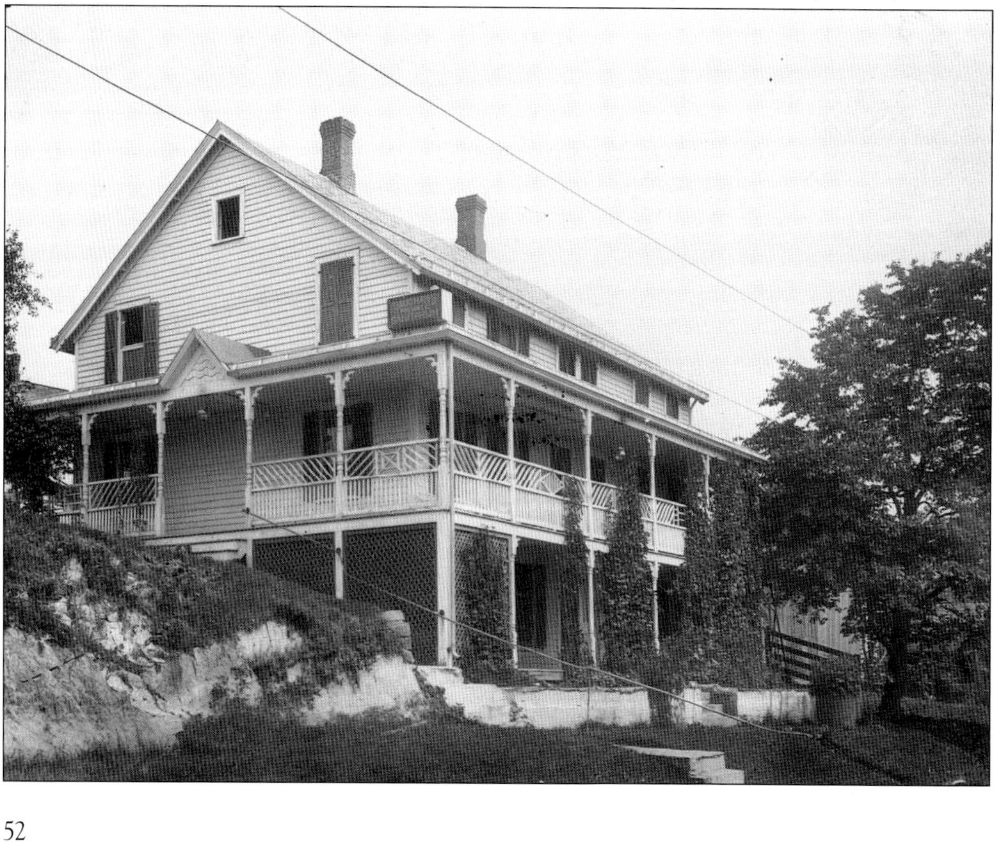

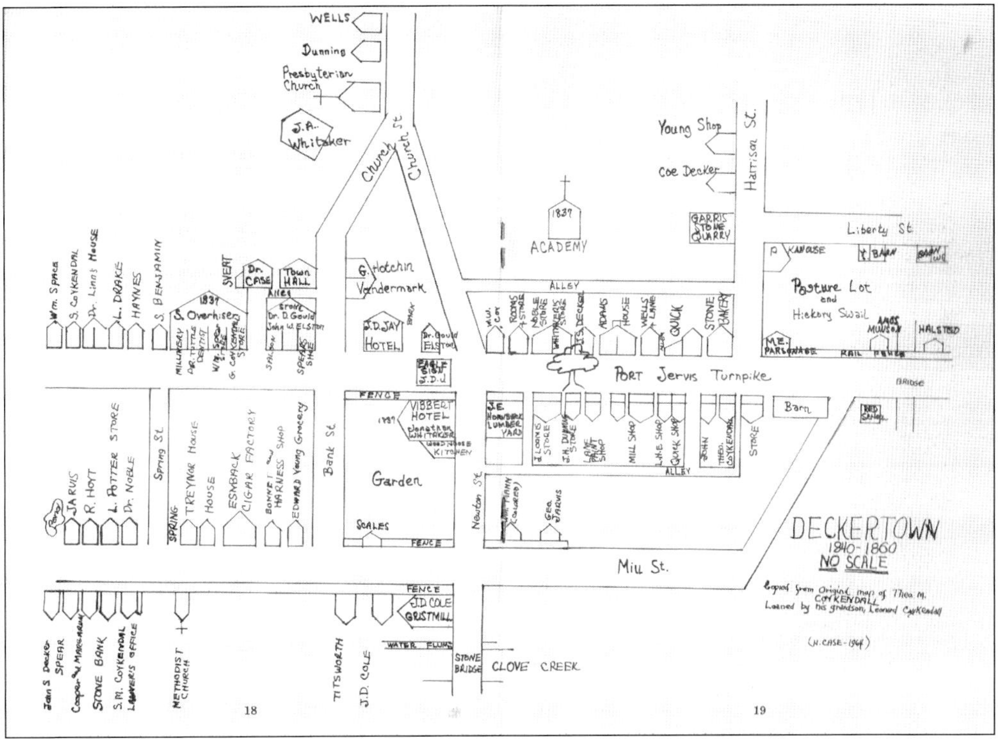

This map is a representation of the dwellings and businesses in Deckertown during the years 1840–1860, reproduced from an original map by Thea M. Coykendall that was loaned by his grandson Leonared Coykendall and provided by town historian Howard Case in 1964. (Courtesy of Howard Case.)

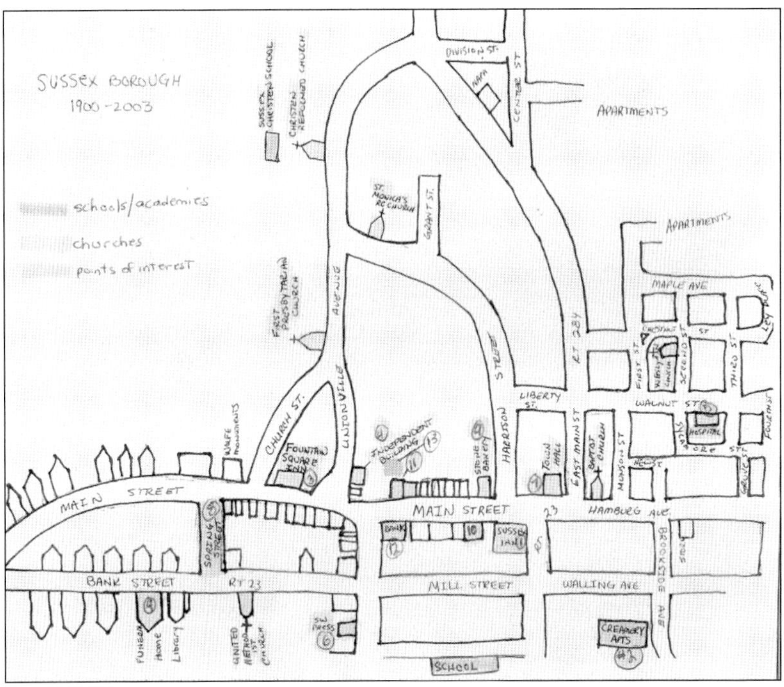

Shown here is a map created by Mary Case that shows a general layout of the dwellings and businesses of Sussex Borough during the 20th century. Several landmarks have remained, such as the Presbyterian church, the Methodist church, and the hotel in the square. (Courtesy of Mary Case.)

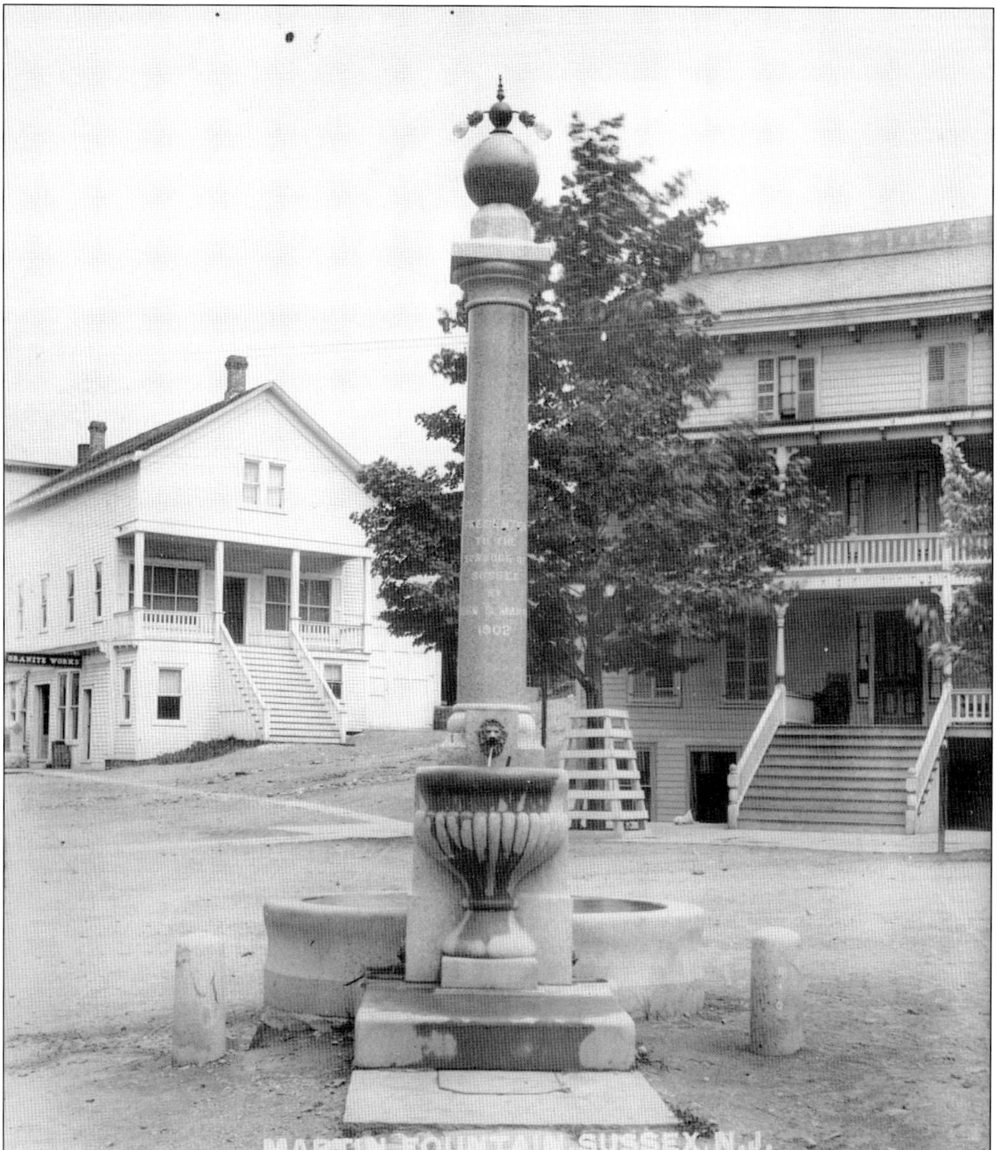

There were three fountains in Sussex, all of which were donated to the town in the early 20th century. Fountain Square's fountain was donated by John F. Martin in 1902 and is located in the middle of town near the Fountain Inn. Thomas Jefferson Dunn donated the other two in 1902 and 1906. The following photographs shows these fountains over time. (Courtesy of Olga Bazylevich Stefkowich and family of Mike the Jeweler.)

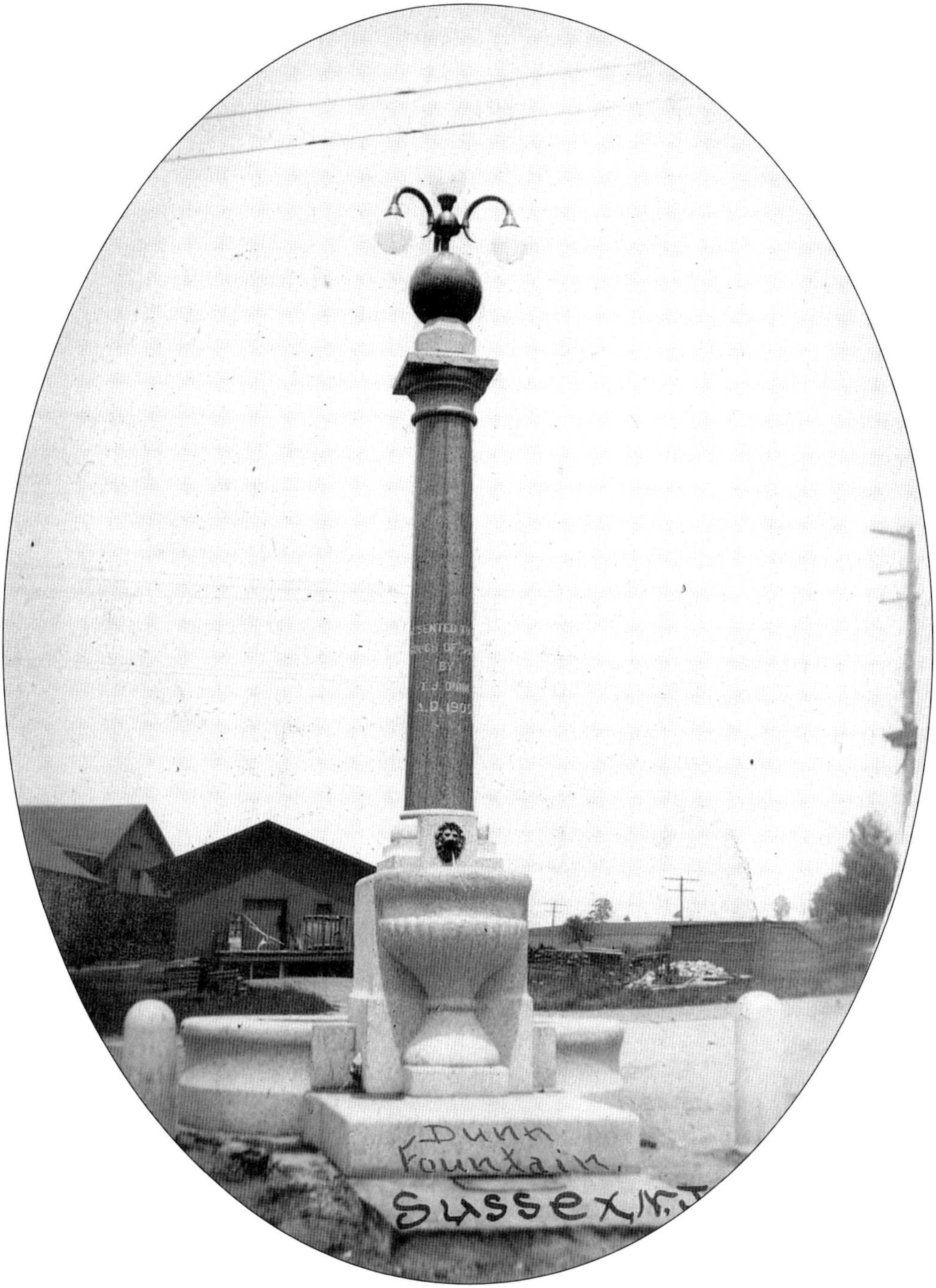

The 1902 Dunn fountain is located uphill to the north on Munson Street near the location of the NYS&W Railroad station and the Harrison House. Neither building is still standing. (From Sparta Public Library.) Here is a poem about the man who gave the fountain, by Peter Lott, Unionville farmer poet: "Generations will go and generations will come / To honor the giver, Jefferson Dunn / We will never forget his generous deeds, / For well he knew our village needs."

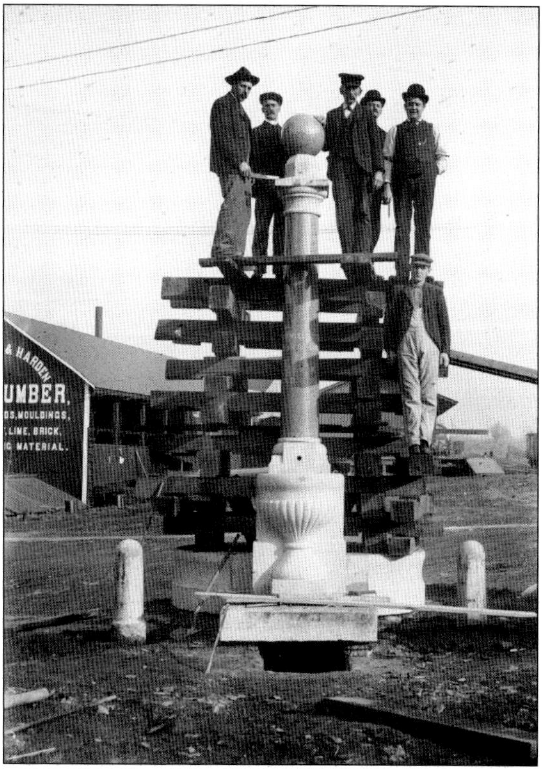

This photograph shows the construction of the Dunn fountain at NYS&W depot in 1904–1906. The man in derby and shirtsleeves is Harry Harrison. The lumberyard and the railroad station can be seen in the background. Here is some insight on how the heavy and bulky fountains were installed.

Of the three fountains, the one in Fountain Square is still a highlighted landmark for the town. The other two have fallen into disrepair. On January 2, 1906, a fountain was recognized at Mill Street, near the creamery complex and the Sussex station of the L&NE Railroad, which came off of a siding from the mainline and has recently been removed.

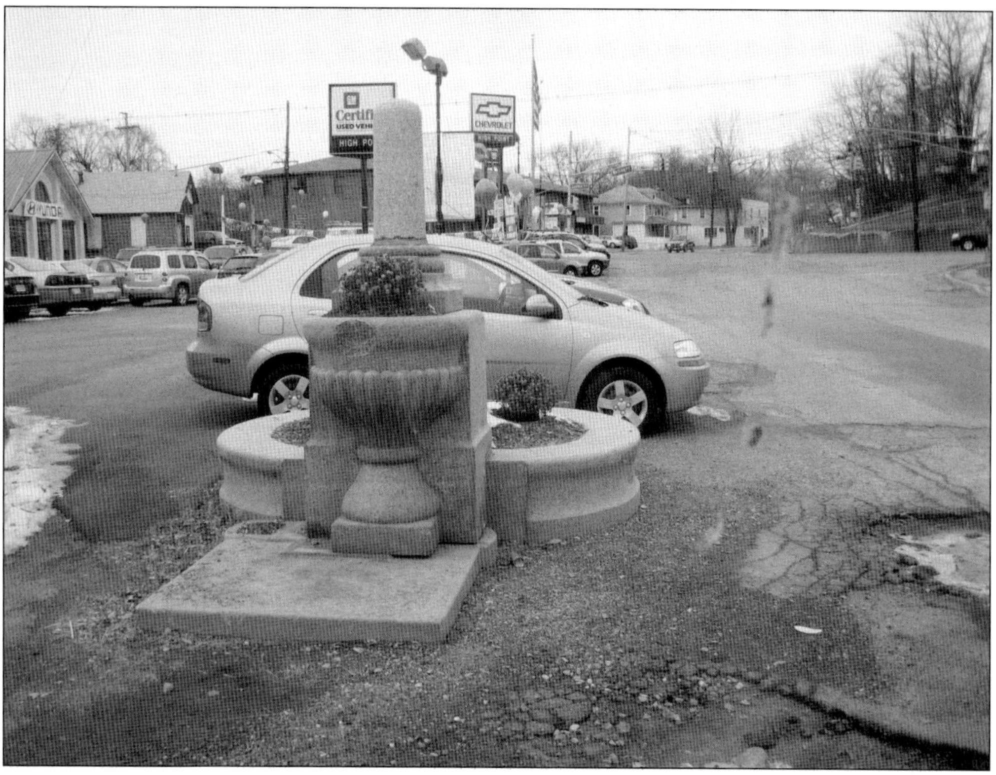

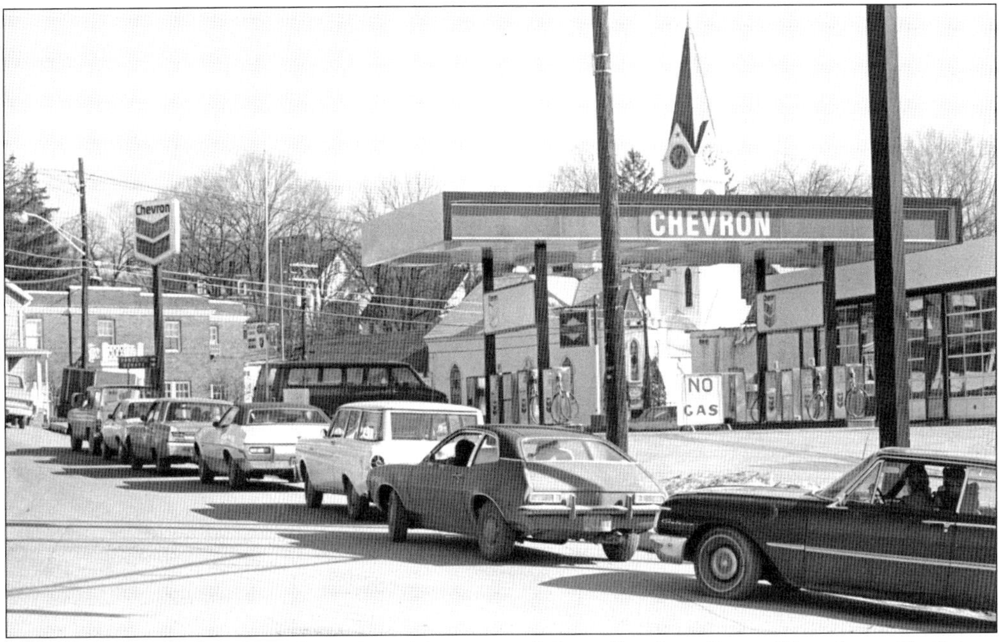

Here is a typical scene from the 1970s of the automobile traffic along Route 23 at the traffic lights. While the cars have changed, the traffic is still abundant. Route 23 and the road to Unionville and also Newton have kept Sussex a hub of transportation throughout the region.

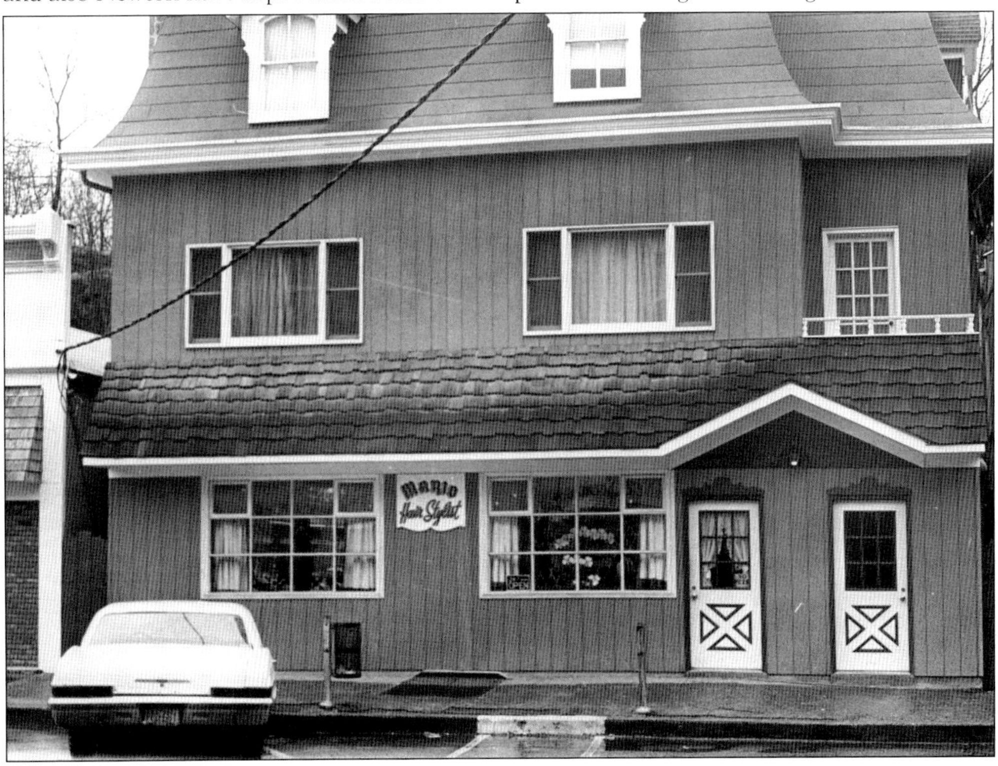

This very old wooden building is one of a few on Main Street, Sussex, that still remain after all these years. Most of the wooden buildings have been replaced with brick or stone.

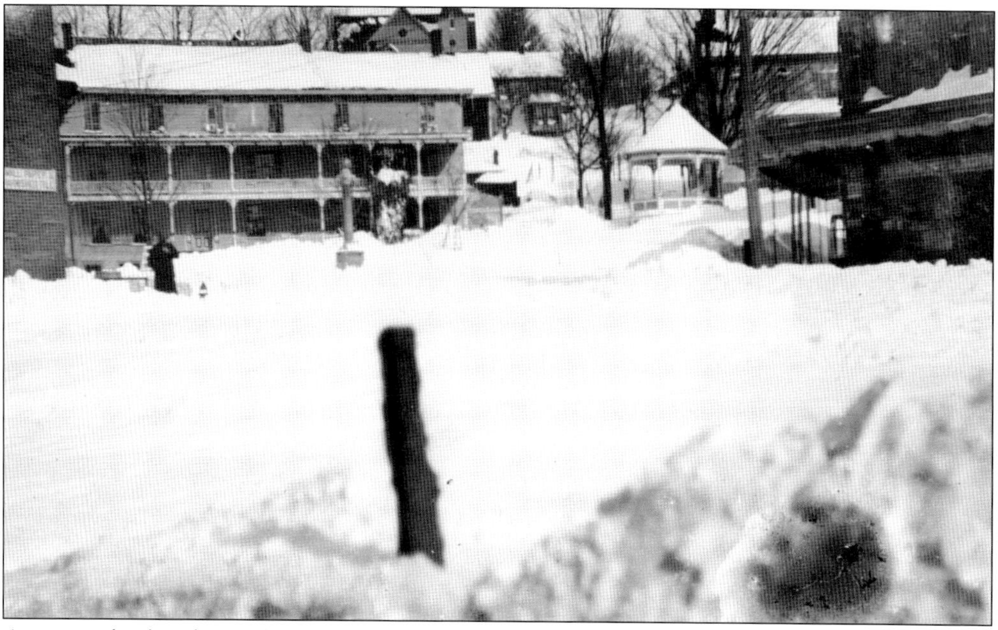

A snowy day breaks, with a view from the hitching post toward Fountain Square. Note that the hitching post has been cleared out for use by a horse and wagon when business starts up for the day.

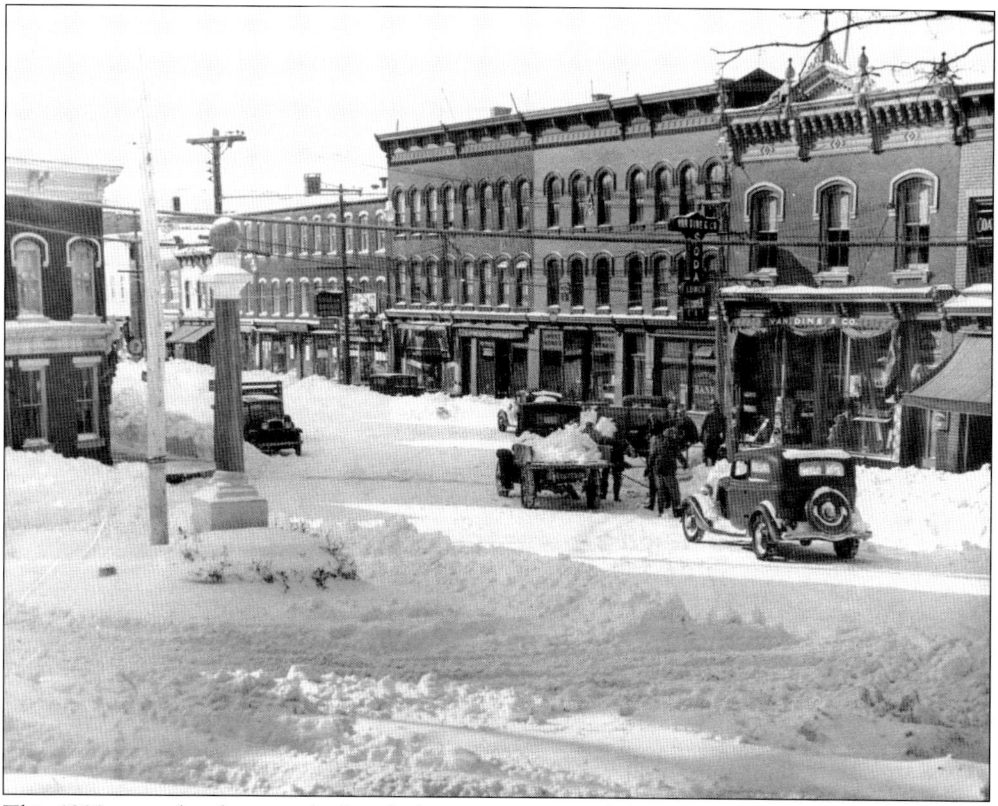

This 1930s snow has been pushed aside for cars to pass and the community to begin its day.

Four

LIFE AROUND TOWN

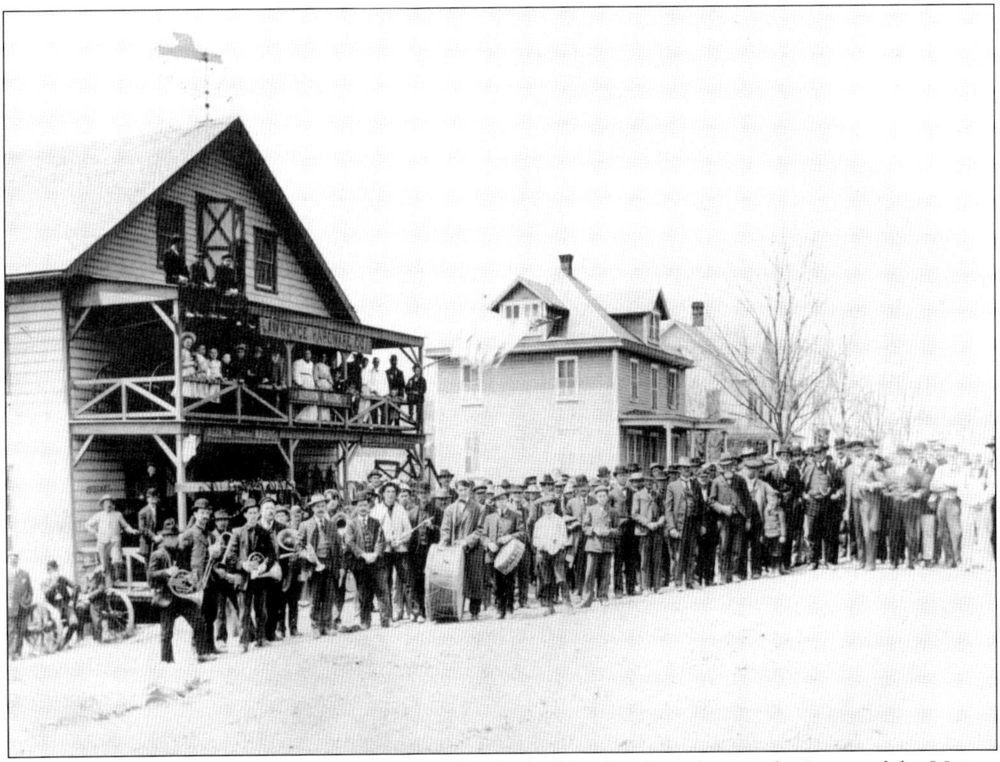

This is an early photograph from Sussex, and it looks like the day of a parade. Some of the Union Band is shown along with other interested men. They are in front of Lawrence Hardware along Hamburg Avenue about 1909. (Courtesy of Haley Dickson Lawrence.)

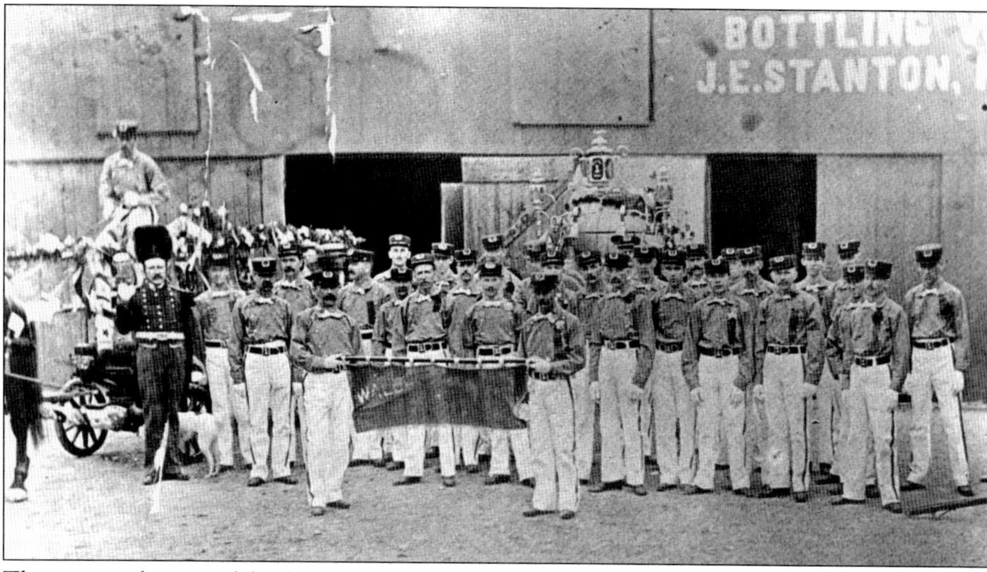

This is an early view of the fire company in Deckertown, shown at the barn off Main Street. The horse-drawn pumper is visible in the background. Note the fancy uniforms. There were horse barns behind the Goble Inn that burned, and a fire engine from Newton was summoned via railroad. This prompted the town to create a fire department. On February 11, 1896, the Wallkill Hose Company was formed in rooms in back of the Wolfe Granite Company, as can be seen in this series of photographs. The Protection Hook and Ladder Company was established just thereafter on February 24, 1896, on Hamburg Avenue.

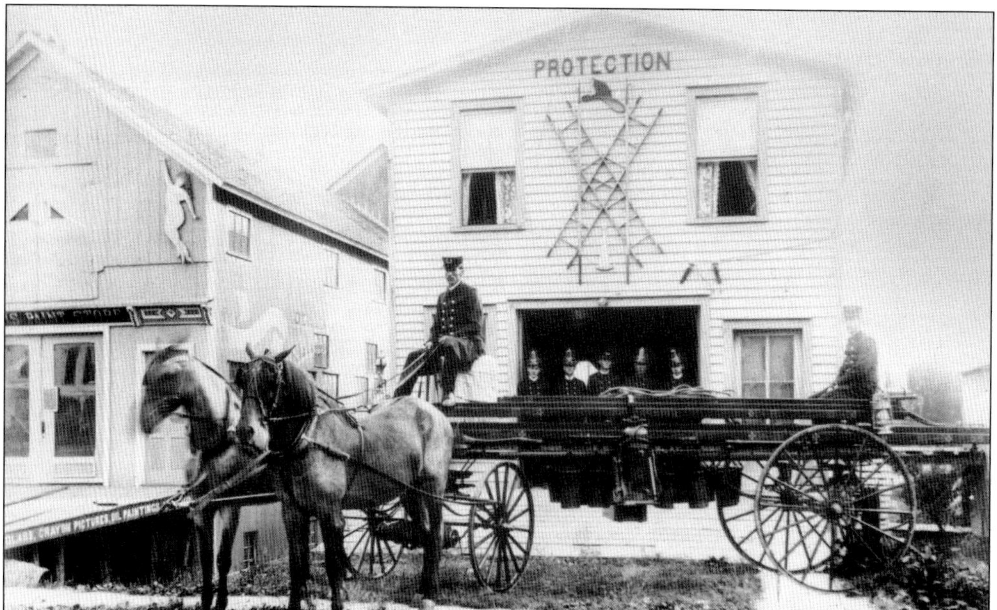

Around 1905, the fire department consisted of a hook and ladder company and also a hose company. Here is a view of the horse-drawn hook and ladder wagon along with the equipment for the bucket brigade. Members of this company were known at the time as the Protection Hook and Ladder Company.

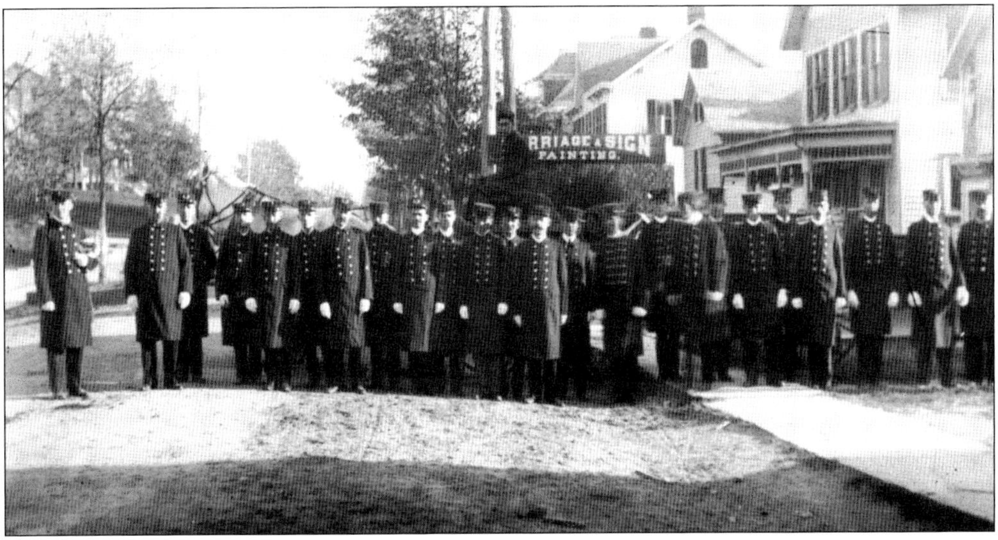

Here are the men who participated in the hook and ladder company on Hamburg Avenue.

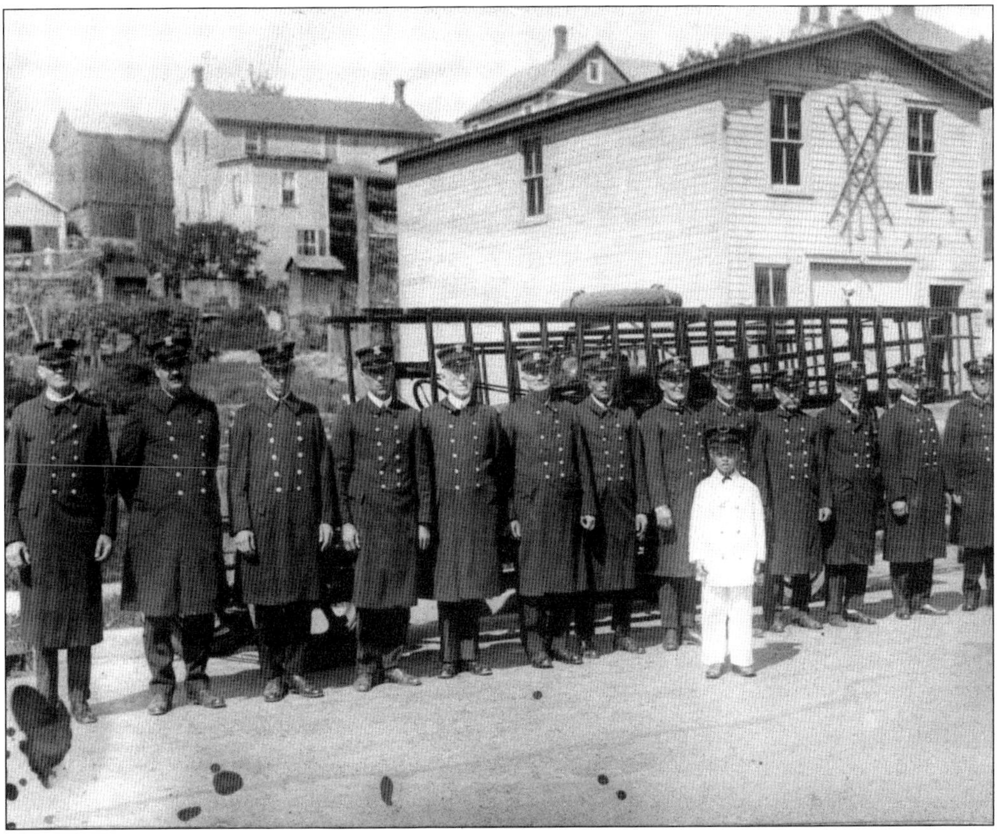

Members of the Sussex Fire Department around 1919 are, from left to right, Charlie Williams, Tom Trudgeon (blacksmith and constable), two unidentified, Jim Adams (barber), Pete Hammond (shoe store), unidentified, Charlie Draper, two unidentified, Carl Becker (Lawrence Hardware employee), unidentified, and Arthur "Art" Henry Crabb, chief of the fire department. The boy mascot is Arthur James "Jim" Crabb, also known as "Art." (Courtesy of Mrs. Theodore Holbert.)

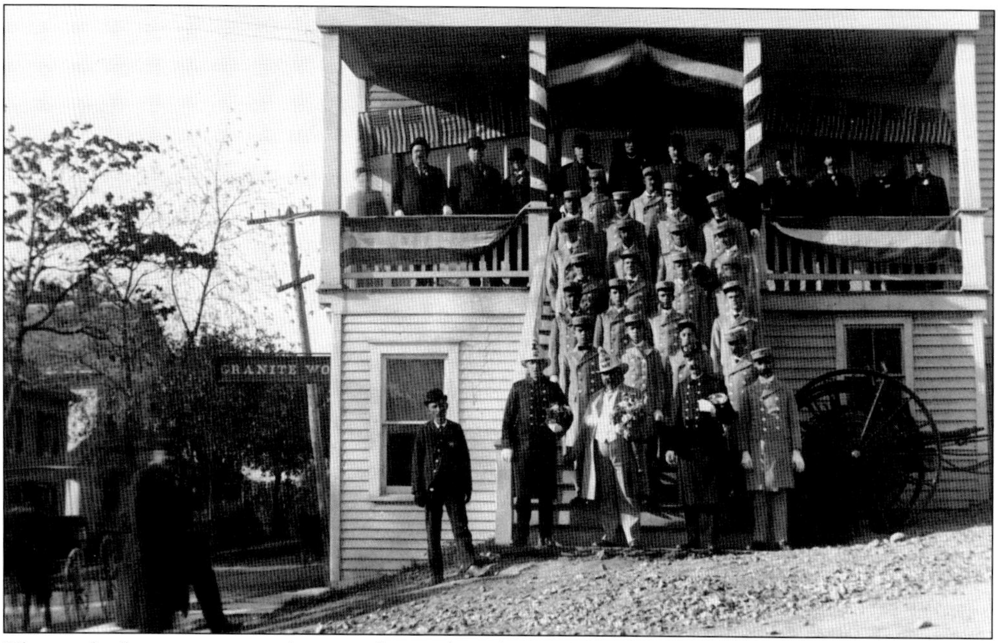

This is the hose company that was located in the middle of town near the Goble Inn next to the Wolfe Granite works. Note the hand-drawn cart that was used to drag the hoses to the fire. The pumper was shown in a previous photograph. Members were known at the time as Hose Company No. 1.

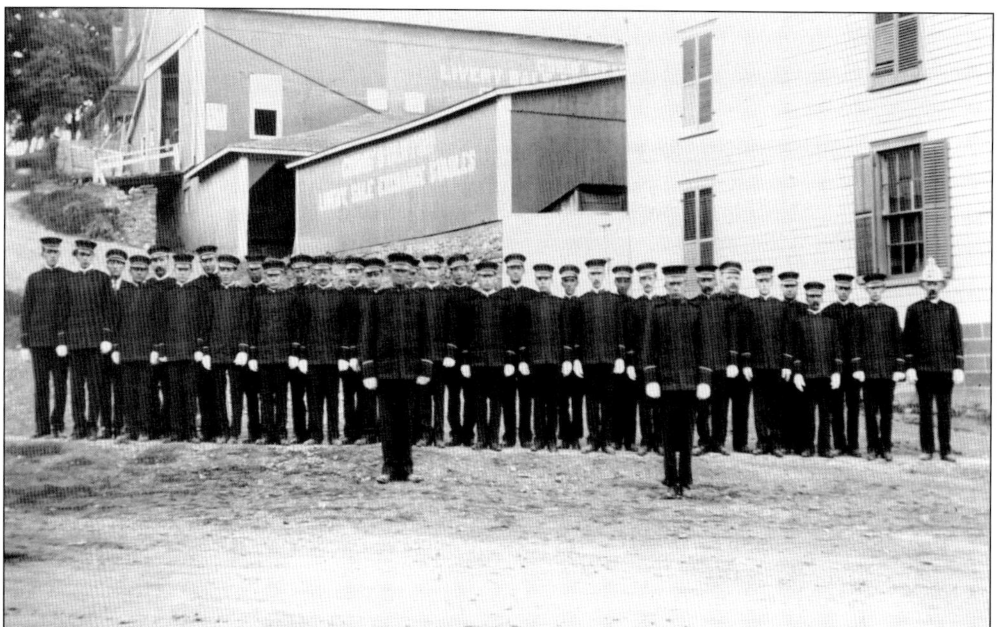

This photograph shows a contingent of men dressed in uniform at the foot of Church Street in Sussex Borough ready for a parade. Note Chris Stanton's Livery—stables for the horses were a part of everyday life. The roadway is very steep for a horse and also a carriage, but this image shows the importance of Sussex Borough where roadways intersected between the city, Port Jervis, Newton, and Unionville and New York state to the north.

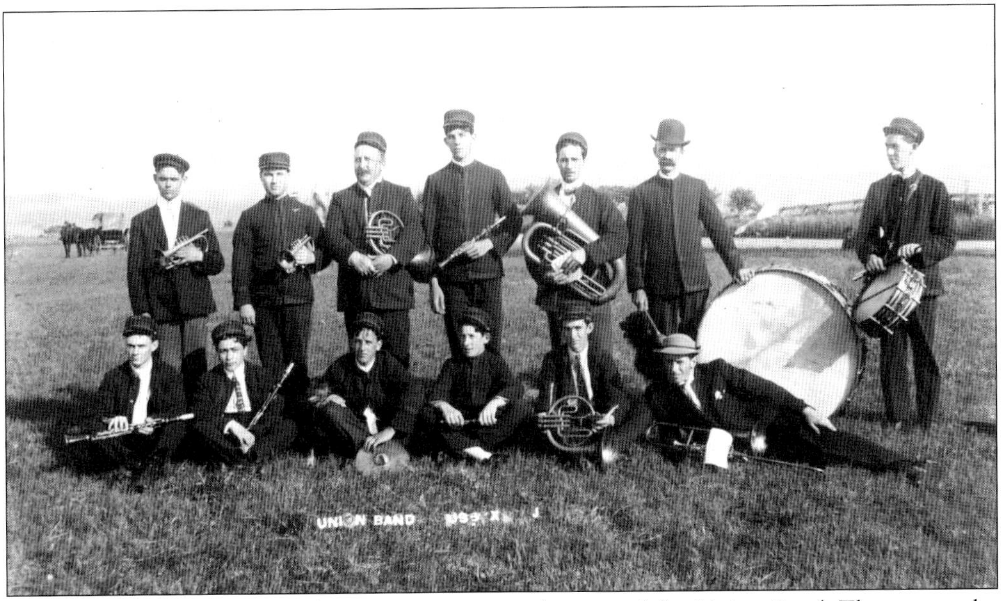

Shown in full uniform with their instruments are the men of the Union Band. They are at the Wantage Driving Park area above Sussex on the way to Unionville, New York, with the view to the east.

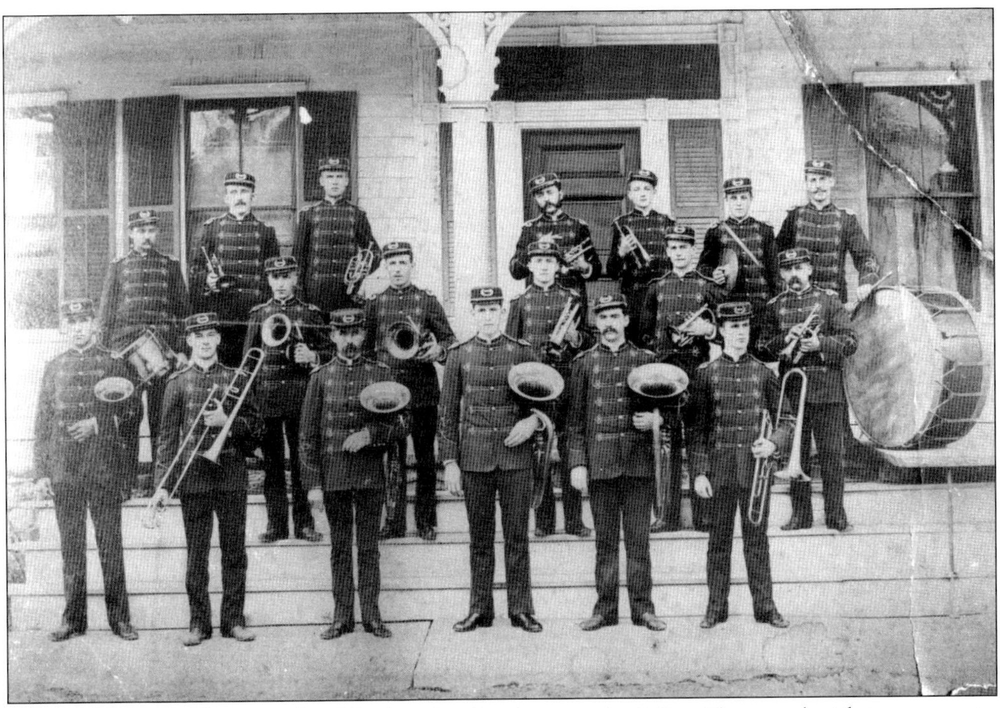

This is a very old photograph of the band at Deckertown in full uniform and with instruments, standing on the steps of the Union House (now Sussex Inn) before the roadway was lowered and the bottom floor revealed.

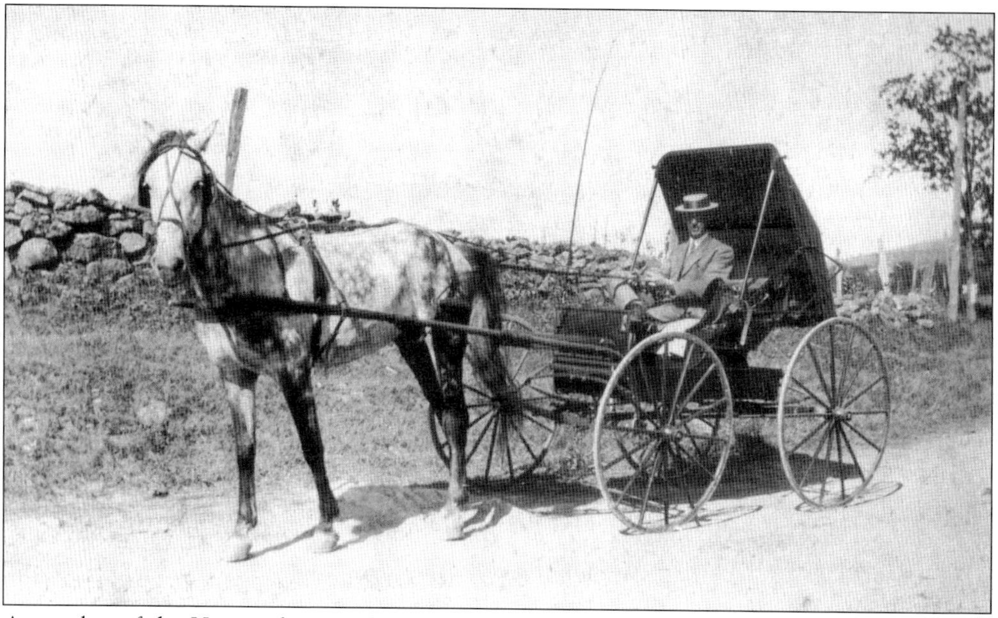

A member of the Havens farming family, and Wantage resident, heads out in his Sunday best with a smartly attentive horse. (Courtesy Havens family.)

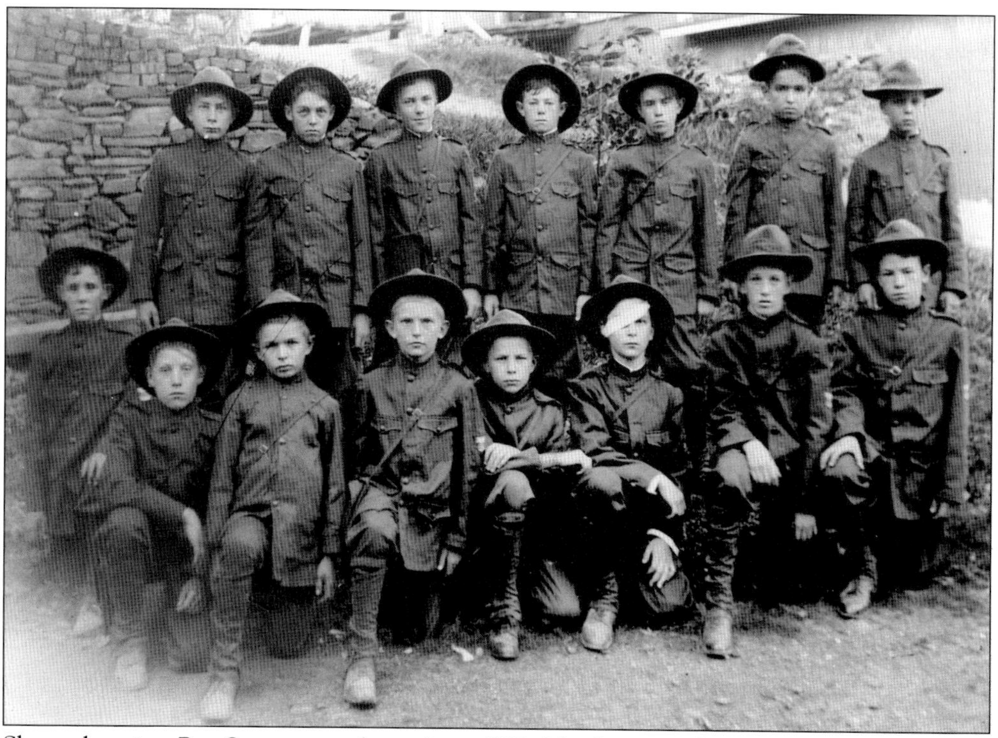

Shown here is a Boy Scout troop from about 1912. Members are, from left to right, (first row) Howard Niles, Everett Babb, Charles McCoy, Jay Wilson, Frawley, Ernest Nass, Jim Williams, and Lee Johnson; (second row) Percy Dunn, DeWitt Wilson, Charles Stanton, Stub Kimble, Harvey Perry, Kenneth McNair, and Larry Wilson.

Here is an early parade coming down the dirt Main Street of Sussex. Note the pumper in the distant background and the teenagers walking alongside the firemen. The horses and carriages are tied up at the hitching posts while the people watch the parade. On September 26, 1902, there was a large parade in Sussex for the veterans of the 15th Regiment of New Jersey Volunteers; these were Civil War veterans.

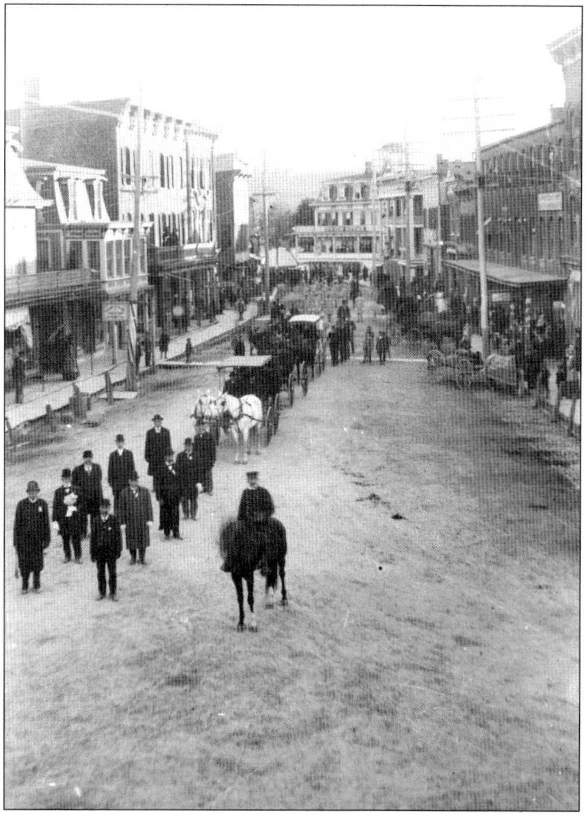

Here is a view of the Union House when the Dicksons were the proprietors. There is abundant bunting for some festive occasion. The brothers of the Benevolent and Protective Order of Elks are invited. Note the sign in the foreground for the Women's Christian Temperance Union (WCTU), which was very prevalent in the early 1900s. This was before Prohibition and also before women could vote. The sign reads that there is free lemonade and ice water.

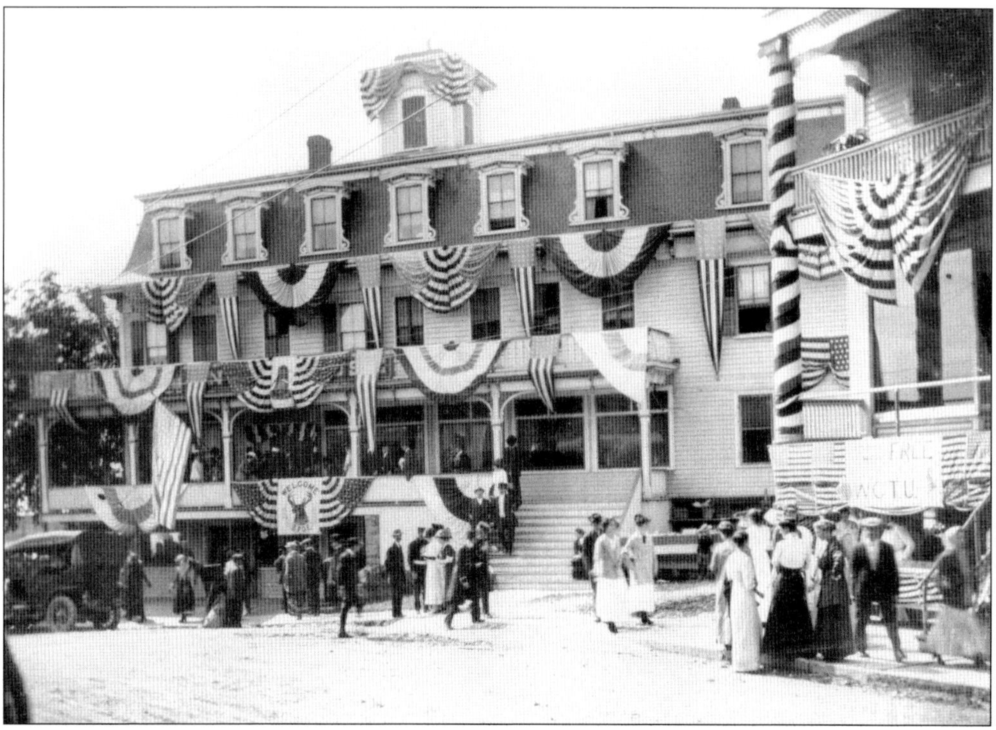

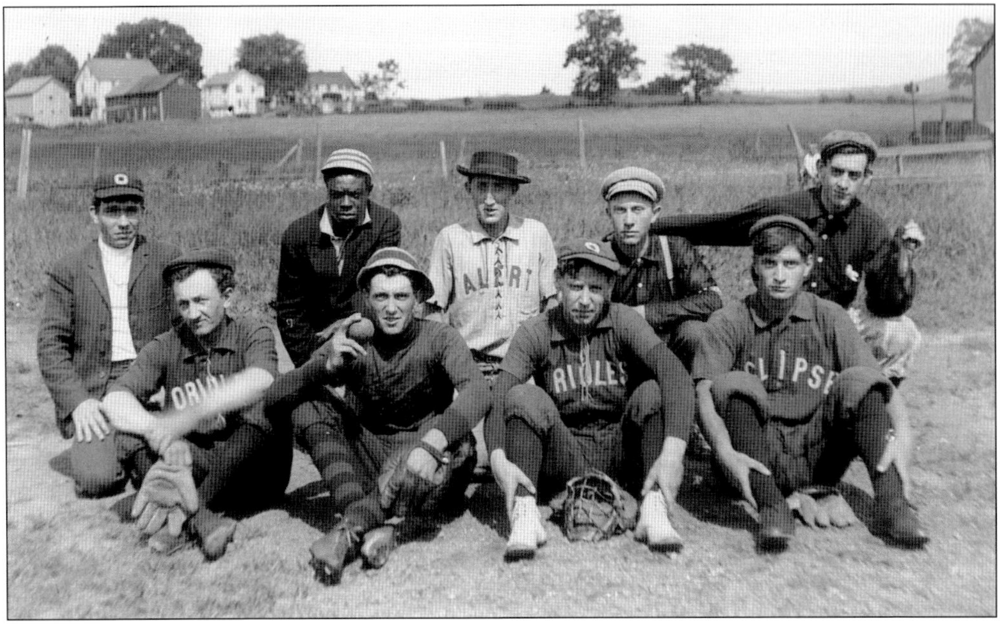

Here is the men's baseball team around 1910. Pictured are, from left to right, (first row) Art Bowman, Harry Sager, and two unidentified; (second row) two unidentified, Matt Van Gelder, John Paugh, and Sief Ray. A small farm boy stands along the fence in the distance.

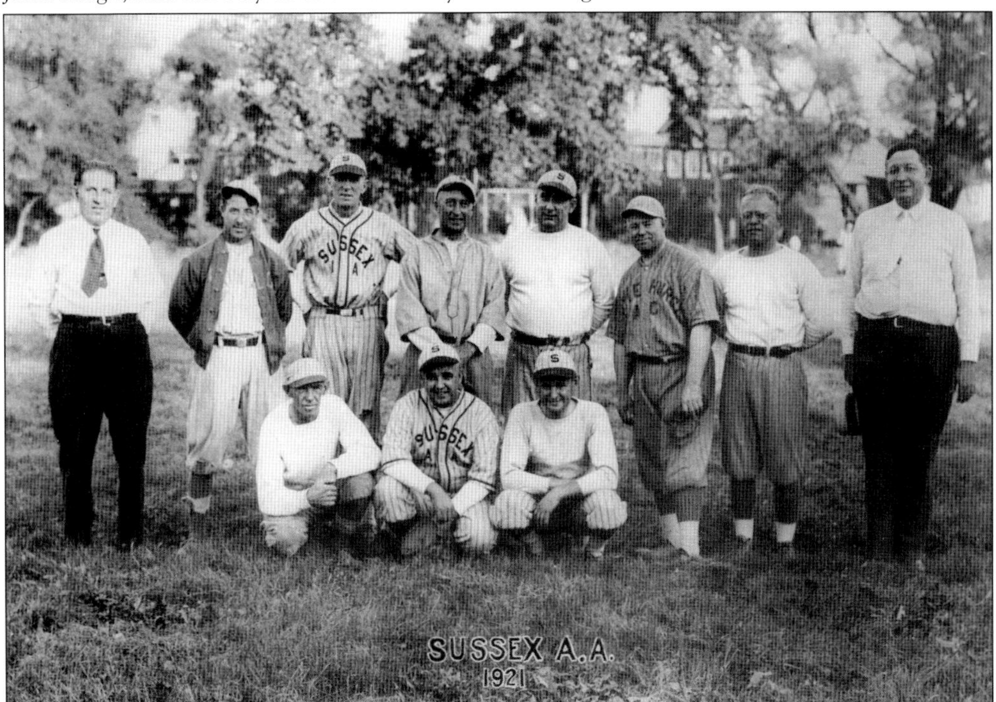

The Sussex Athletic Association is shown in its glory in 1921; pictured are, from left to right, (first row) Lou Van Riper, Hipe Runyon, and Harvey Dickson; (second row) Nick Jonson, Bunny Standfield, Harry Sager, Everitt "Polly" Paulson, Frank Simon, Stub Kimble, Claude Pinkle, and Irv Shorter. (Photograph by Walter Freck.)

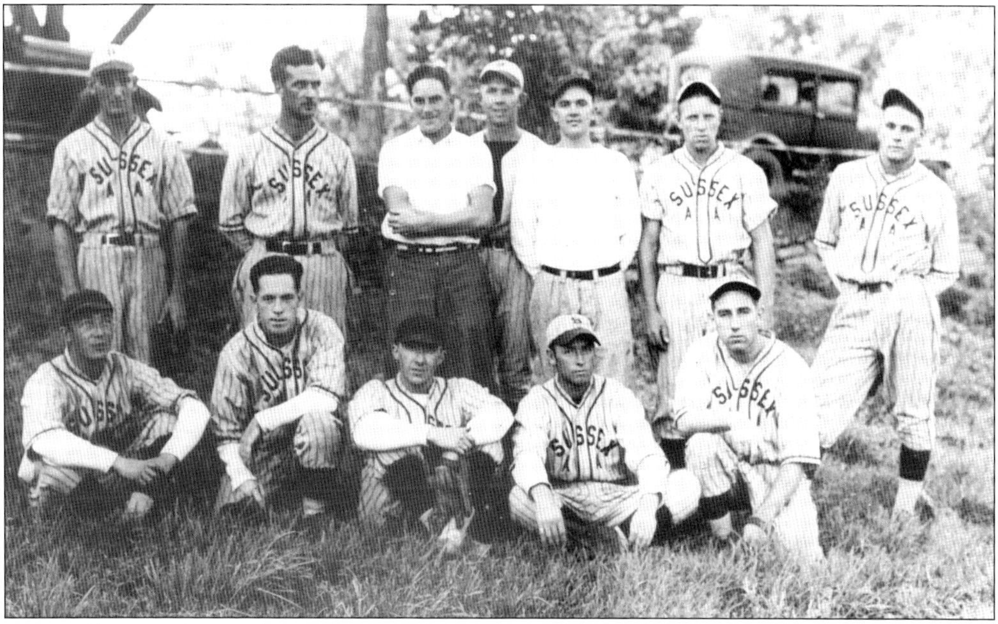

Pictured here on September 13, 1932, is the Sussex Athletic Association baseball team. Pictured are, from left to right, (sitting) Paul Harrison, Willard French, Harry Harrison, Bill Bird, and Walt Lewis; (standing) Fini Knapp, Scott McKee, Don Henderson (killed in a car accident five hours after the picture was taken), Chas Miller, Don Christie, Bucky Beemer, and Pres Conklin. (Photograph by Walter S. Fresh.)

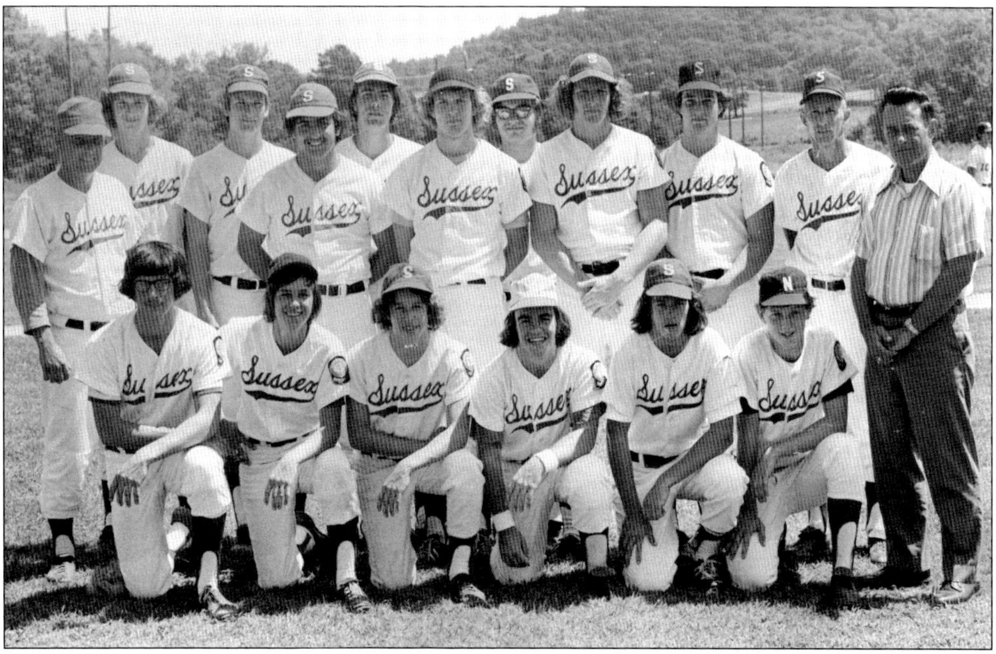

Here is a Sussex baseball team from the 1970s. This team included some students from the high school. The school had moved over the years from on top of the hill above Main Street, down to the field alongside the Clove Brook, and then, in the late 1960s, up to the hill above the present-day Sussex Airport in the locality of Woodbourne.

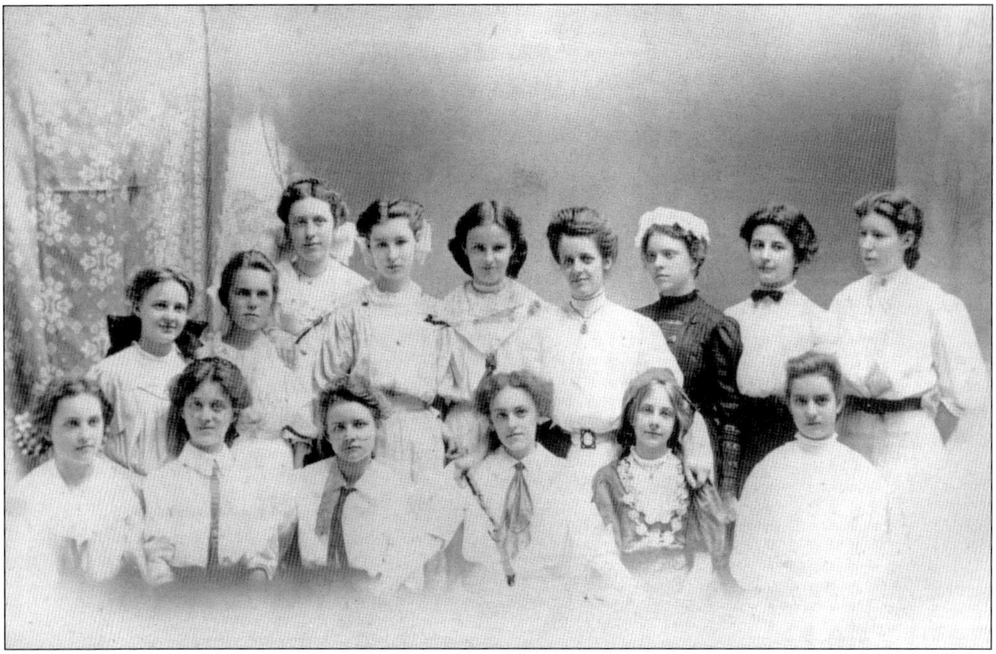

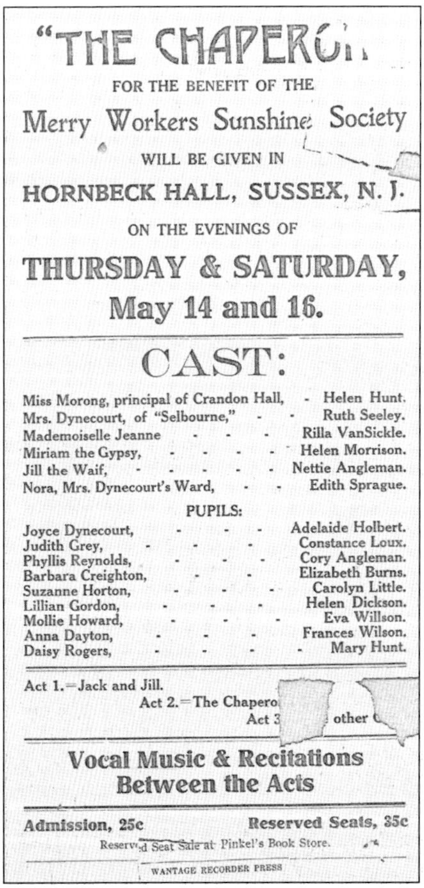

"THE CHAPERO[...]

FOR THE BENEFIT OF THE

Merry Workers Sunshine Society

WILL BE GIVEN IN

HORNBECK HALL, SUSSEX, N. J.

ON THE EVENINGS OF

THURSDAY & SATURDAY,

May 14 and 16.

CAST:

Miss Morong, principal of Crandon Hall,	Helen Hunt.
Mrs. Dynecourt, of "Selbourne,"	Ruth Seeley.
Mademoiselle Jeanne	Rilla VanSickle.
Miriam the Gypsy,	Helen Morrison.
Jill the Waif,	Nettie Angleman.
Nora, Mrs. Dynecourt's Ward,	Edith Sprague.

PUPILS:

Joyce Dynecourt,	Adelaide Holbert.
Judith Grey,	Constance Loux.
Phyllis Reynolds,	Cory Angleman.
Barbara Creighton,	Elizabeth Burns.
Suzanne Horton,	Carolyn Little.
Lillian Gordon,	Helen Dickson.
Mollie Howard,	Eva Willson.
Anna Dayton,	Frances Wilson.
Daisy Rogers,	Mary Hunt.

Act 1.—Jack and Jill.
Act 2.—The Chapero[...]
Act 3[...] other [...]

Vocal Music & Recitations Between the Acts

Admission, 25c — Reserved Seats, 35c

Reserved Seat Sale at Pinkel's Book Store.

WANTAGE RECORDER PRESS

In times before radio, television, computers, cars, and, for many people around here, before telephones and electricity, one might wonder what they did for entertainment. While the men attended their clubs and societies, some of the women became immersed in plays. Here is a photograph from around 1905 of one such event at Hornbeck Hall. Those pictured are, from left to right, (sitting) Rilla Van Sickle, Hattie Angleman, Adelaide Holbert, Constance Loux, Carolyn Little, and Eva Willard; (standing) Helen Hunt, Helen Morrison, Edith Sprague, Ruth Seeley, Helen Dickson (Lawrence), Mary Hunt, Grace Elizabeth Burns, Frances Wilson, and Cory Angleman.

Here is the program for the play performed by the cast in the photograph above. According to an advertisement in the *Wantage Recorder*, "The Chaperone" was a three-act play.

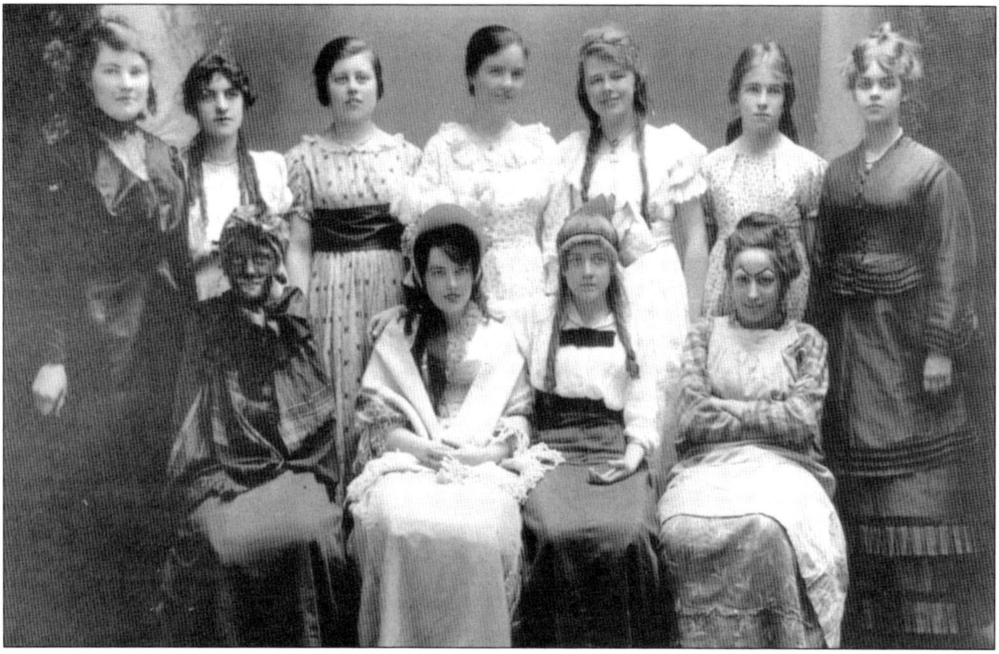

In 1916, the play "The Sunshine Girls: A Fightin' Event" was put on by the Sunshine Society, Laura B. Clark's project. Pictured are, from left to right, (first row) unidentified, Ruth Harrison, Peggy Miller, and Rose Botti; (second row) Viola Neilson, Urena Van Dine, Marie Kimble, Mary Stanton, Lucy Morrison, Ida Harden, and Emma Kerchman.

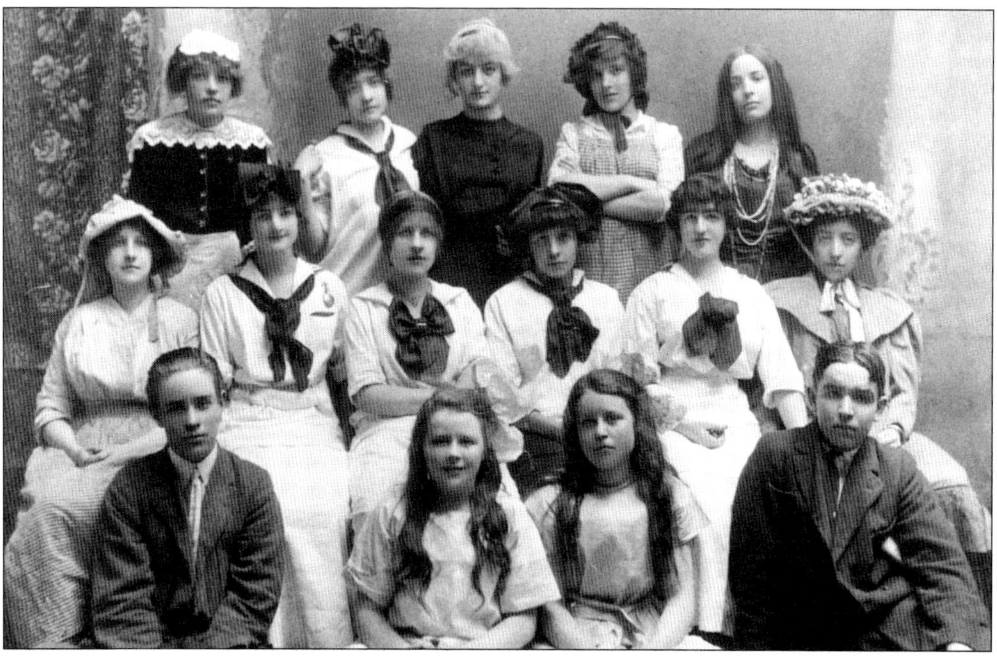

The Sunshine Girls from 1914 are, from left to right, (first row) Lee Perry, Lucy Morrison, Marie Kimble, and Kenneth McNair; (second row) ? Brown, May Bloom, ? Brown, Katherine Botti, Alberta Ward, and Margaret Botti; (third row) Bertha Texton, Peggy Miller, unidentified, Ruth Harrison, and Rose Botti.

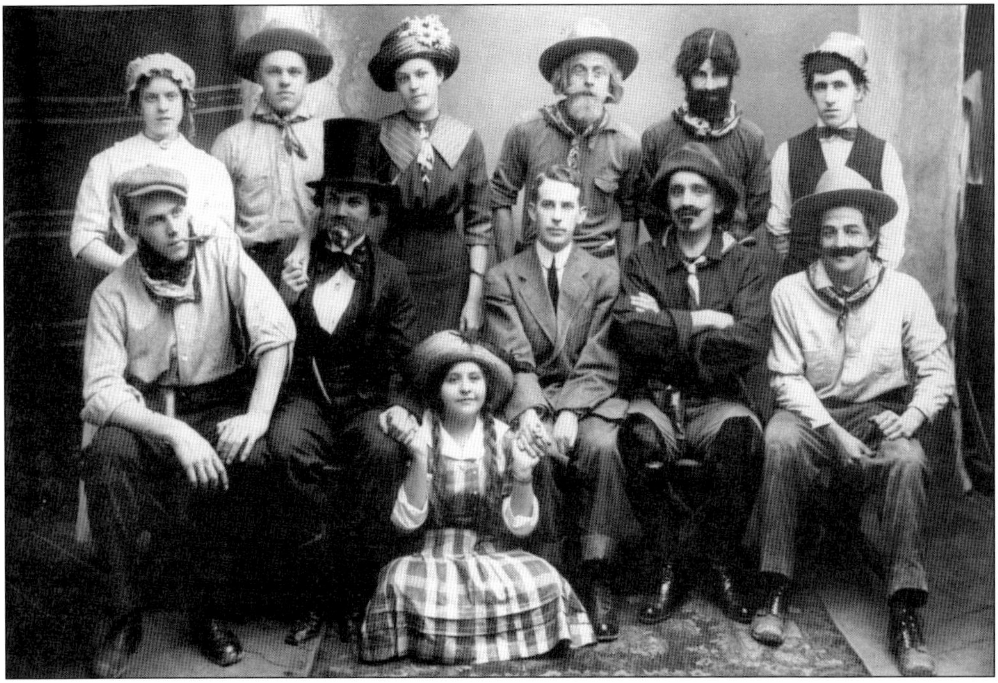

This is the Home Talent Show. Pictured are, from left to right, (sitting) Floyd Youmans, Theodore Holbert, unidentified, Willie Pinkel, Sam Newman, and William Dymock; (standing) Edith Buss, Claude Pinkel, Helen Youmans Wilson, Bile Lawrence, unidentified, and Pee Wee Johnson.

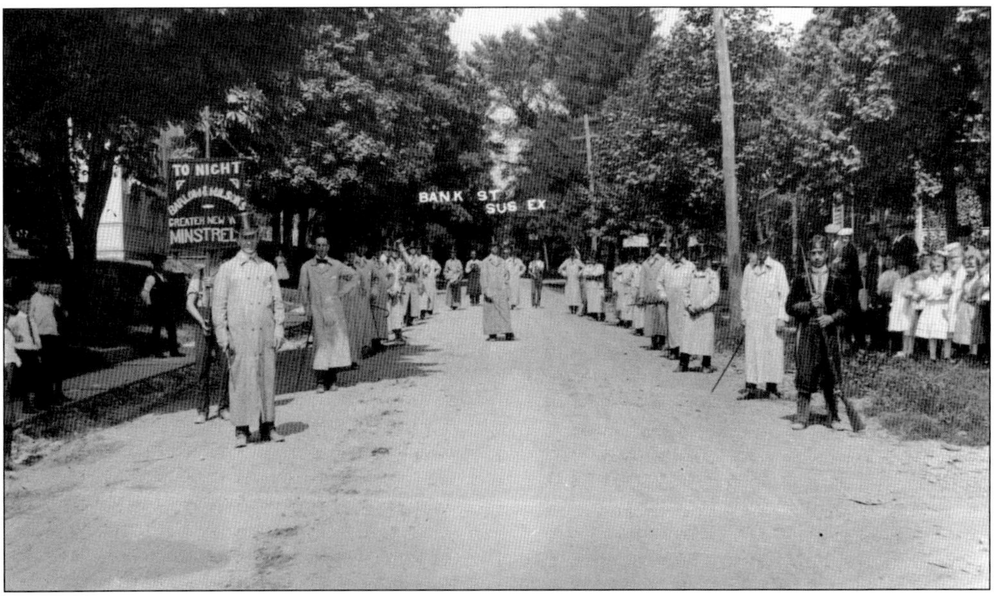

A big event that would pull into town during the summer months was the traveling minstrel show. Traveling minstrels frequented the Northeast during the latter part of the 1800s and provided entertainment for the community before there was much of any other outside influence, except for the telegraph message, stagecoach, and train. Minstrel shows were sort of the forerunner to the circuses that came to town and the vaudeville acts of the city. This particular group is the Barlow and Wilson's Greater New York Minstrels.

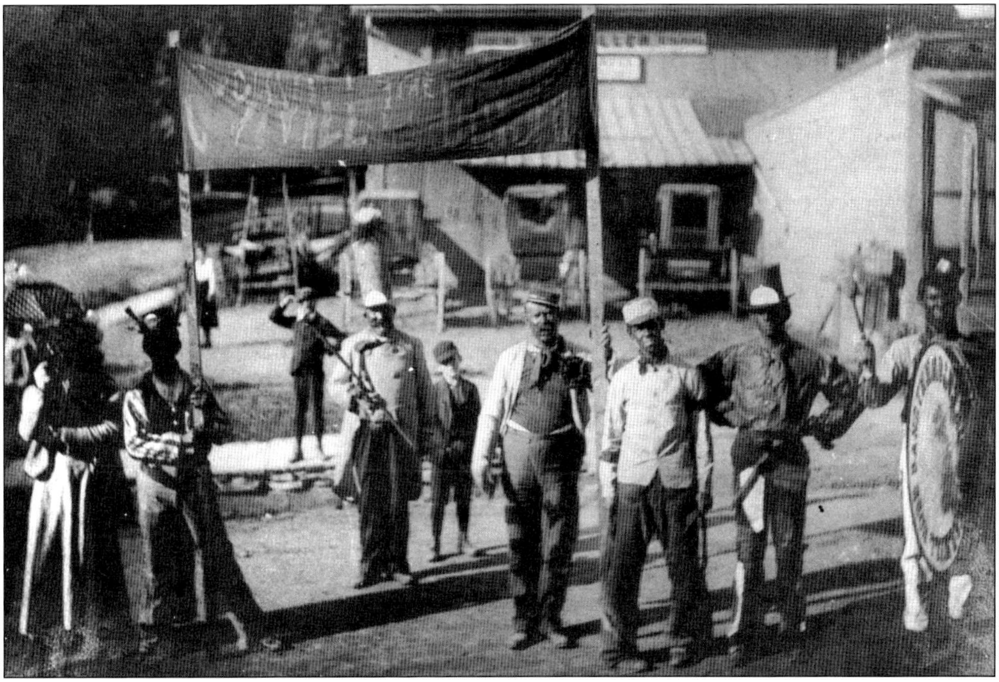

The location of this makeshift minstrel show is by the blacksmith and carriage shops along Newton Avenue and Bank Street. The minstrels brought bands, music, bicycle-riding tricks, jokes, skits, and shows.

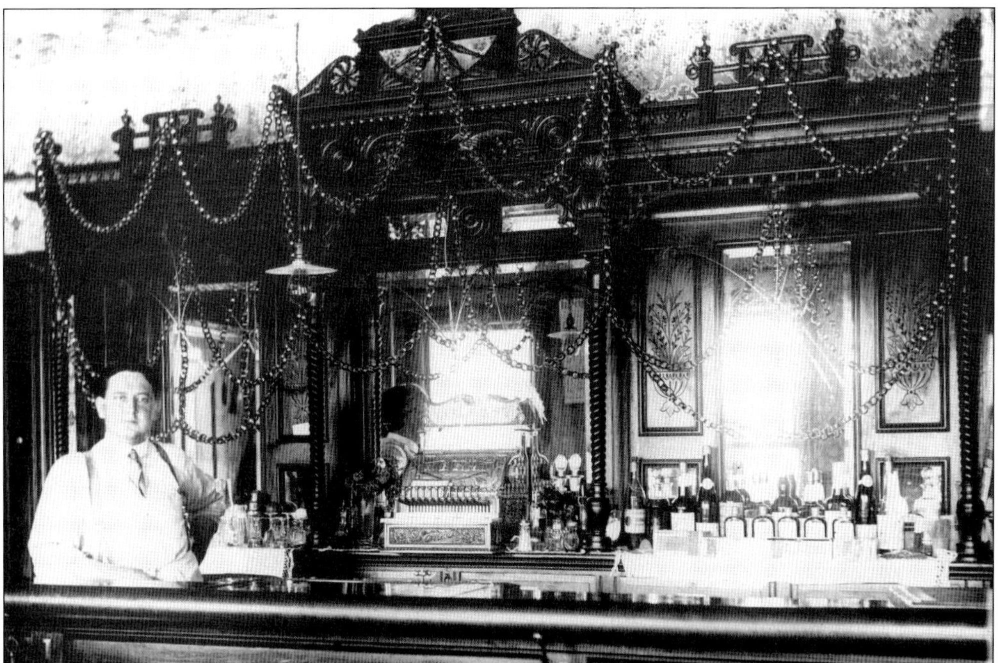

At the top of the hill in Sussex next to the NYS&W Railway station stood the Harrison House, with rooms for travelers and stables in the back for the horses. Taken from a glass-plate negative, this image is of the Harrison House Bar with Harry Harrison in 1904.

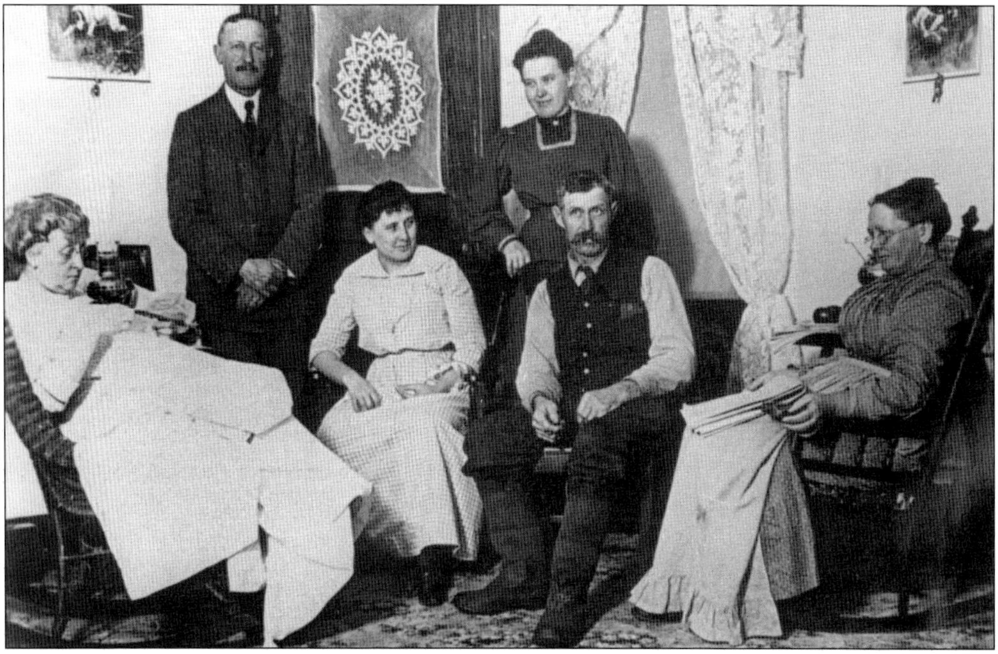

Taken about 1905 at the Goble Inn, this photograph is of the Goble family, with Mrs. Dexter Goble. This was at a time before electricity, as can be determined by the oil lamps for light.

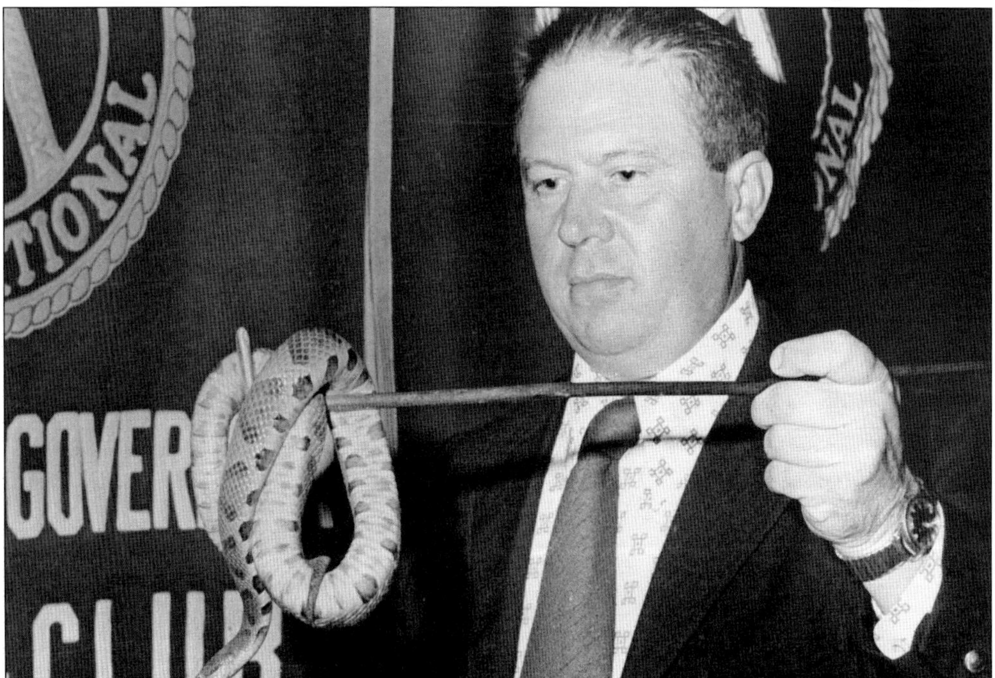

Fred Space Jr. is shown with a live snake at a local Kiwanis Club meeting in the 1960s. Space Farms is the home to many types of animals from around the world. Space Farms is a 100-acre park with over 500 animals, both live and preserved, of more than 100 different species. There are also many buildings dedicated to showcasing American history collections.

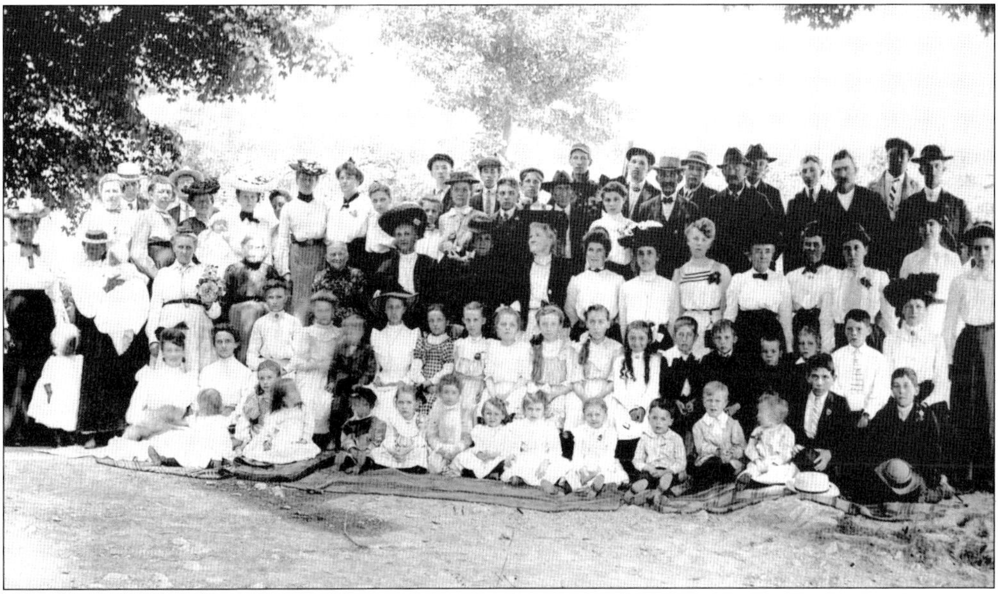

A family outing, either a reunion or picnic, is shown in this picture. According to the notes accompanying the photograph, it was probably taken at the Mount Retirement School site, also known as the (Stiles) Millens farm, around 1903–1904.

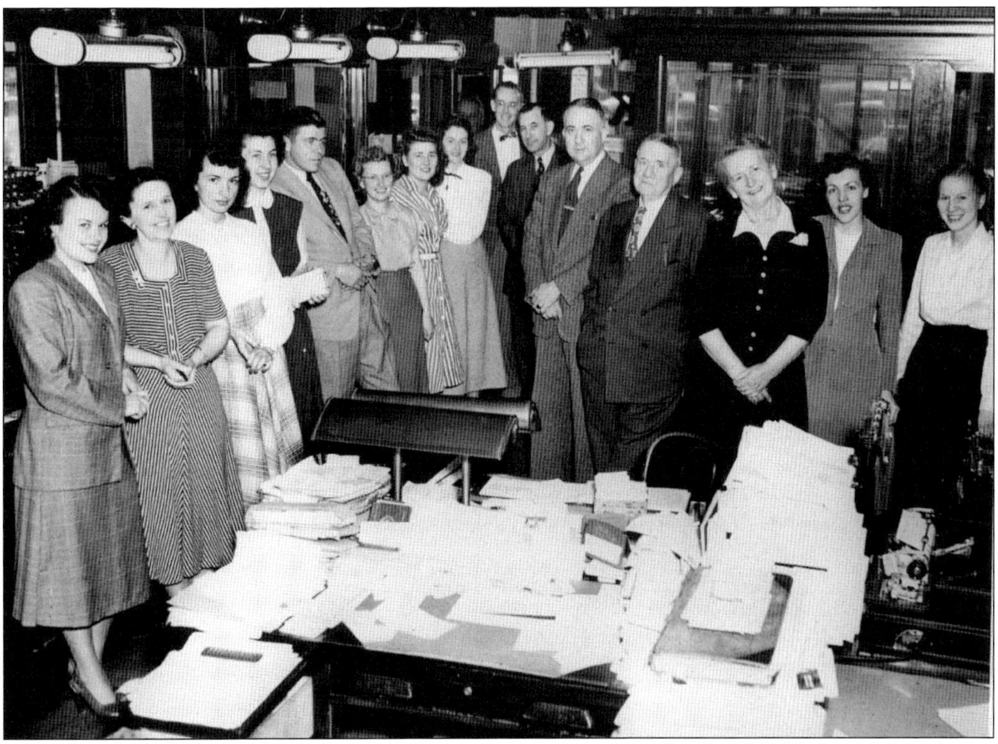

Here are the employees of the Farmers National Bank at the time of remodeling the bank. From left to right are Marilyn Fusco, Frances NcNally (Osborne), Betty Jane Claus (Freck), Cosh, Fred Margarum, Willeta DeGroat (Hillard), unidentified, Strongan, unidentified, Ted Holbert, Burton Wilson, Jub Pellow, Ford Margarum, Beatrice Smith, Madeline Johnson (Decker), and unidentified.

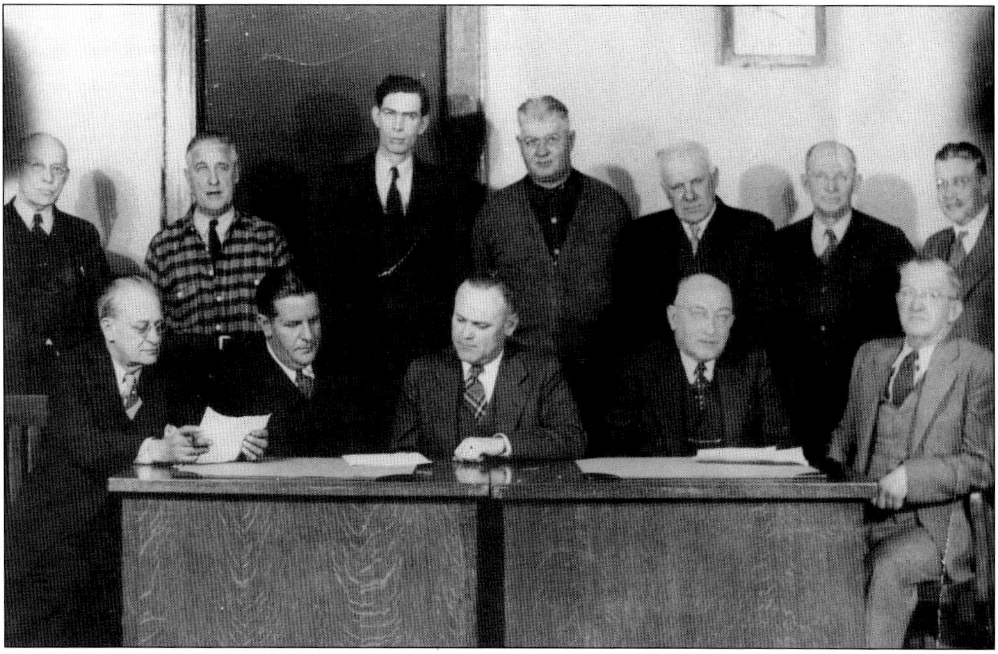

Some of the town fathers of Sussex are shown in this photograph; from left to right are (sitting) Dr. John D. Haggerty, unidentified, Mayor Theodore Holbert, Charlie Writer, and Charles Wolfe; (standing) Tom Sutton, Wallace Hartford, Dr. Bailey, Tom Trudgeon, unidentified, Albert Havens, and Dr. Keyes.

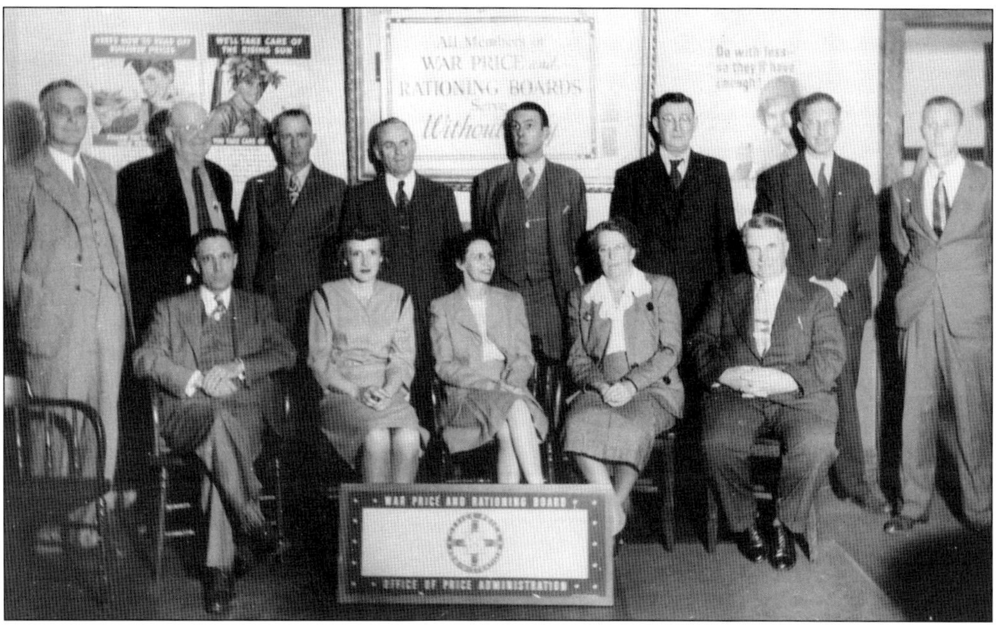

The War Price and Rationing Board from World War II is shown here. Sussex, as the rest of the country, felt the effects of the war effort. Sussex even had airplane spotters in case of enemy bombing. From left to right are (sitting) Benton Armstrong, Anabel Norman, Cara Adams, Helen Wilson, and Miles Masker; (standing) Clifford Ryerson, Milt Southard, Frank Davenport, Ted Holbert, Adrien Hommell, Marshal Hunt, John Whitfield, and Richard Renhardt.

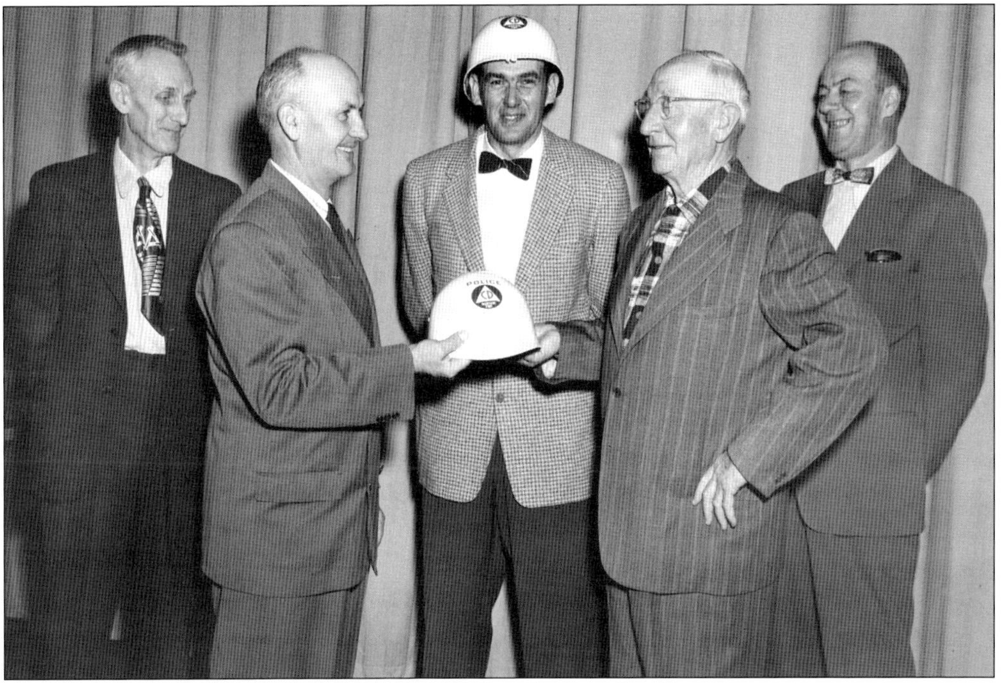

Following World War II rationing, there was a need for the Civil Defense in the 1950s and 1960s. Shown here with their white CD helmets is a group of Sussex citizens preparing to protect the town in the modern era.

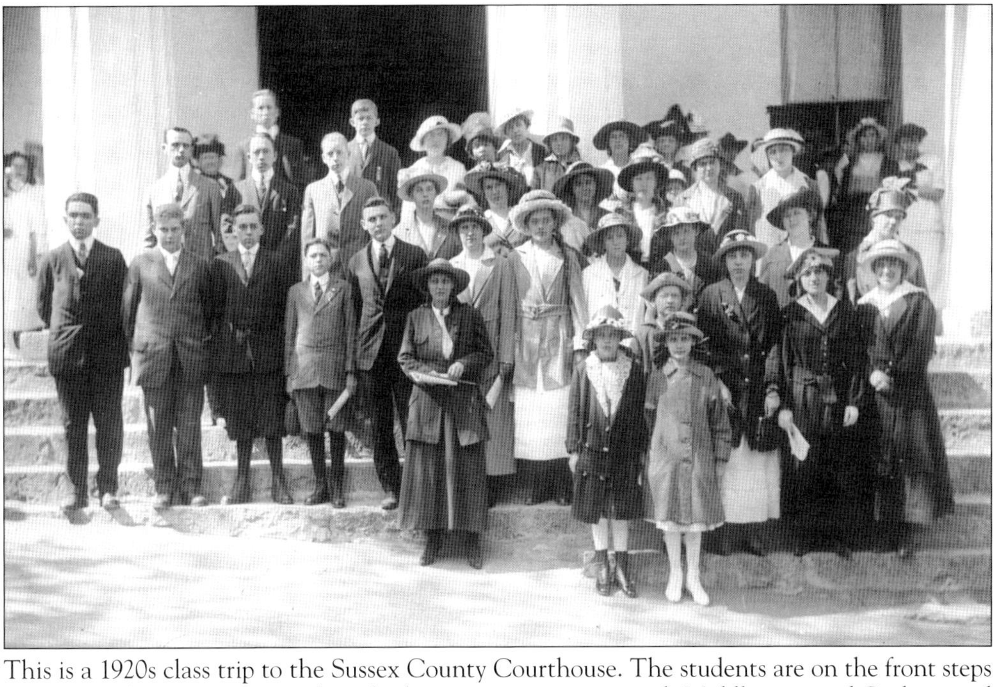

This is a 1920s class trip to the Sussex County Courthouse. The students are on the front steps of the courthouse. Sussex residents had a strong connection with Middletown and Goshen, and also New York. Identified in this photograph are Kenneth McNair, Si Wilson, Jack Holbert, Alice Decker, Lucy Morrison, and Urena Van Dine.

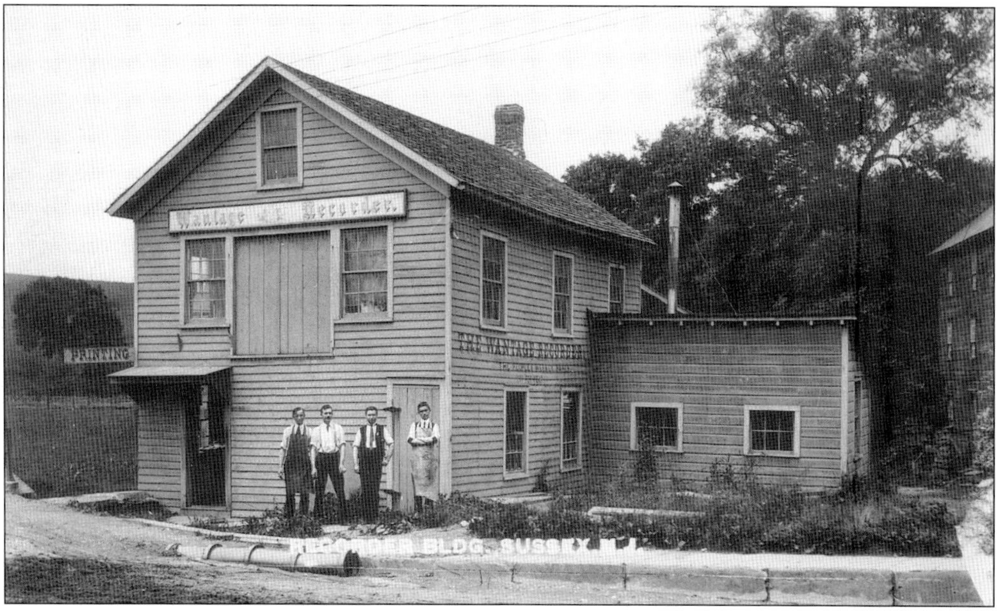

Besides the *Sussex Independent*, another newspaper was in town, the *Wantage Recorder*. Shown is the staff of the newspaper at the front of the building, which still stands at the edge of the Clove Brook. The brook once supplied energy to a previous business. (Courtesy of Olga Bazylevich Stefkowich and family of Mike the Jeweler.)

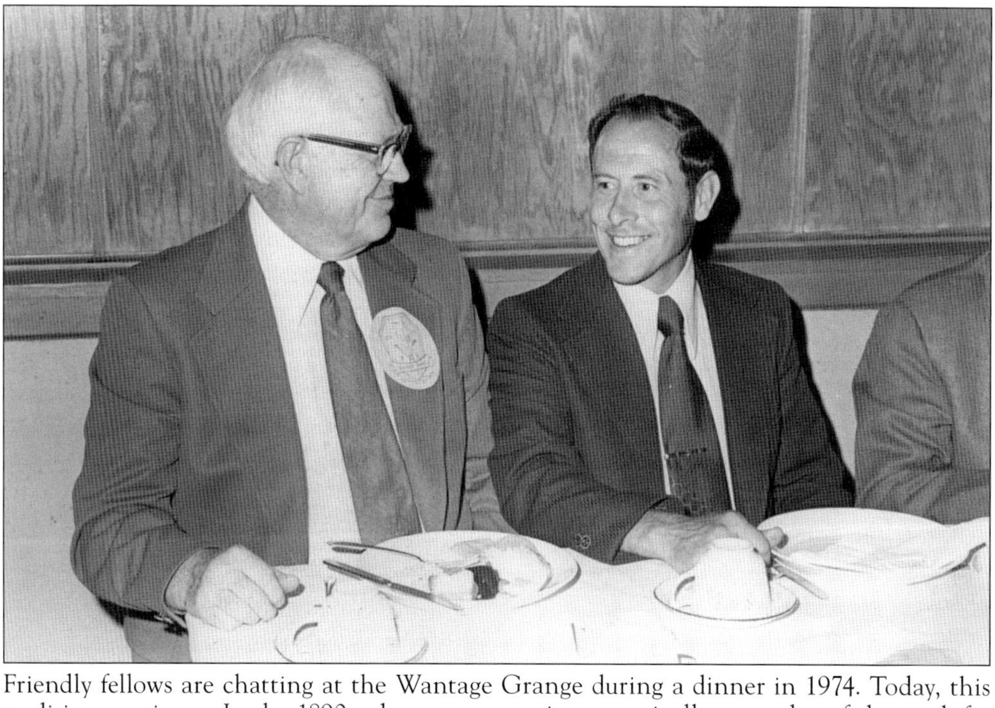

Friendly fellows are chatting at the Wantage Grange during a dinner in 1974. Today, this tradition continues. In the 1890s, there were meetings practically every day of the week for the following organizations: the Grange, the Odd Fellows, Kilpatrick Council of the Royal Arcanum, Rebeccas, Sons and Daughters of Liberty, Ku Klux Klan, and the Wantage Council No. 207 of the Junior Mechanics.

Huge amounts of snow are not just associated with the blizzard of 1888; heavy snowfalls have also been seen in recent years, too. Here is the result of a great snowfall in the early 1970s. This photograph is probably from the parking lot of the present A&P shopping center.

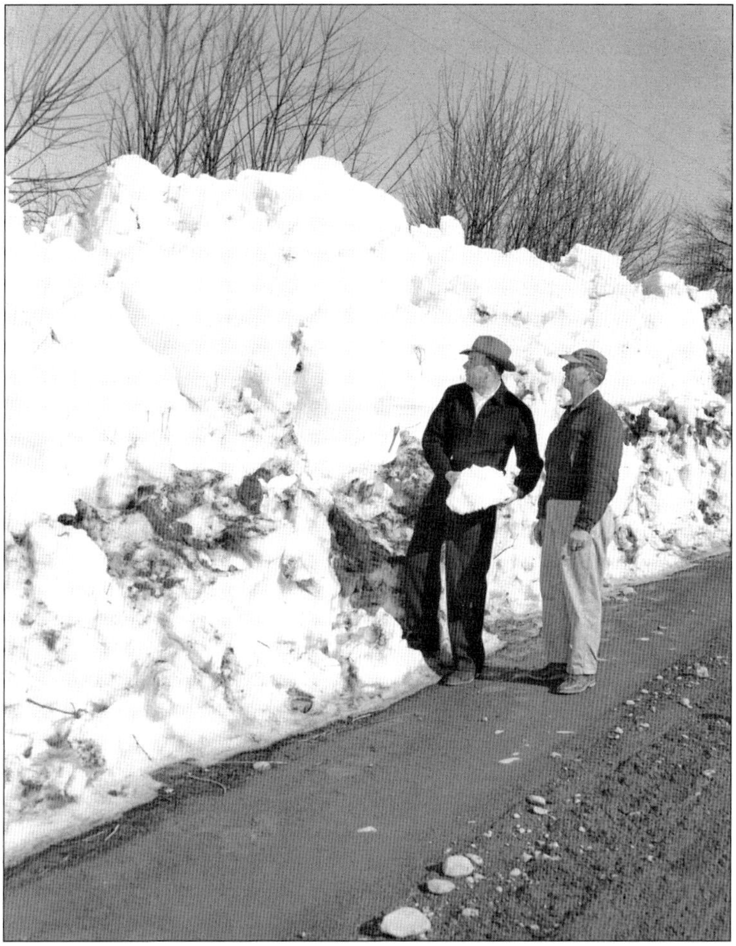

A patron is seen posing for the camera outside of Sutton's about 1895 in an early view of the town of Deckertown and its businesses.

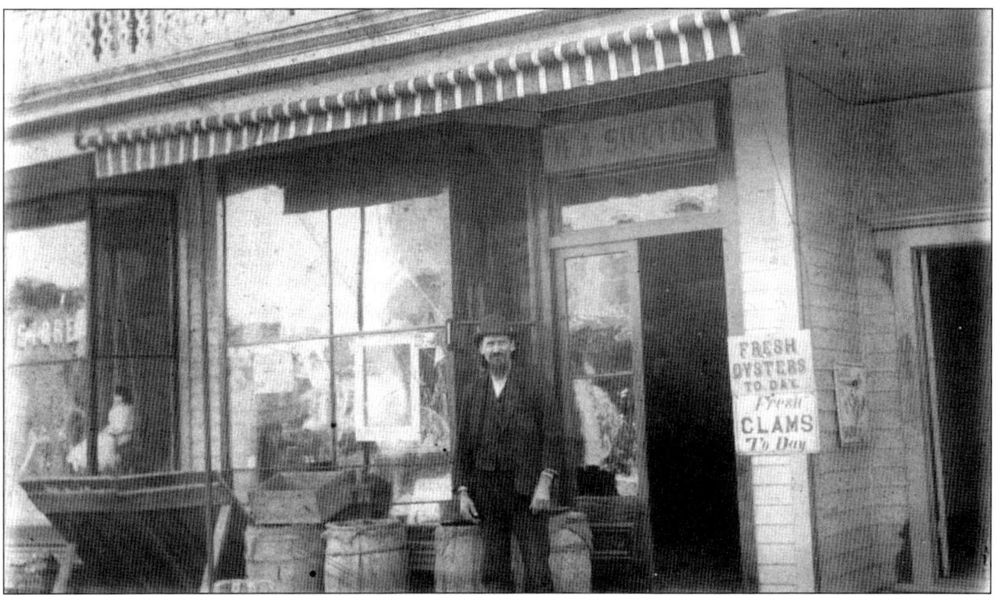

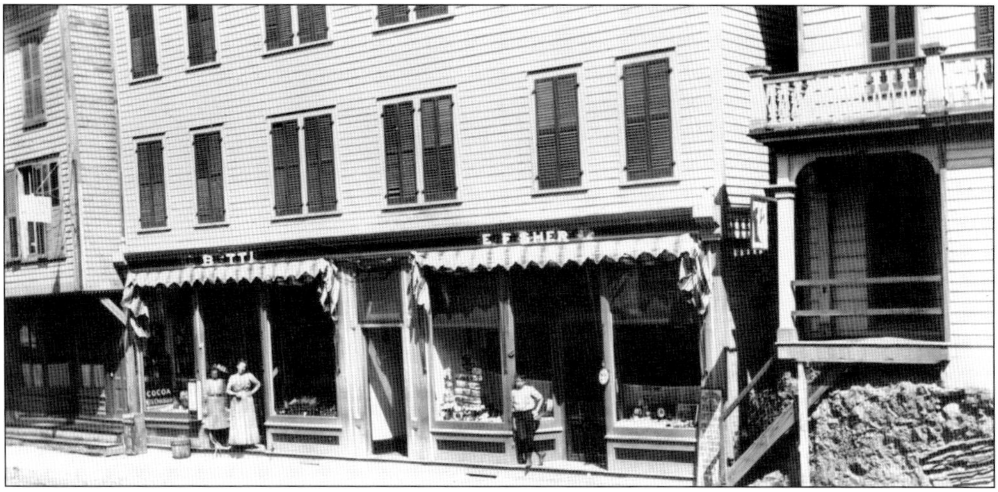

Several patrons are seen looking out from the establishments of Botti and Fisher along Main Street in Sussex about 1910.

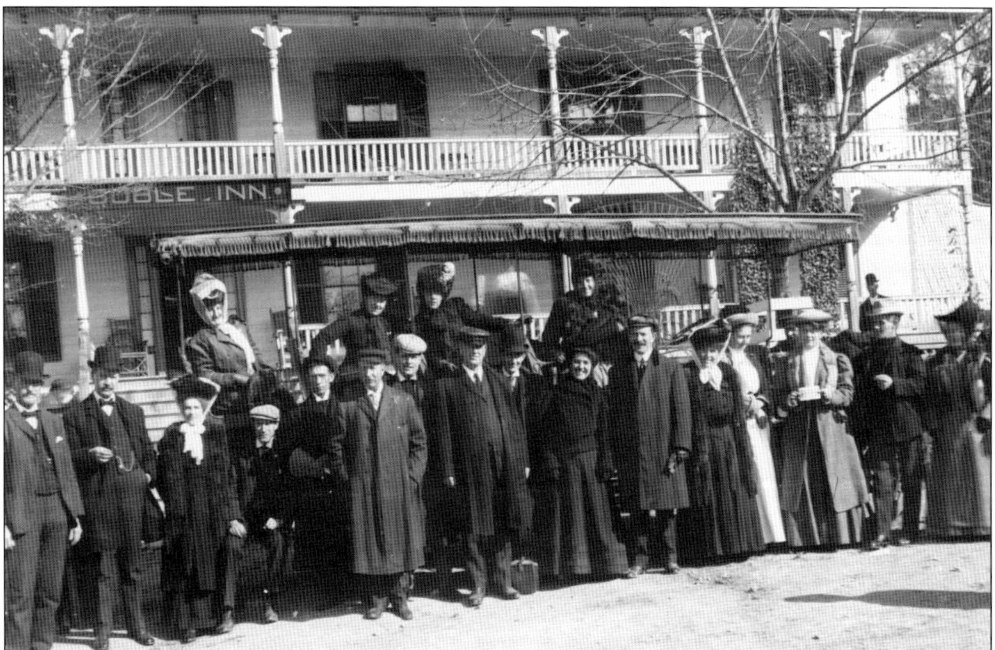

Here, some folks are getting ready to say goodbye and depart on an outing or perhaps a train ride to the city. Leaving from the Goble Inn, these Sussex-Wantage residents will be traveling in a large surrey with a fringe on top.

Five

SCHOOLS

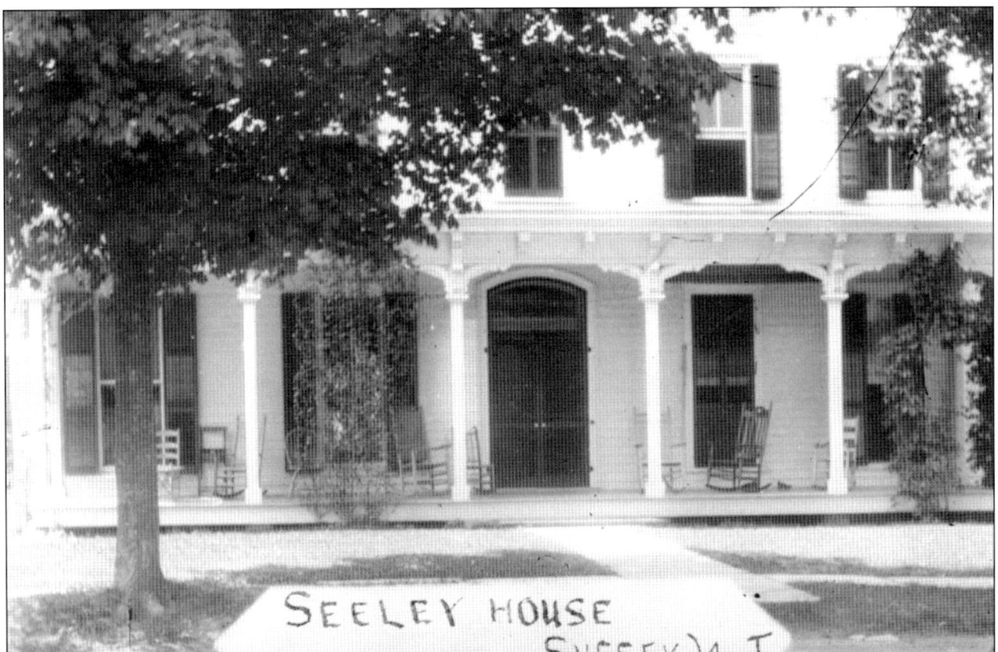

The wooden building of the Seeley School became the home of the Alexander Linn Hospital. The hospital continues today on the same site but is now housed in a brick structure. (Courtesy of the Sussex Fire Department Museum.)

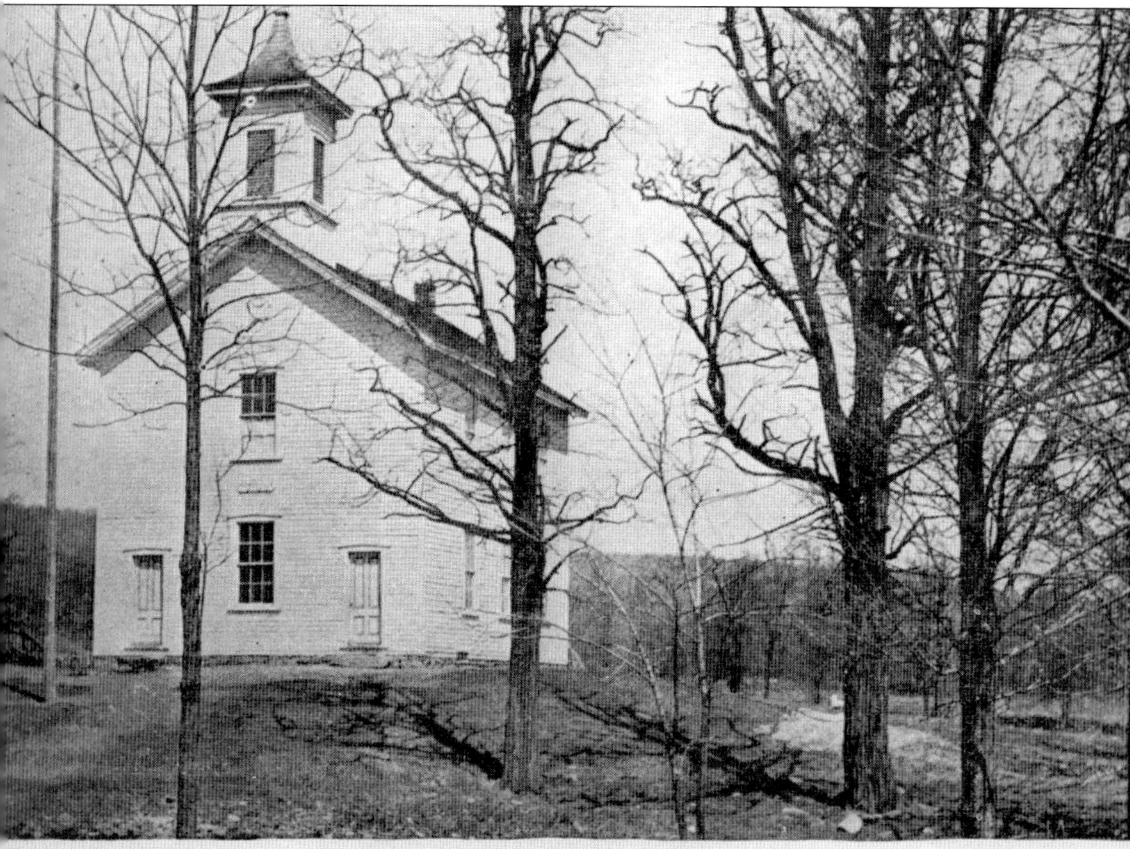

THE SCHOOLHOUSE, BEEMERVILLE, N. J.

The Beemer School was a one-room schoolhouse, located north of Beemerville on the old Deckertown Pike. Across the street from the Libertyville school, which is still standing today, one can see the old marker that identified the turnpike. Turnpikes were authorized by the New Jersey legislature in 1804 and were an important part of the growth of America, stimulating the growth of stagecoaches in the years before the arrival of railroads around 1870.

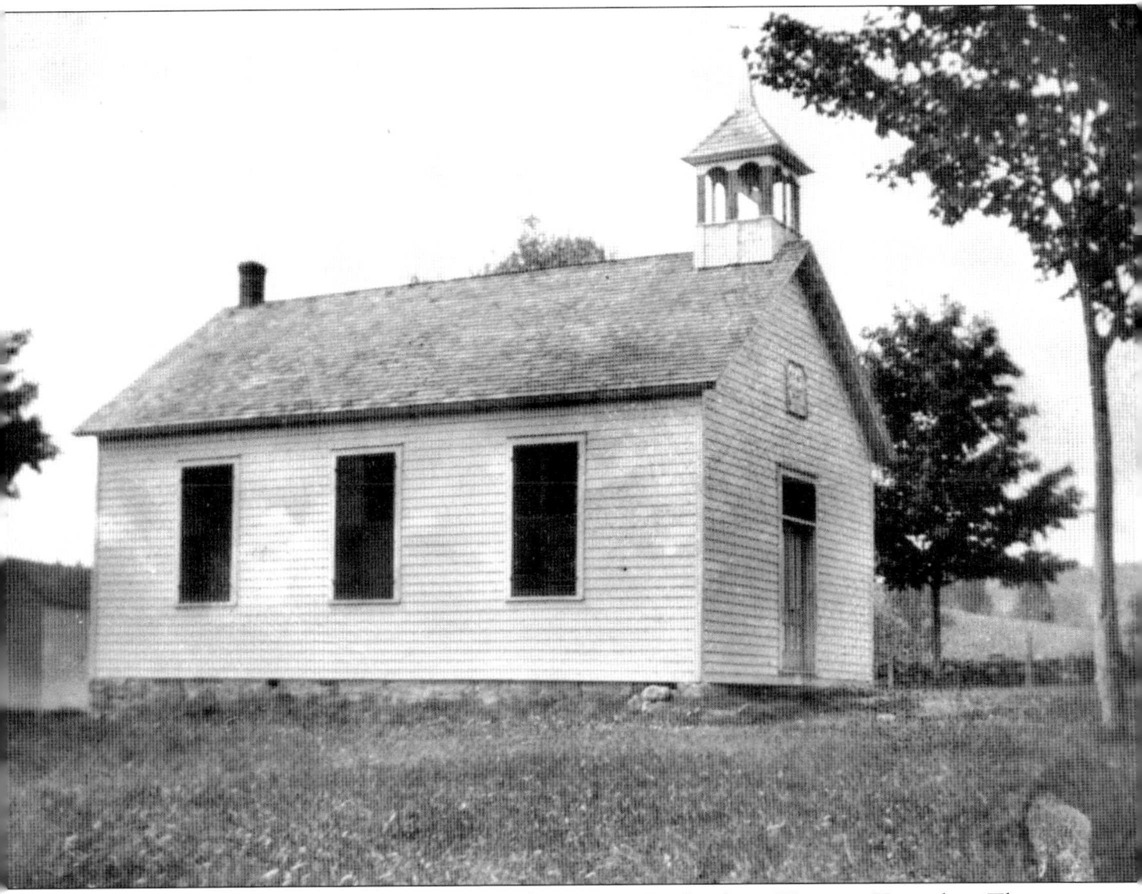

This is a view of the Pond School. In 1902, there were 17 schools in Wantage Township. These included: Dunnvale, Dunning (Plumbsock), Wolf Pit, Mount Salem, Jacksonville, Colesville, Quarryville, Libertyville, Central School, Van Sickle, Woodbourne, Lewisburg, Clove, Pond, Blooming Grove, Union, and Beemerville. As the population of Wantage Township grew, the number of schools did also to accommodate the students. However, since the township was so large, transportation was often slow, with many rural communities lacking the means to take the kids to school. (Courtesy of Jennie Sprague Henderson.)

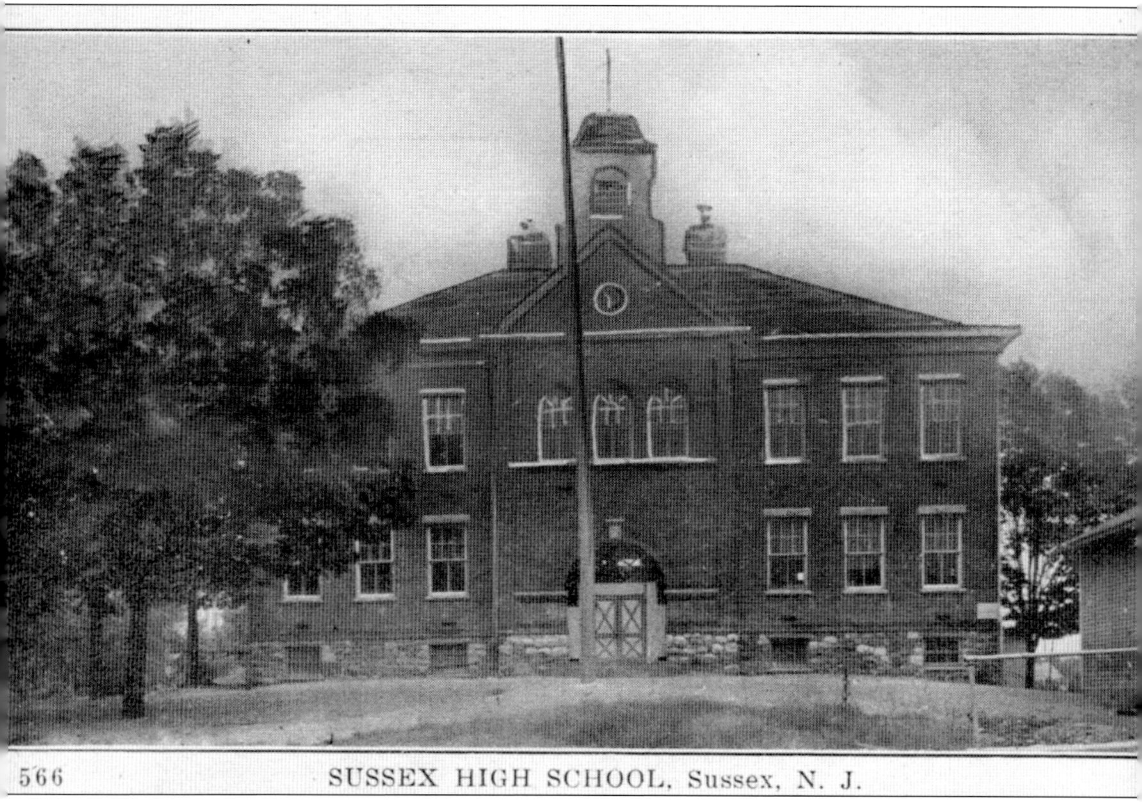

The building shown here was the home of the Rankin School, the town school. It consisted of five rooms and was made of wood. This school had a course of study that went up to the junior high level. The wooden building on top of the hill in Sussex was torn down and replaced by a brick elementary school, erected in 1903. An additional annex of two rooms was later added and served the town for all school purposes until the high school was built on Loomis Avenue. Over the years, consolidation of the schools took place, as follows: Van Sickle (1912) with Libertyville, Blooming Grove (1912) with Lewisburg (1912), Jacksonville (1917) with Colesville, Clove (1917) sent their pupils to Sussex, Pond (1917) sent their pupils to Sussex, Woodbourne sent pupils to Sussex, and Libertyville and Central both sent pupils to Sussex (1919). All students went to the Wantage Township Consolidated School in 1937, which is located just north of town on Route 23. (Courtesy of Mary Eleanor Eppler.)

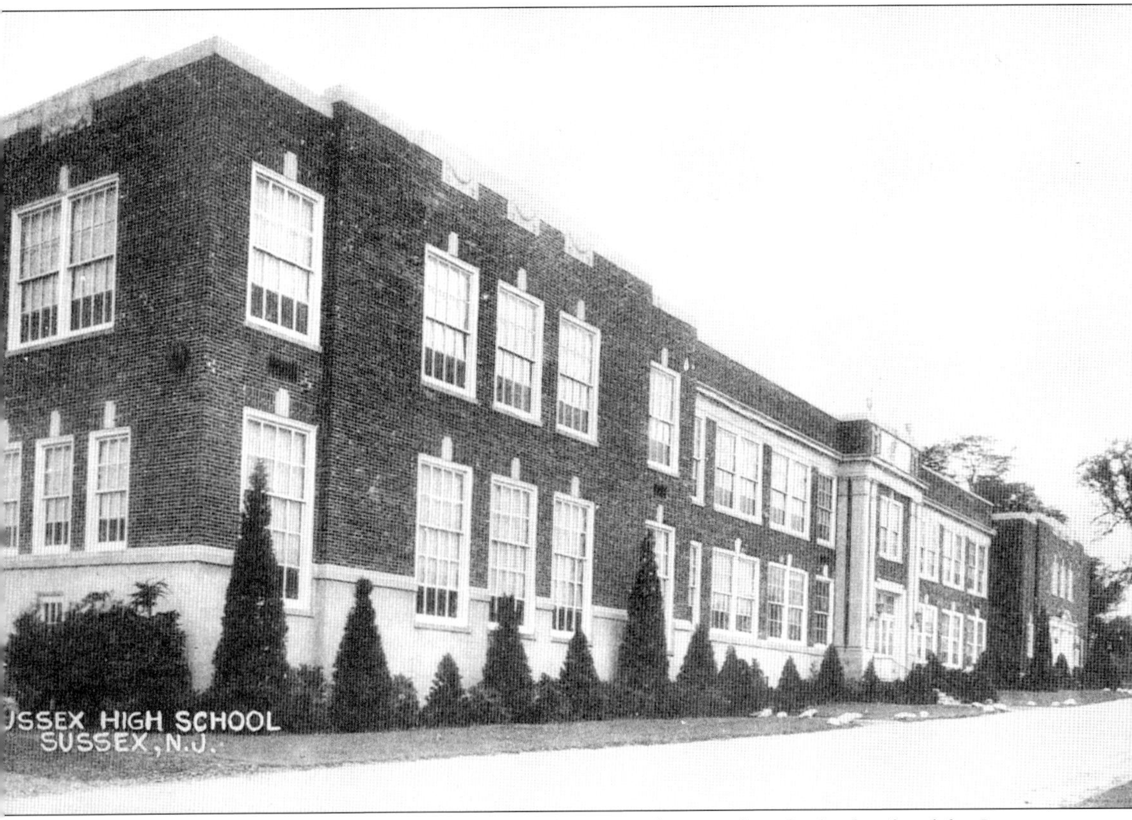

This brick building on Loomis Avenue, beside Clove Brook, served as the high school for Sussex until the late 1960s, when High Point Regional High School was built to serve the larger area. The enrollment in 1902 was 296 for both the elementary school and the high school. That enrollment grew to 202 elementary and 227 high school students in 1940. (Courtesy of Mary Eleanor Eppler.)

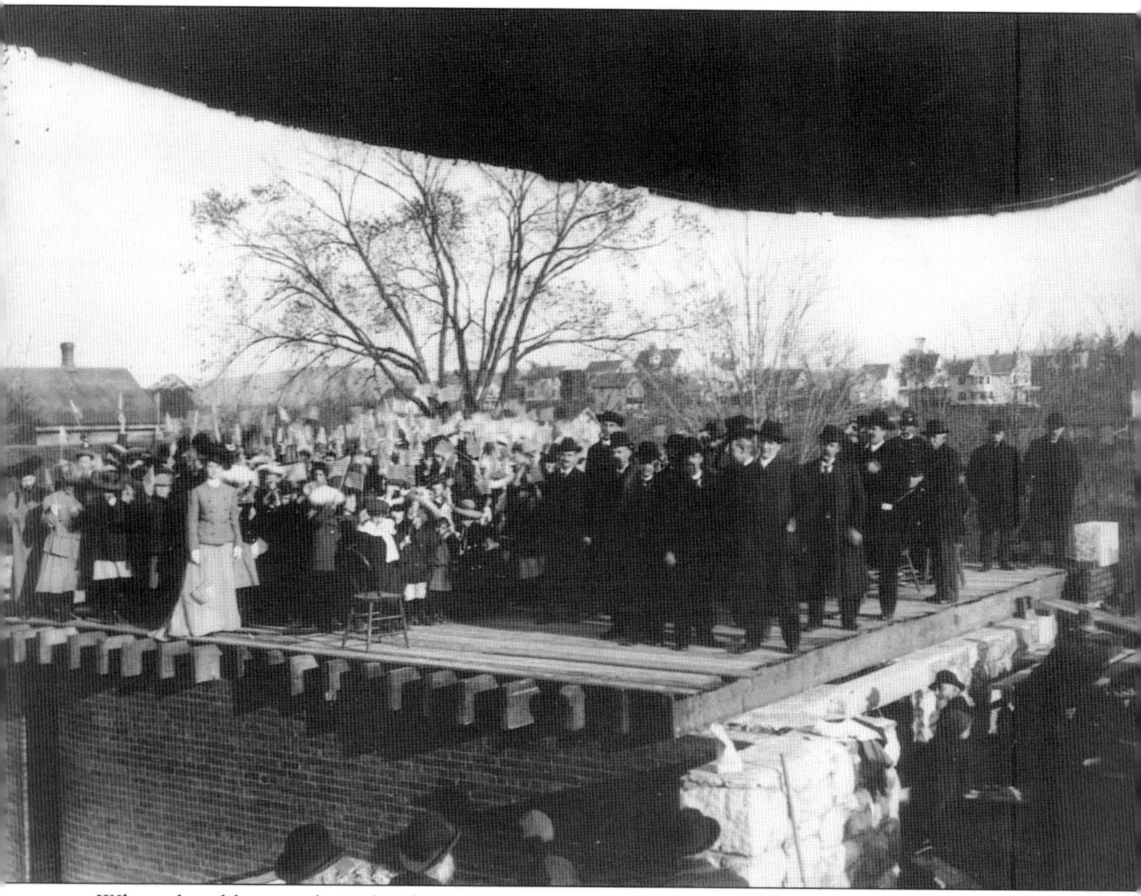

When the older wooden school on Academy Hill was torn down, a new brick structure replaced the building. As reported in a news article on October 28, 1904, the cornerstone was laid for the Harrison Street School that remained a town school until 1976. Note the children all waving American flags and the white stone with the year on it on the right. (Courtesy of Olga Bazylevich Stefkowich and family of Mike the Jeweler.)

Six

CHURCHES

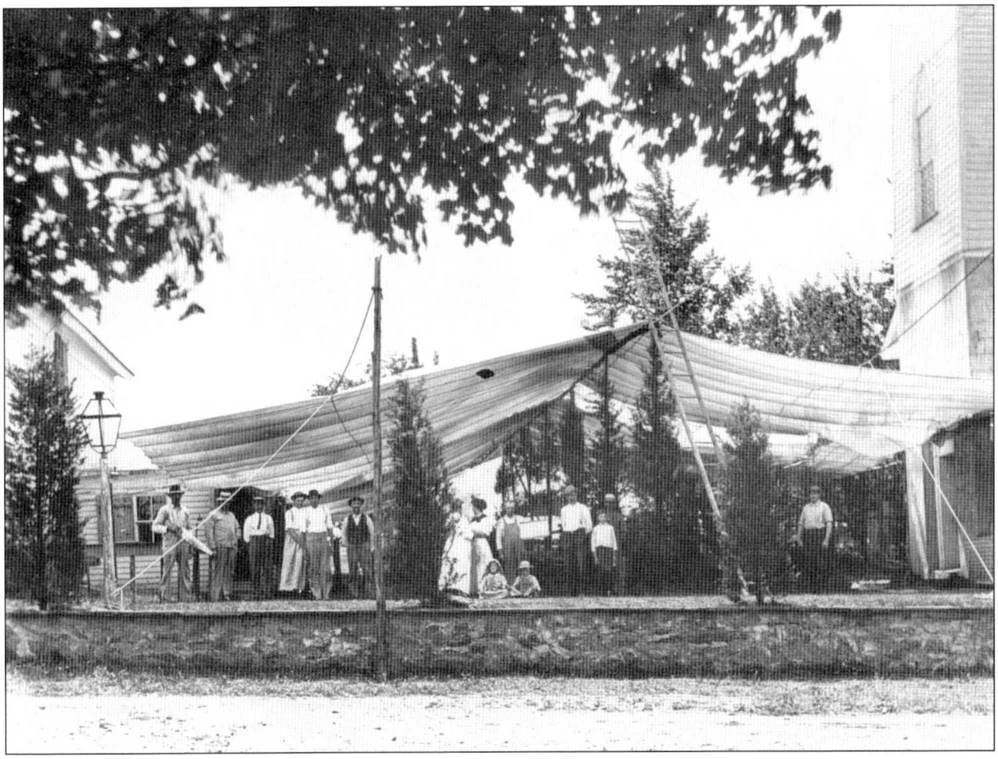

Welcome all to the Beemerville Harvest Home. Pictured around 1905 under a canvas tent beside the Beemerville Presbyterian Church are, from left to right, (sitting) Lena Johnson and an unidentified boy; (standing) Will Wolfe, Frank Meddaugh, Dave Truex, Charlie Couse, Howard Ayers, John Beemer, Mrs. Net Meddauge, Ethel Hockenberry, Rev. William Westervelt, Charlie Couse Sr., Clinton Mars, unidentified, and Steve Mars, the operator of the Beemerville Creamery. Events similar to this continue to this day in the Sussex-Wantage area.

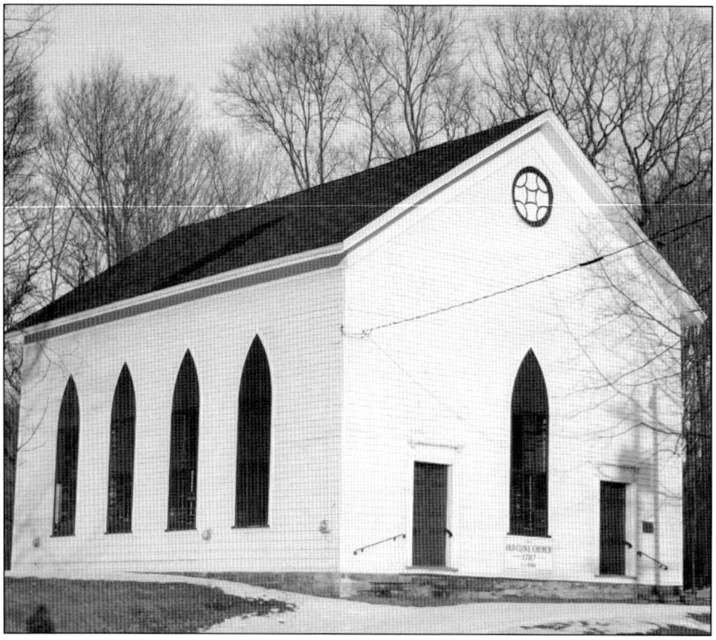

The Old Clove Church is a landmark. The congregation formed as early as 1741 with the Minisink Dutch Reformed Church, formally organized in 1787. In 1818, a merger united several congregations. Over the years, there were three locations of the church, with two being close to cemeteries. The church was purchased by the Sussex County Historical Society in 1972 and is now owned by the Friends of the Old Clove Church. (Author's collection.)

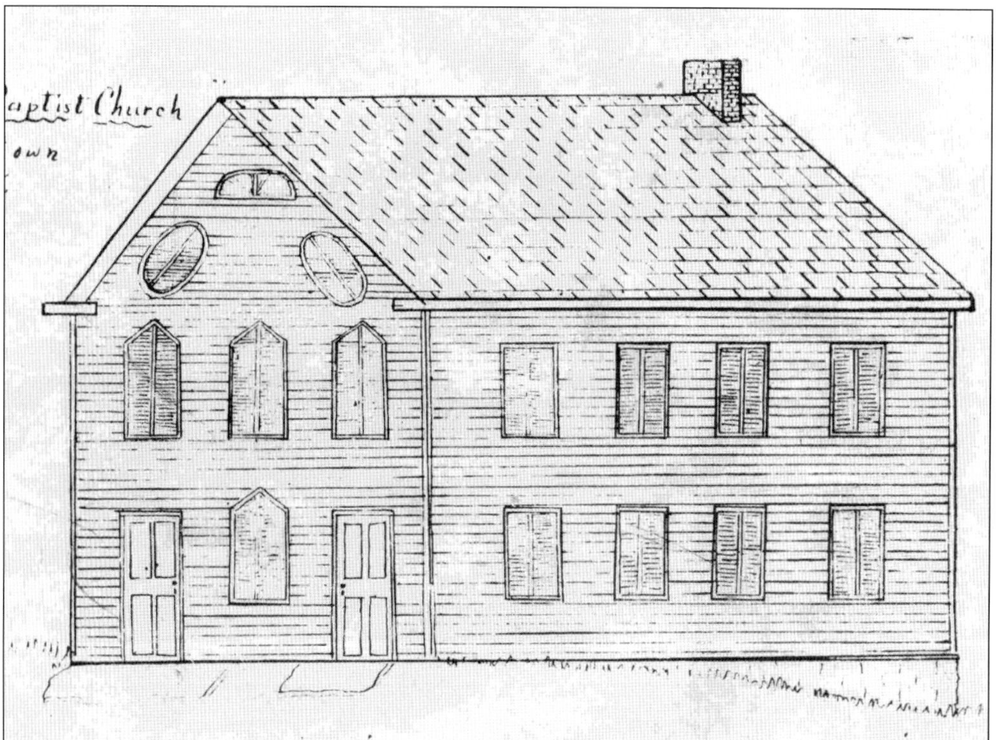

The Baptist church in Sussex has a storied past. The church reputedly began in the late 1700s on the Morrisvale estate, near Hamburg, along today's Route 94, which, at the time, was called King's Highway (after the king of England), and near where there was an encampment of General George Washington's Revolutionary War troops. The congregation then built the structure depicted here in the 1800s. The church congregation was moved again in the late 1800s to Sussex, where it remains today.

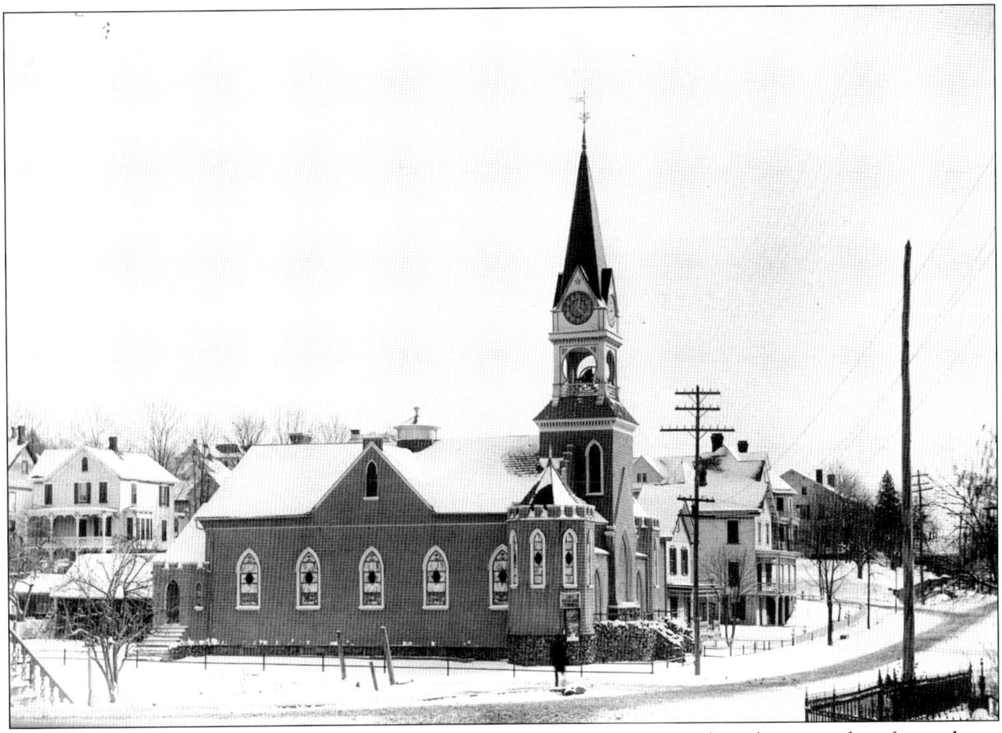

Here is a view of the exterior of the First Baptist Church of Sussex. This photograph is from about 1905, but the structure looks about the same today. Shown prominently is the church steeple, with the clock and bell tower. Local Thomas Jefferson Dunn donated the clock, along with a monument. He donated a similar monument and clock to the Unionville, New York, Church, which is found just over the border from New Jersey.

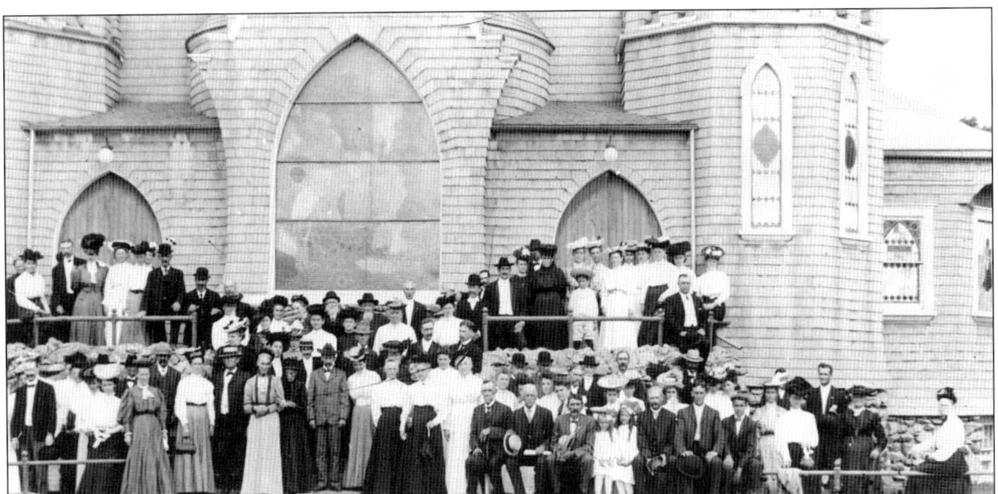

Seen at the front entry to the first Baptist Church of Sussex is the congregation decked out in their Sunday best. Note the ornate hats of the women and that all the men are dressed well and richly. This photograph is from about 1915 or before and is a good representation of the population of the town at that time.

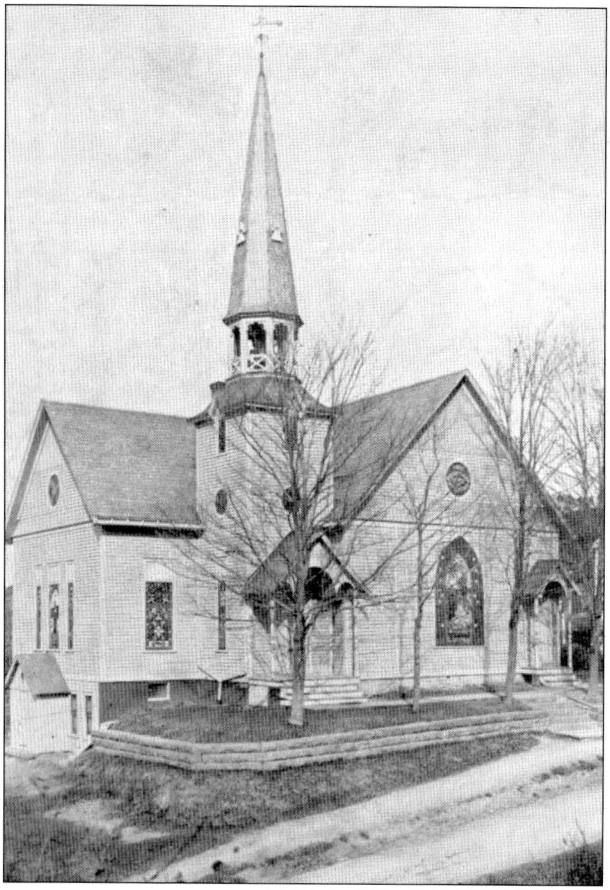

The Presbyterian Church of Sussex was built in 1839. A weeklong observation for the 140th anniversary was held in 1979. Some of the windows were stained glass and dedicated to individuals. Among those honored are James A. Wood, Martha Ecob Hamilton, Samuel Whitaker, John Loomis, Abram and Jane Smith, Lewis and Anna Wintermute Whitaker, Bennie Simmons, and Elizabeth Munson. These were prominent people and family names in the Sussex-Wantage area. The church began with meetings in a log cabin on property owned by Peter Decker in 1818. (Author's collection.)

The Presbyterian church has always been located in an outstanding location—at the top of Church Street on the hill above the town center of Sussex. The building can be seen on the earliest woodcut images of the town by Barber and Howe, dating from the mid-1840s. (Author's collection.)

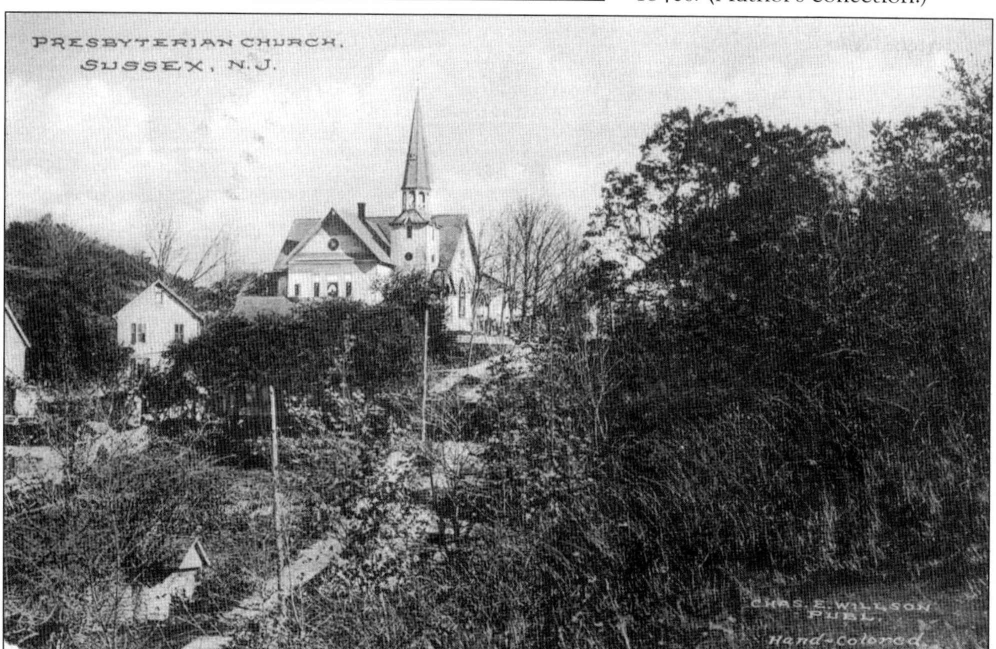

This is the first Methodist Episcopal Church of Sussex. There is also a Methodist Episcopal church in Wantage that served Libertyville and Colesville that was formed on October 16, 1860. Another Methodist Episcopal church served an area of Wantage just north of Sussex; this one was formed in 1831 and is now gone, but the Wantage Cemetery along Route 284 was left behind. The picture was taken by Thomas L. Smith and Clarence Ayers about 1900. (Courtesy of Olga Bazylevich Stefkowich and family of Mike the Jeweler.)

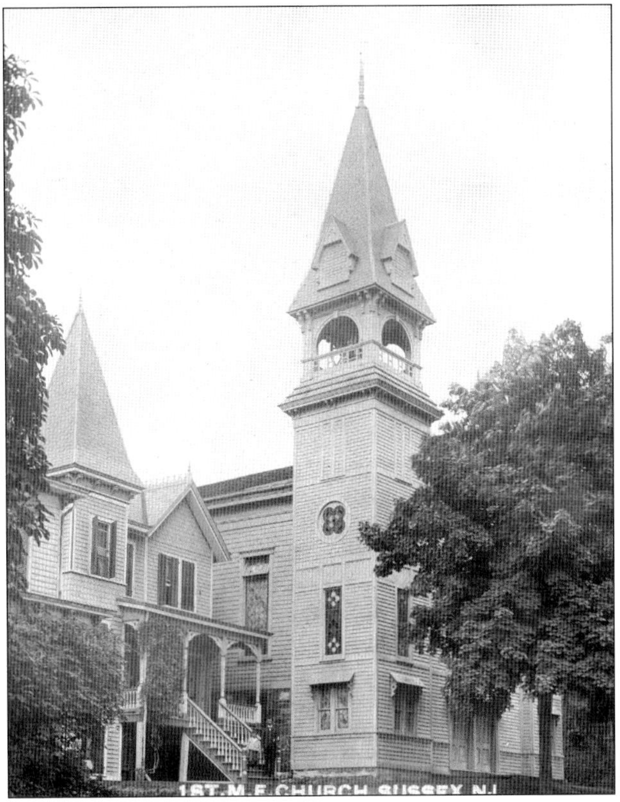

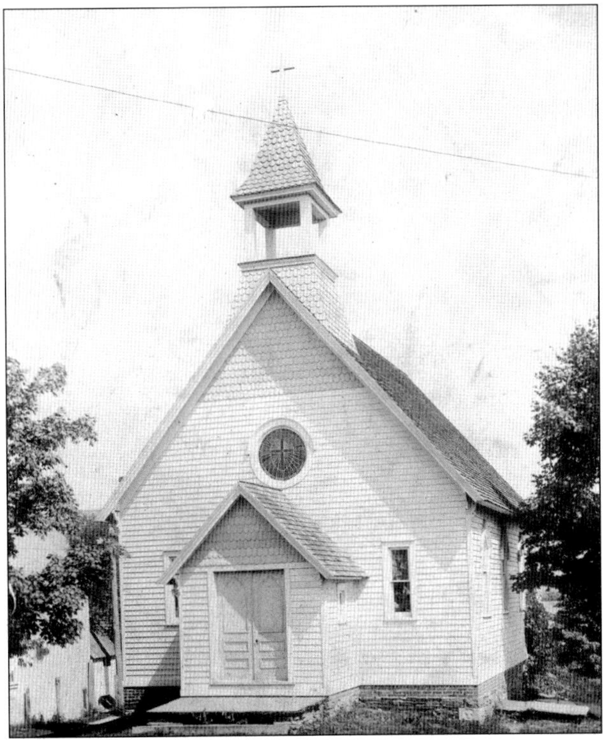

This is St. Monica's Roman Catholic Church parish. This church building was later replaced by the present brick structure. Records seem to show that the first Roman Catholic service in the locality of Deckertown began in a private home on what is now East Main Street in 1855. The cornerstone was laid on May 4, 1881. The picture was taken by Thomas L. Smith and Clarence Ayers about 1900. (Courtesy of Olga Bazylevich Stefkowich and family of Mike the Jeweler.)

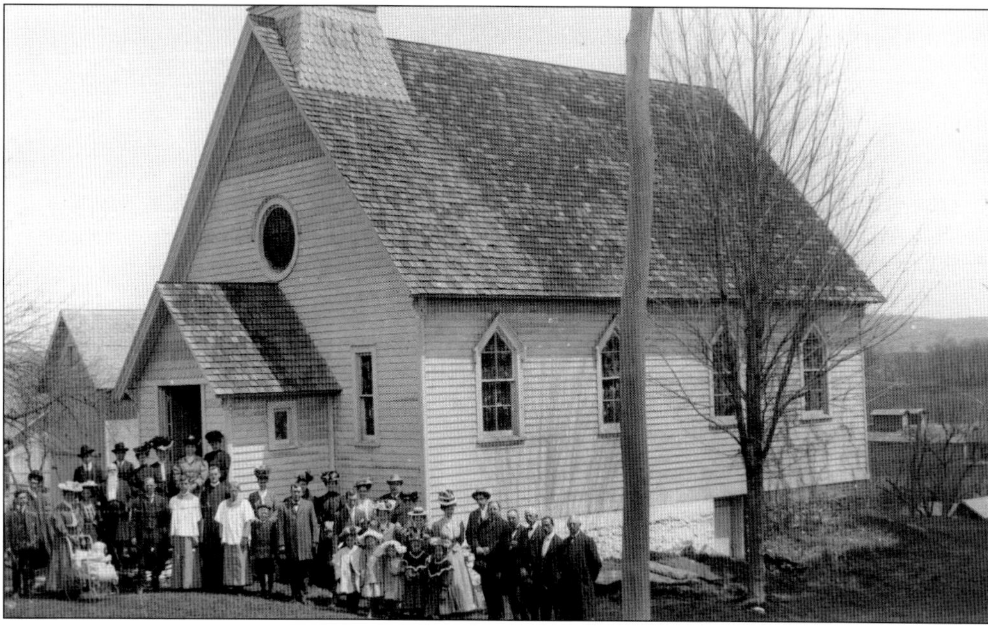

Another view of the Catholic church in Sussex is shown in this photograph. Its location was and is on Harrison Street atop the hill above the town. (Courtesy of Olga Bazylevich Stefkowich and family of Mike the Jeweler.)

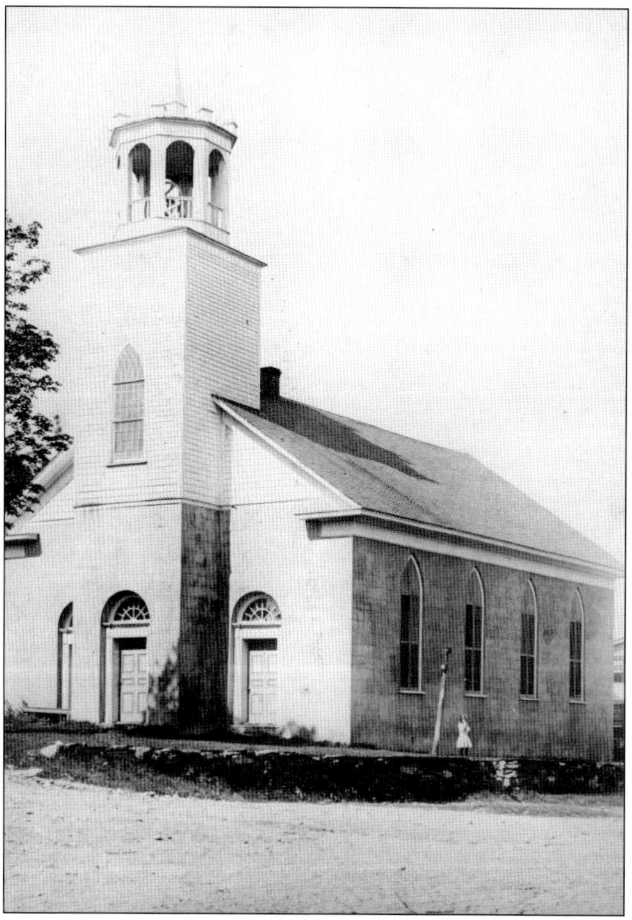

The Beemerville Presbyterian Church is seen in a classic glass-plate negative print from about 1902. The church still stands in the middle of Beemerville with an active congregation. (Courtesy of Olga Bazylevich Stefkowich and family of Mike the Jeweler.)

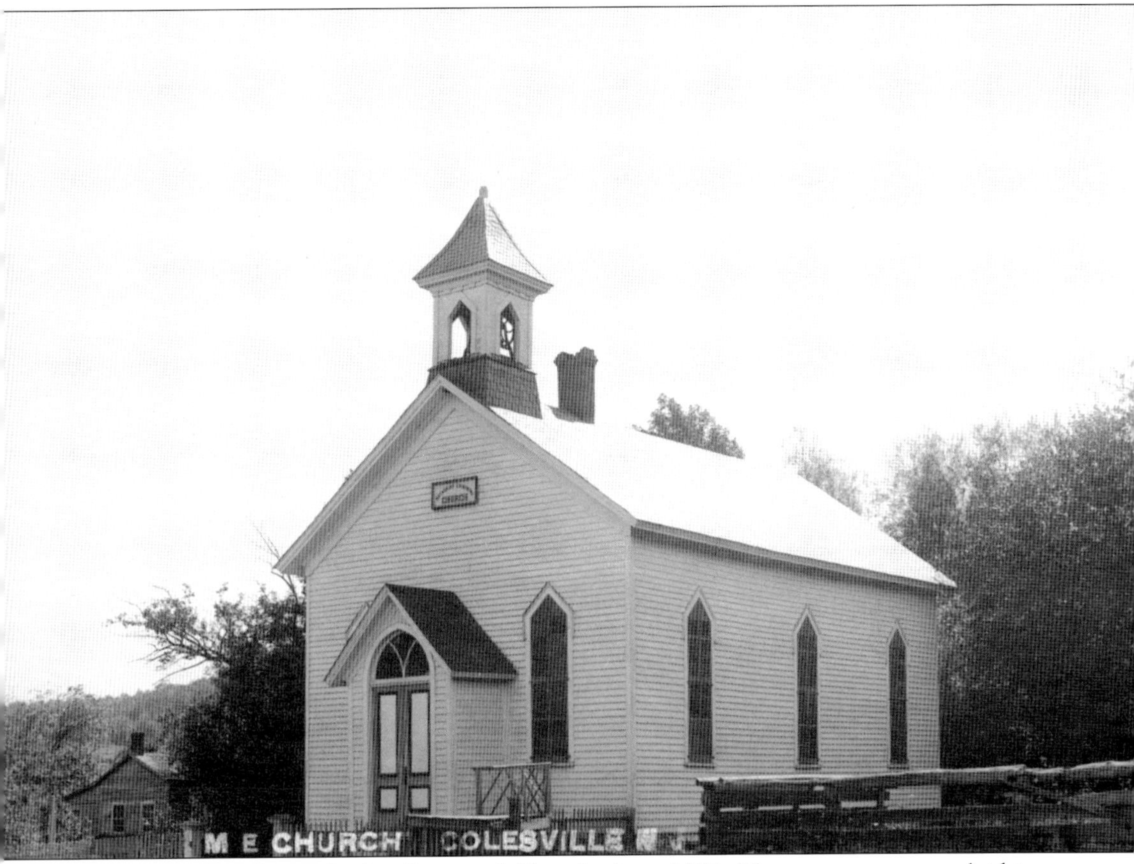

This is the Colesville Methodist Episcopal Church about 1900. The cornerstone was laid in October 1887. Around 1895, the nearby Old Red Church closed its doors; lumber from it was used for the parsonage. The photograph was taken by Thomas L. Smith and Clarence Ayers. The building still exists but is no longer a church. (Courtesy of Olga Bazylevich Stefkowich and family of Mike the Jeweler.)

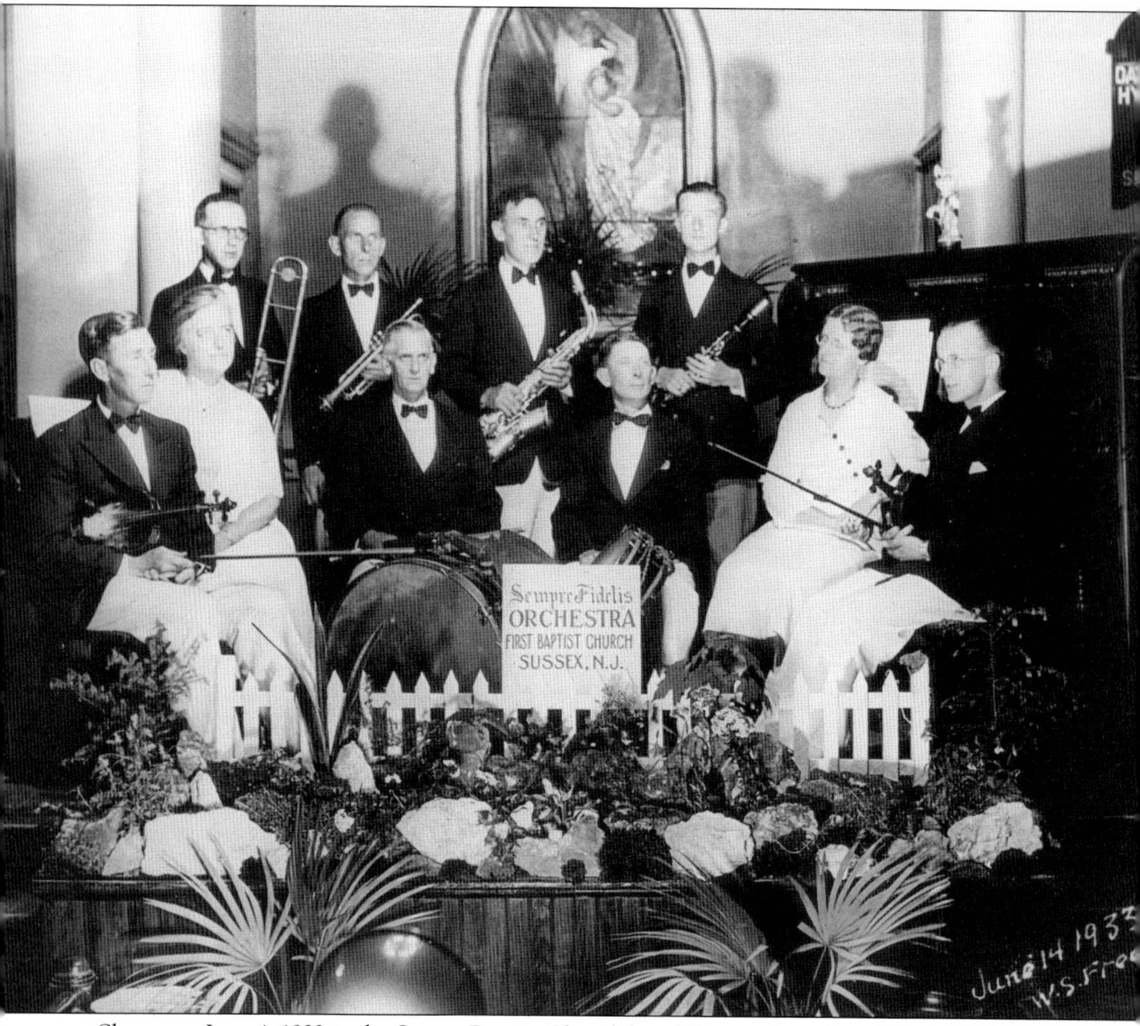

Shown on June 4, 1933, is the Sussex Baptist Church band. Pictured are, from left to right, (sitting) Harry Beemer, Carrie Smith, Walter Freck, Namon Sutton, Emma Roome, and unidentified; (standing) unidentified, Jake Nyhius, Fritz Nyhius, and unidentified.

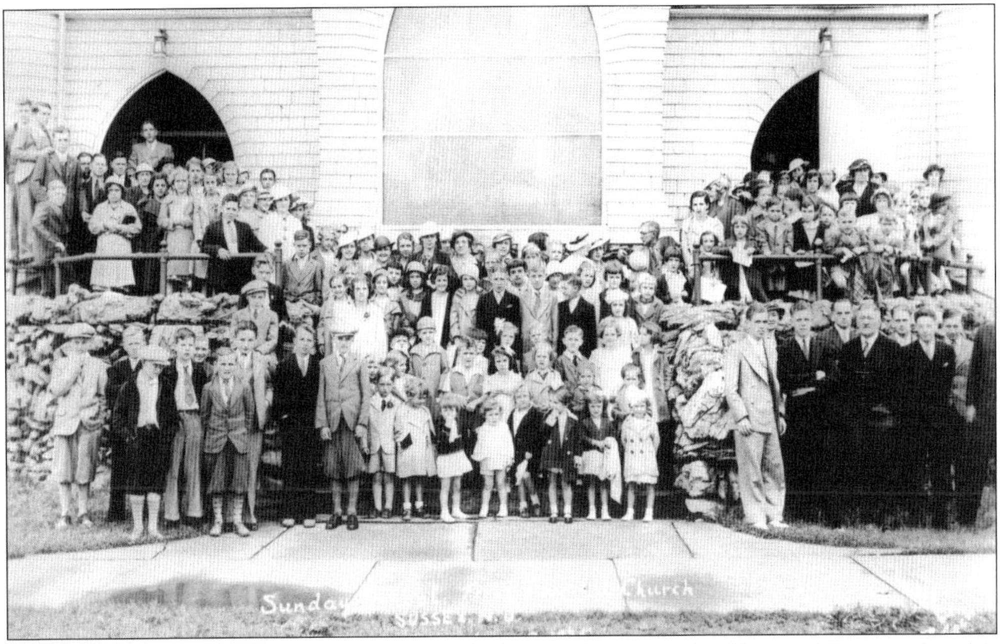

Here are members of the congregation of the Sussex First Baptist Church. The date for this photograph is June 9, 1935, and the people have a generally more youthful appearance than the other photograph from the same church some 20 years earlier. This shows a good cross section of the people, including how they dressed and who they were, in the town in the mid-1930s. It is not a stretch to say that most of the people who have been long-term residents of the town have some relatives present in this photograph.

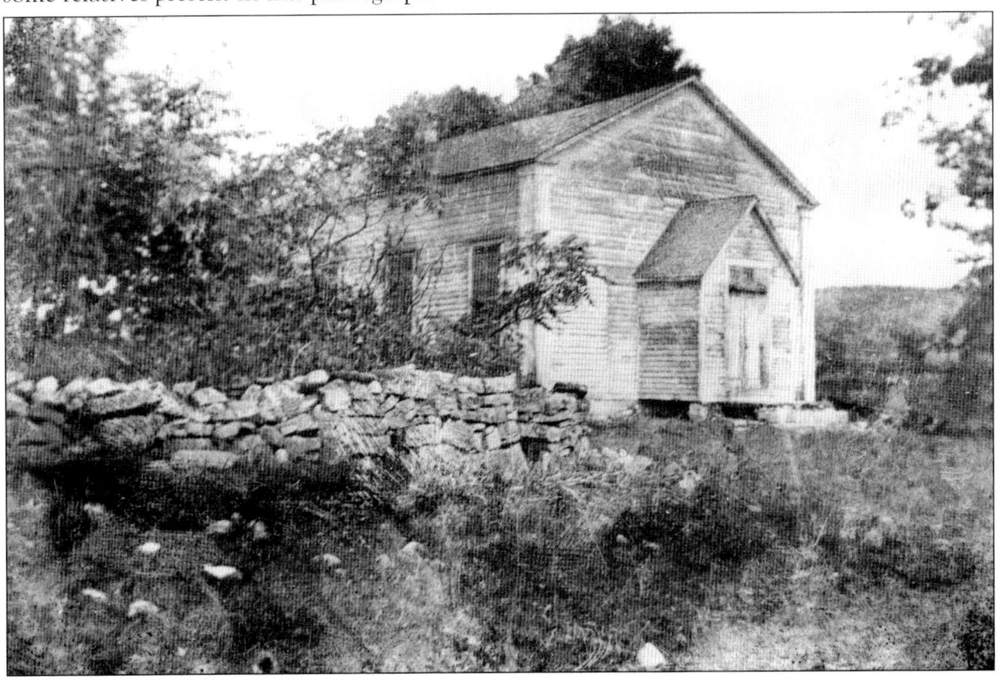

Here are the remains of an old church as it appeared about 1910. This photograph is from the Wantage archives. The church was known as "the Lord's House."

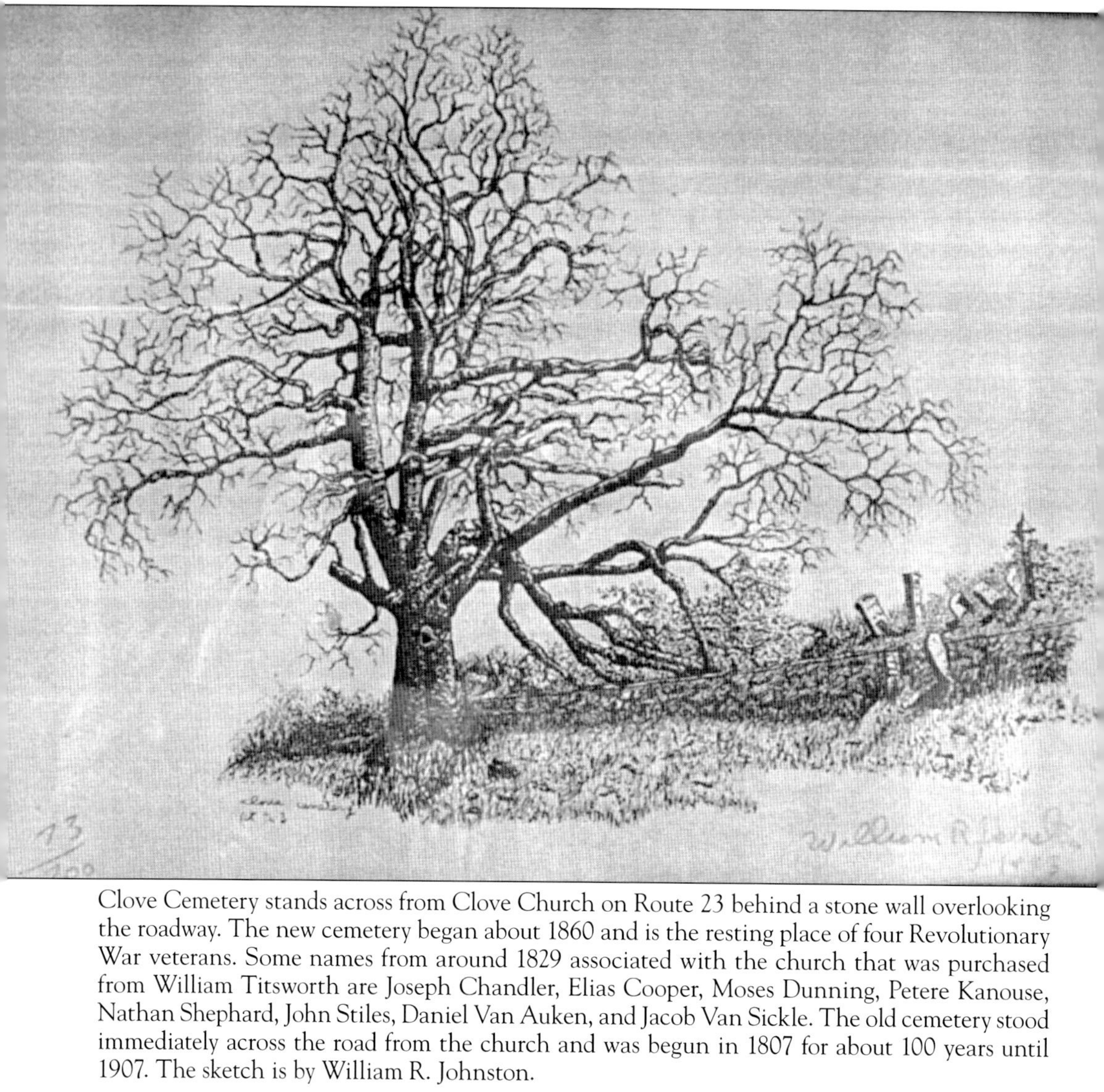

Clove Cemetery stands across from Clove Church on Route 23 behind a stone wall overlooking the roadway. The new cemetery began about 1860 and is the resting place of four Revolutionary War veterans. Some names from around 1829 associated with the church that was purchased from William Titsworth are Joseph Chandler, Elias Cooper, Moses Dunning, Petere Kanouse, Nathan Shephard, John Stiles, Daniel Van Auken, and Jacob Van Sickle. The old cemetery stood immediately across the road from the church and was begun in 1807 for about 100 years until 1907. The sketch is by William R. Johnston.

Seven

HORSES

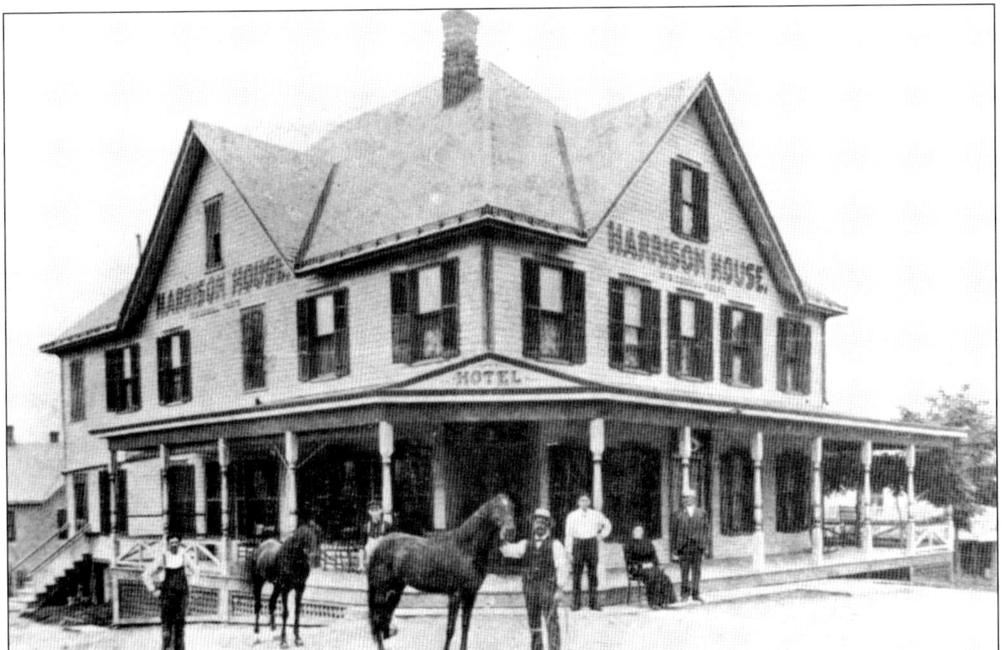

Deckertown had a most famous horse—perhaps the best trotter ever—Goldsmith Maid, "Queen of the Trotters." Goldsmith Maid (1857 to September 23, 1885) was a national hit in one of the nation's premier sporting events, trotting. Here is a local gentleman showing off his horse with another man at the ready. Events like this were available in the town of Sussex at the horse-racing park.

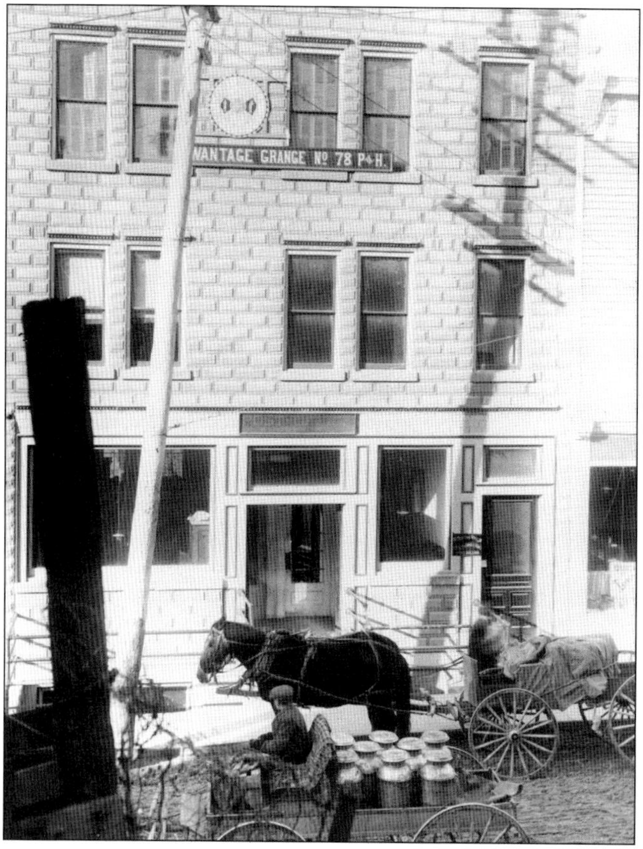

This image is looking out onto Main Street in Sussex about 1905. One can see the horse and wagon at the post office, with the driver reading the news and the ever-present milk cans in the back of a farmer's wagon. These cans of milk would be brought into town on a daily basis from the nearby farms to be processed; most of it was then sent by rail to places far away in need of fresh dairy products.

Some happy passengers pose here in Fountain Square in Sussex Borough. This "station wagon" will pick up passengers from the train and bring them to the De Camp Hotel for lodging. Directly behind the wagon is the Victorian gazebo used as a bandstand and a means for addressing the public.

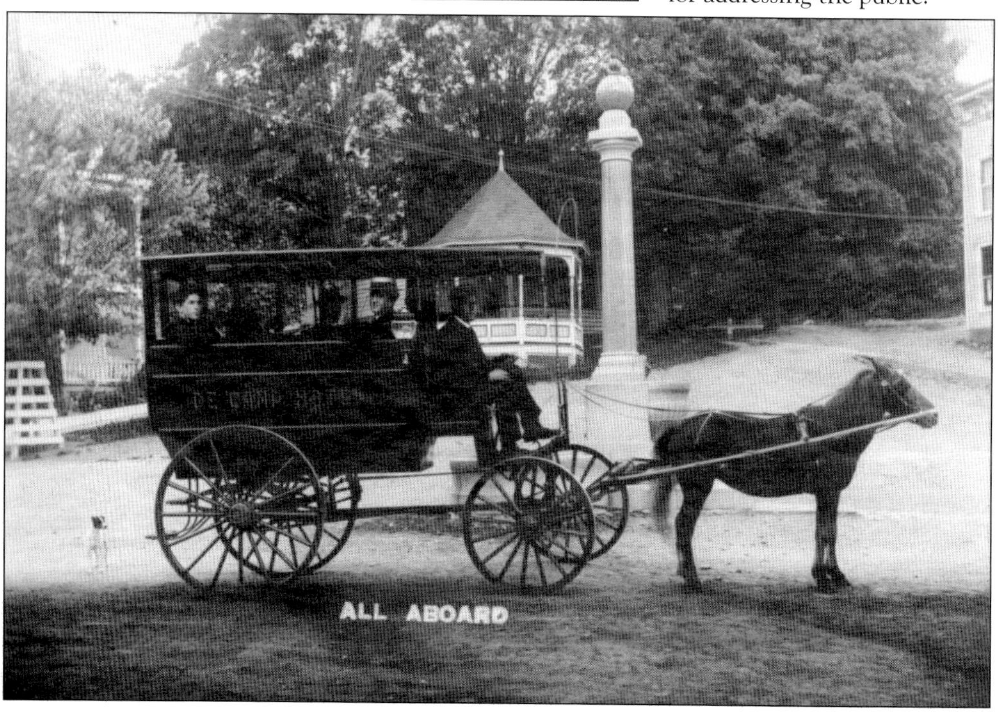

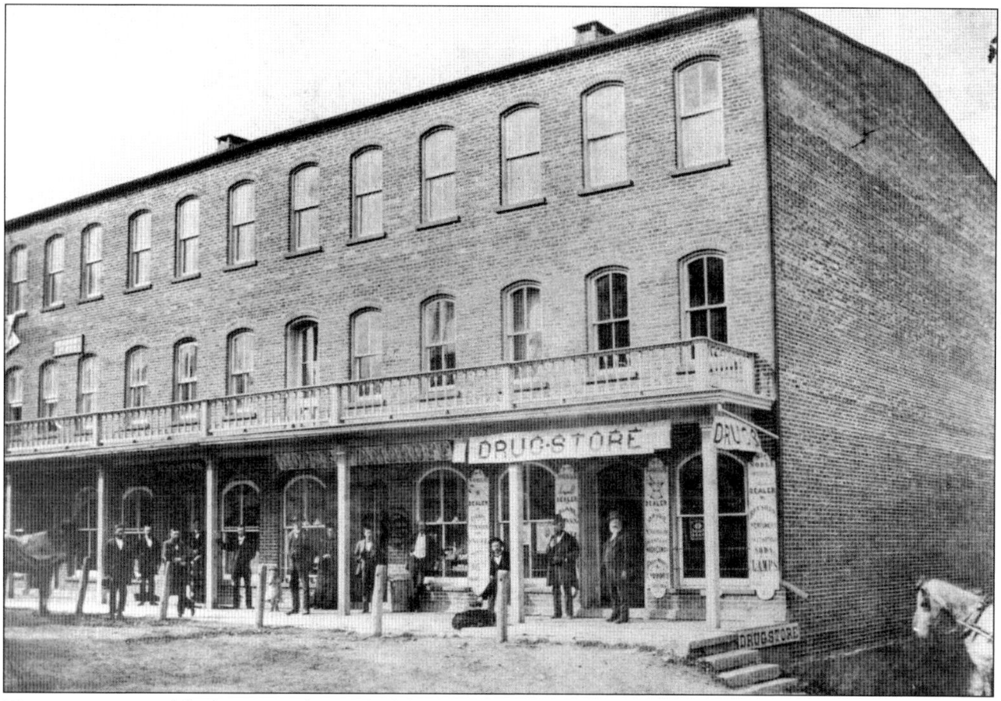

Here is a very old photograph, probably from the 1880s, showing the life and times outside of the Hornbeck Block on Main Street in Sussex. This is before the Union Block was added at the end on the right. Of note are the hats and dress of the men, the hitching posts, and hound dog sleeping on the walkway beside the dirt roadway. From looking at the signs, store patrons were able to buy snuff at the Couse Vandruff Drugstore.

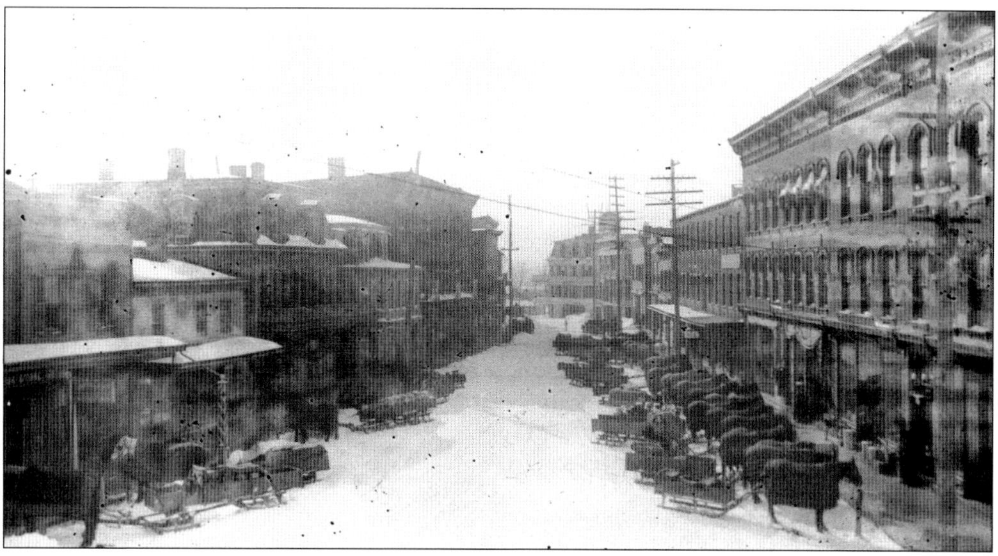

This is a very nice winter scene on Main Street in Sussex. The sleighs indicate that a sizeable snowstorm has taken place, and the roads are passable by the sleighs with their smooth runners. It is still chilly, as seen by all of the horses with blankets on them. Milk cans are evident on the work sleighs, some with two sets of runners, an omnipresent sight in this hard-working farming community.

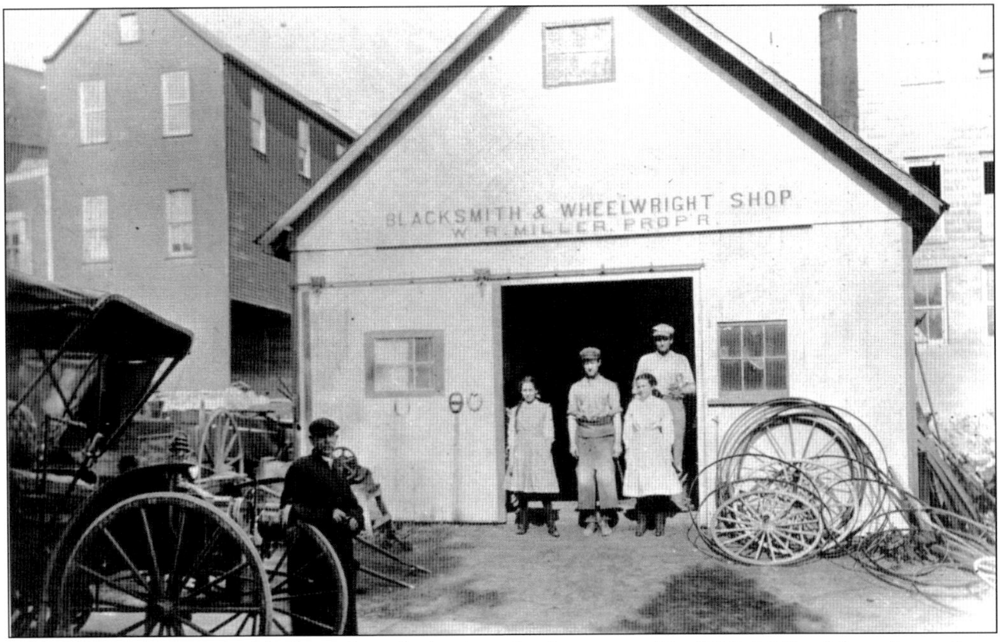

Off Bank Street was the blacksmith and wheelwright shop owned by W.R. Miller. He is shown here with his family. Note the results of his trade in the photograph—the attractive new wooden wheels and the metal for the outer covering of the wheels to help them last longer. A handsome carriage can be seen to the left with vulcanized tires that had taken the place of the older iron rims.

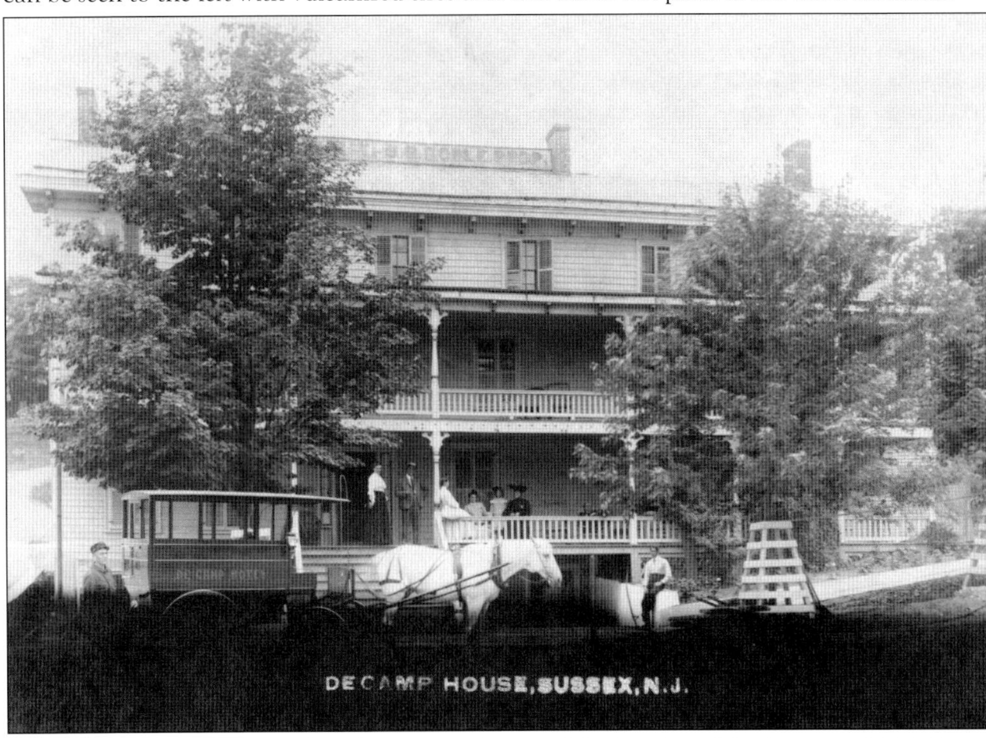

This image depicts the time when there was a change of the De Camp Hotel and the Goble Hotel. The wagon stands out front waiting to go to the train station.

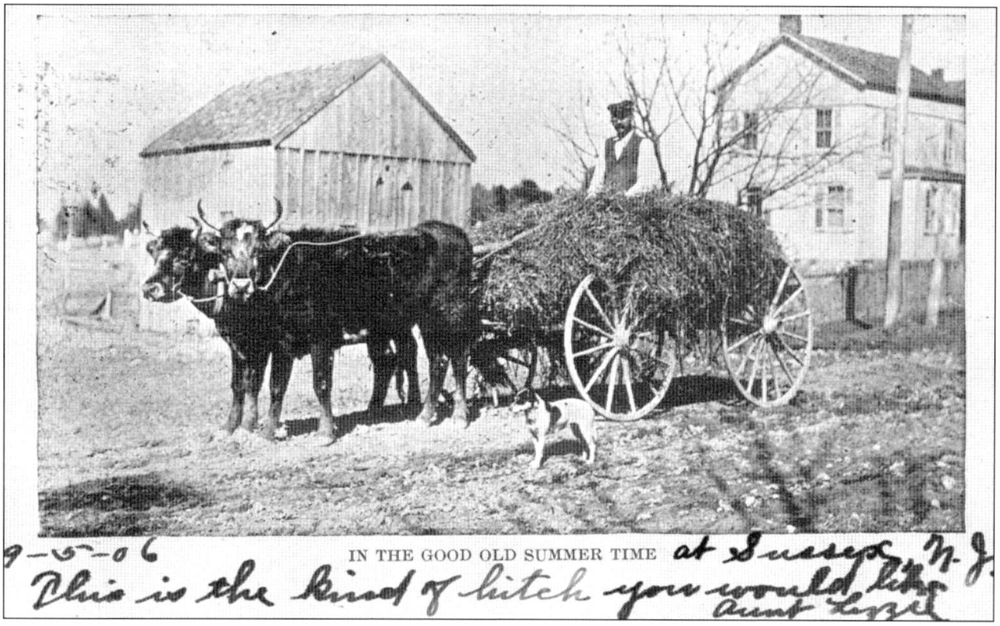

In addition to horses, other transportation included oxen. They were probably among the earliest beasts of burden in the area of Sussex-Wantage, being able to pull more weight and being perhaps easier to care for. Oxen could not haul as far or as fast as horses but had a place here in the rural country of Sussex County. (Courtesy of Mary Eleanor Eppler.)

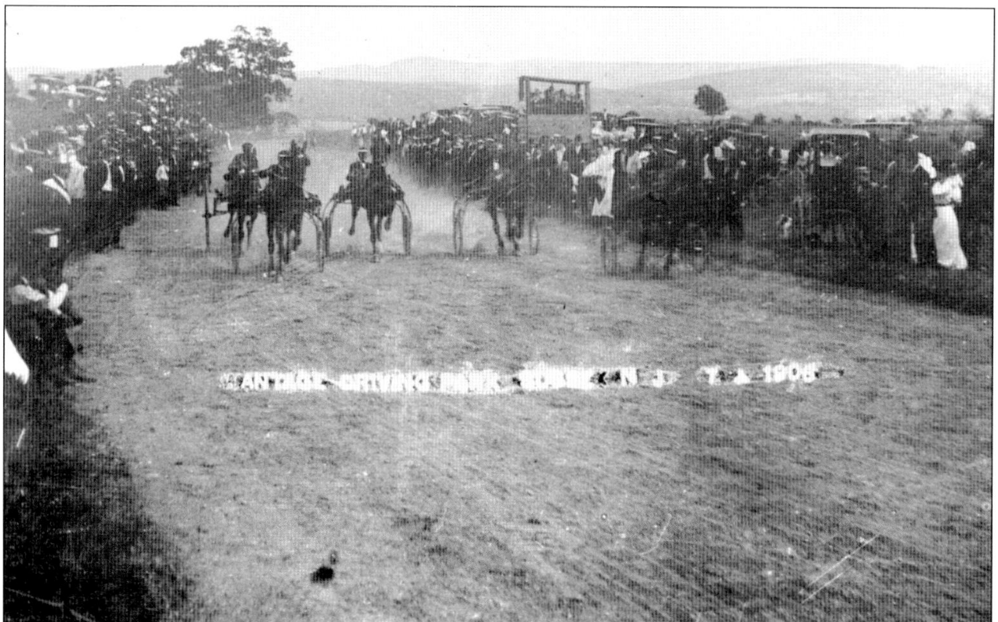

Welcome to the Wantage Racing Park in 1908! There were perhaps 1,500 people here at the track on any given day. The track was located just north of Sussex Borough across from today's Fairview Cemetery. Pictured here is the beginning of a race, the first of a series of distinctly and exclusively Sussex-Wantage horse-racing images. A day of racing would start at the Harrison House. Then the participants would bring their steeds to the nearby track and prepare. And they're off!

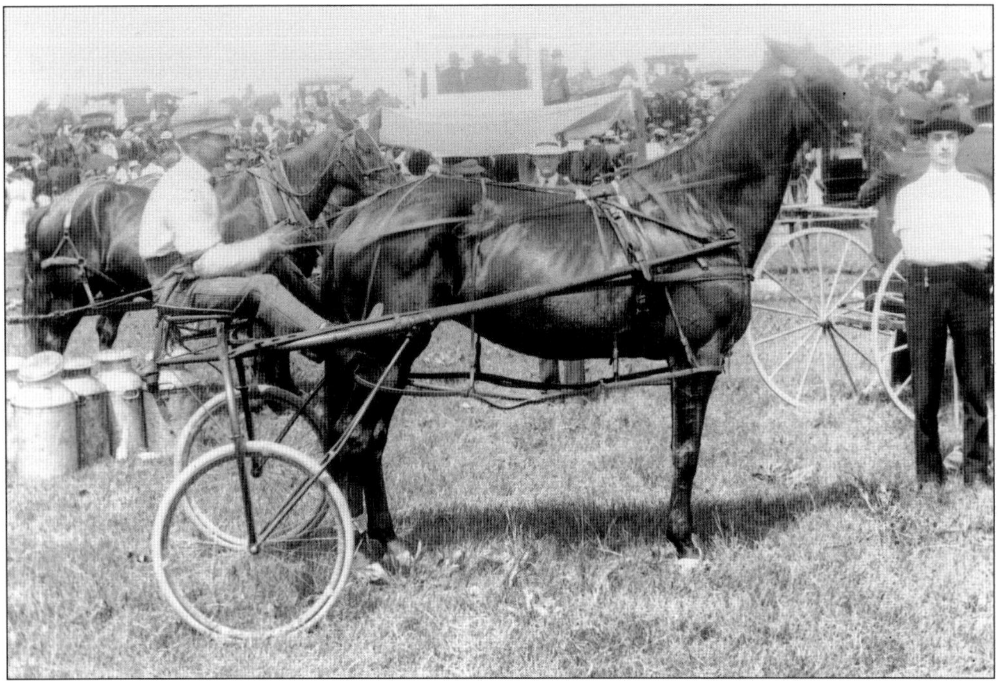

Here is the paddock of the Wantage Racetrack on race day with a large crowd gathered around. This is "Doc" McCoy. Doc owned a horse known as Dorothy S., presumably shown in the photograph. The crowded racetrack surrounding the paddock area with the booth at the finish line is visible. Note the many parasols, carriages, and nicely dressed residents of Sussex-Wantage attending this outstanding event. (Photograph by LMH.)

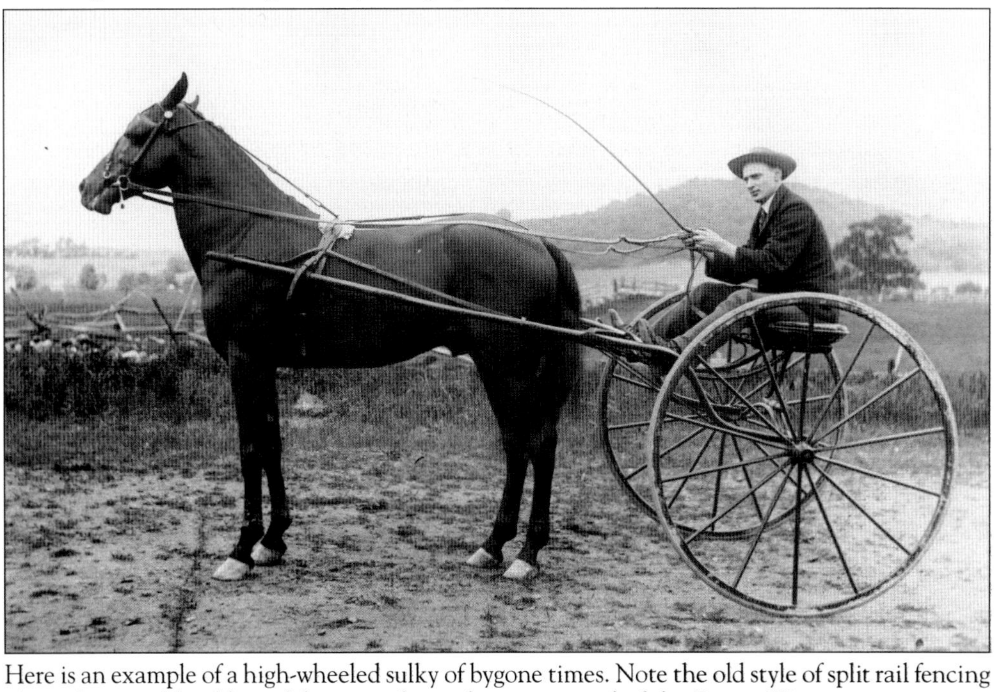

Here is an example of a high-wheeled sulky of bygone times. Note the old style of split rail fencing along the round boulders of the stone fence that are typical of the Sussex-Wantage area.

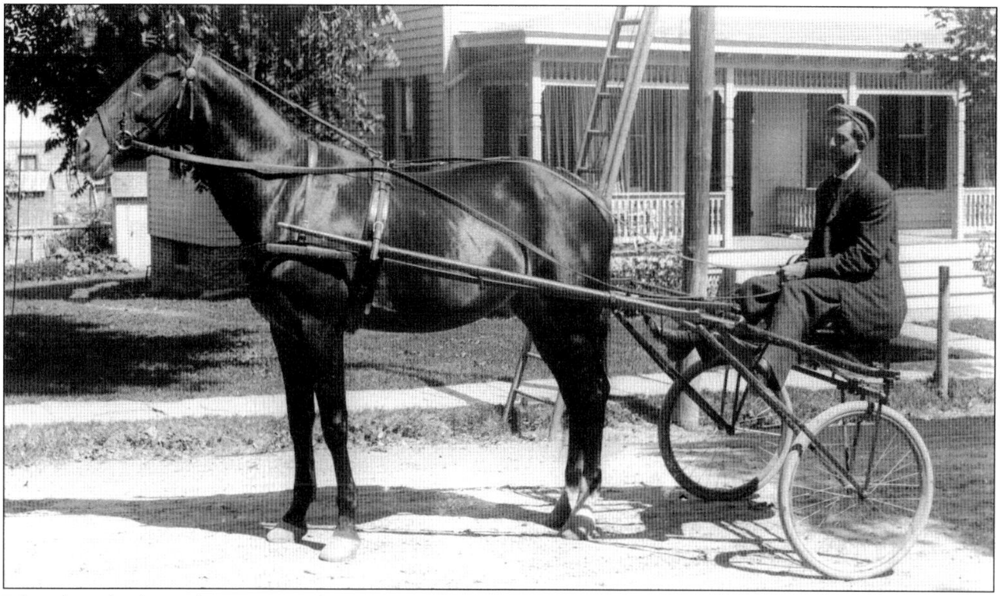

This fine looking horse is on his way to the racetrack on a dirt road in Sussex. Note the slate walkway leading around the house to the privy (outhouse) and the cabbage patch nearby. A ladder is up against the pole where first the telegraph was run, then the telephone on party lines, and then electricity later on.

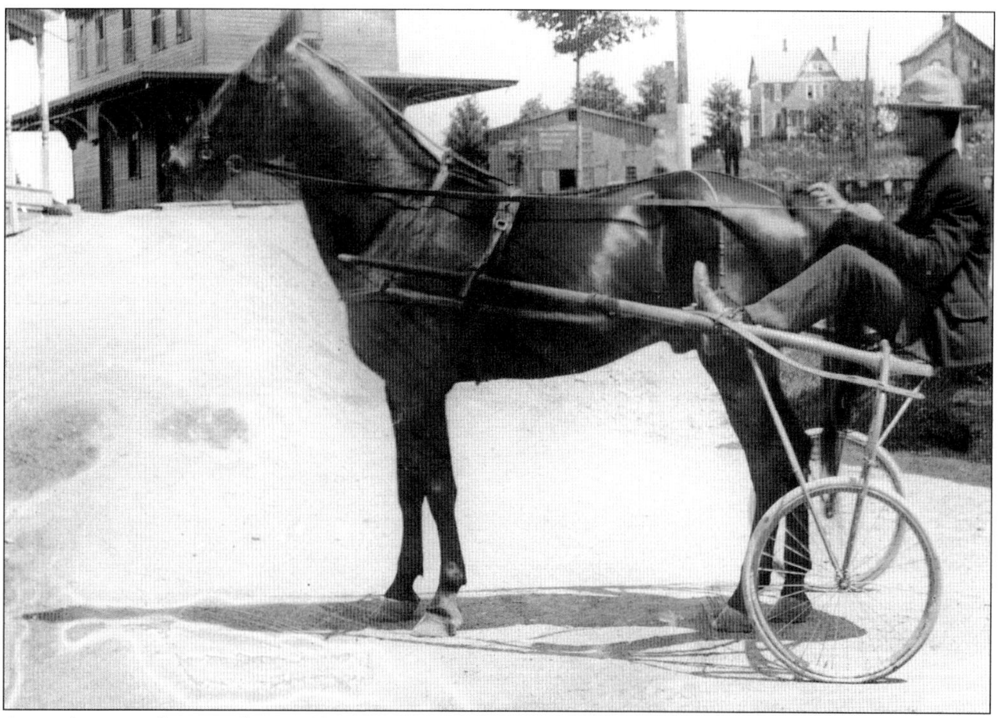

A racehorse is showing his stuff at the Harrison House with the Sussex Station in the background and the porch of the Harrison House to the left. The driver is wearing a campaign hat, perhaps from the Spanish-American War, and has the look of a no-nonsense driver. Fred Ayers took this photograph.

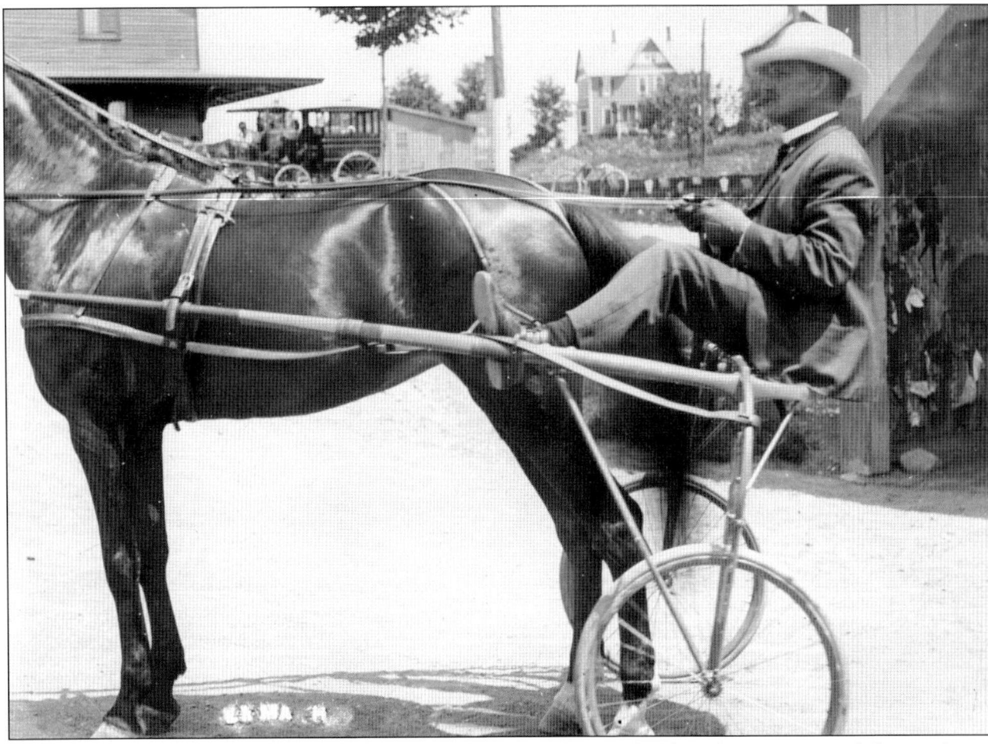

With a cigar in his mouth and a bright white Stetson hat on his head, a very proud driver drives this sleek racehorse, known as Erma H. He is confident but perhaps not the fastest in the sulky. This may actually be Austin Van Sickle. The time of this photograph may be late afternoon and the station wagons and horses may be awaiting the arrival of the NYS&W passenger train on its eastbound route, due at 5:33 p.m.

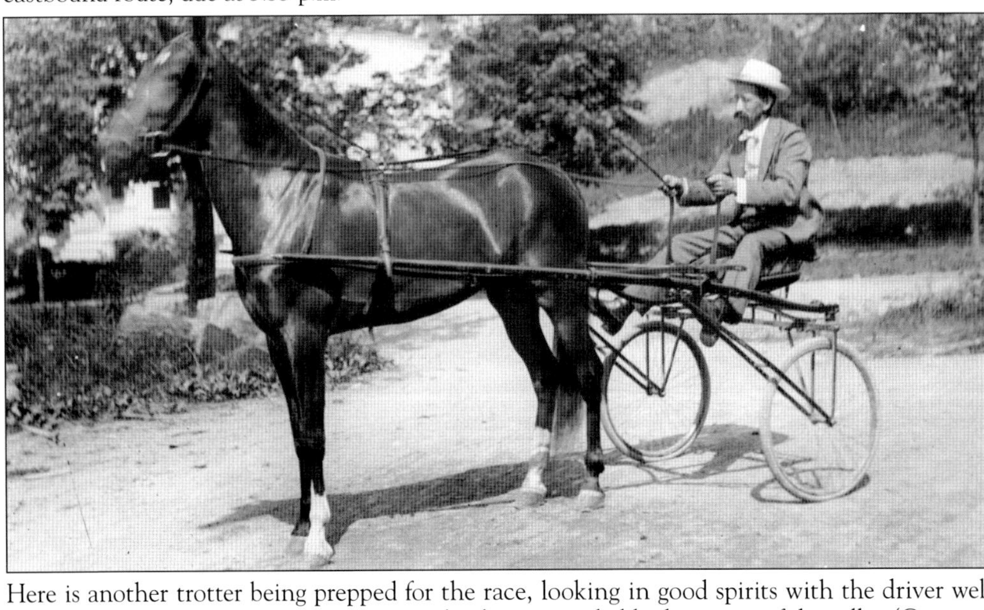

Here is another trotter being prepped for the race, looking in good spirits with the driver well dressed with a bow tie and white Stetson. The driver is probably the owner of the sulky. (Courtesy of LMH.)

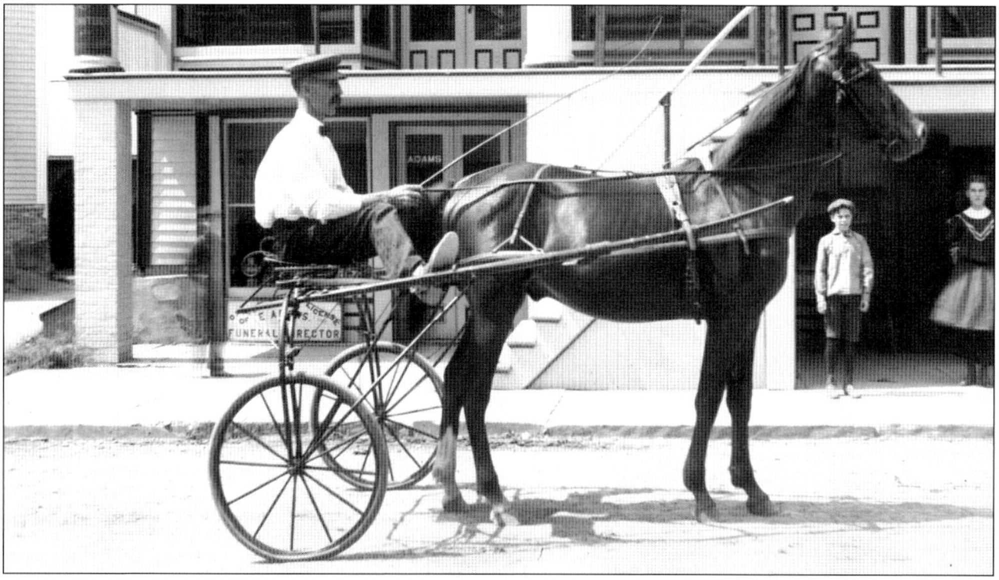

Dawson Van Sickle, a horse trainer, is shown in a racing pose outside of the funeral home on Main Street in Sussex. Also seen here is his daughter Rilla. (Courtesy of Fred Ayers.)

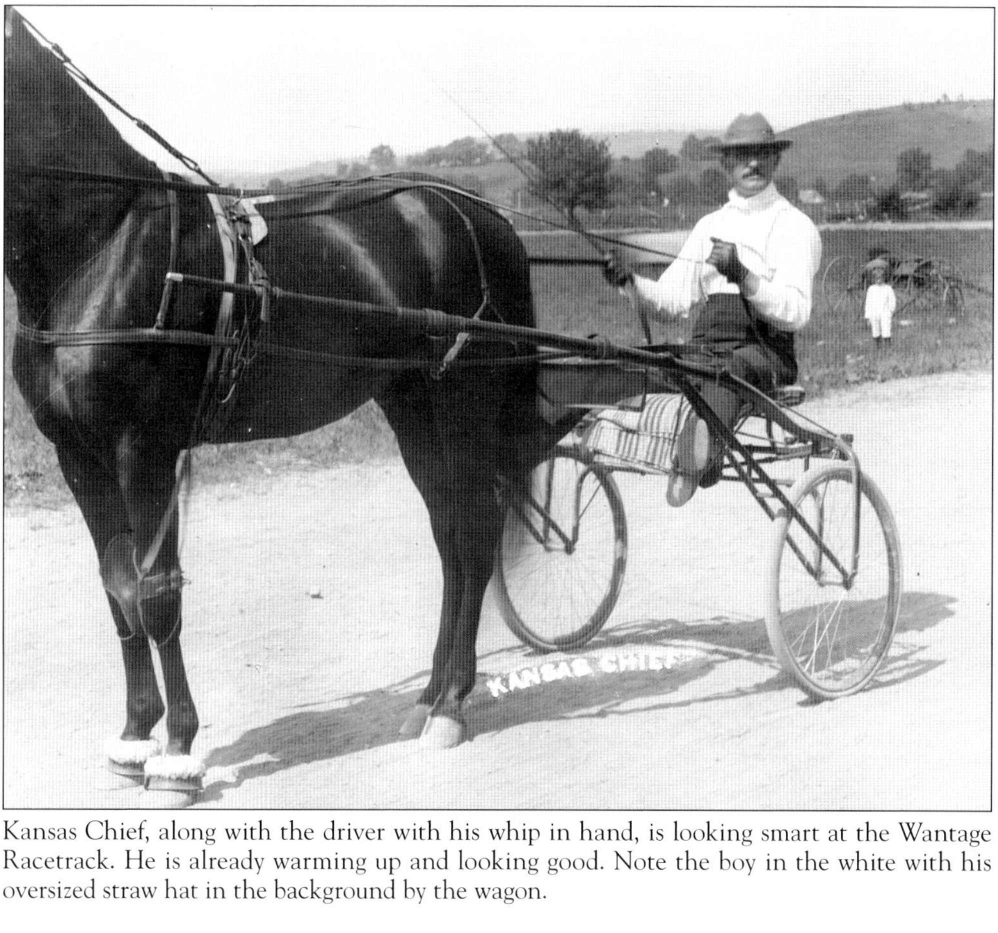

Kansas Chief, along with the driver with his whip in hand, is looking smart at the Wantage Racetrack. He is already warming up and looking good. Note the boy in the white with his oversized straw hat in the background by the wagon.

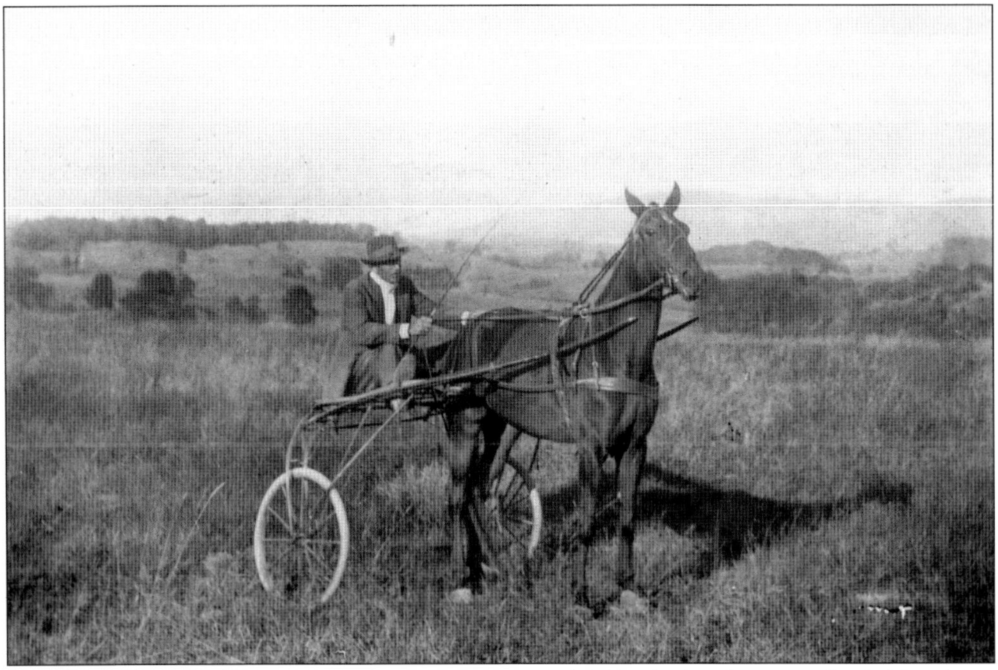

The local Renaissance man from Wantage, Peter Lott (1865–1914) is shown in the field with his racing horse and sulky. He was not only a Unionville farmer but also a poet. The horse's name was Babe. Here is part of one of Peter's poems: "Our wild flowers, like the bloom of childhood, / Strewing our pathway for a day / Along sunny rivers and dark wildwood, / They quickly fade away." (Photograph and poem courtesy Peggy Checkur and Gilman and Lott family.)

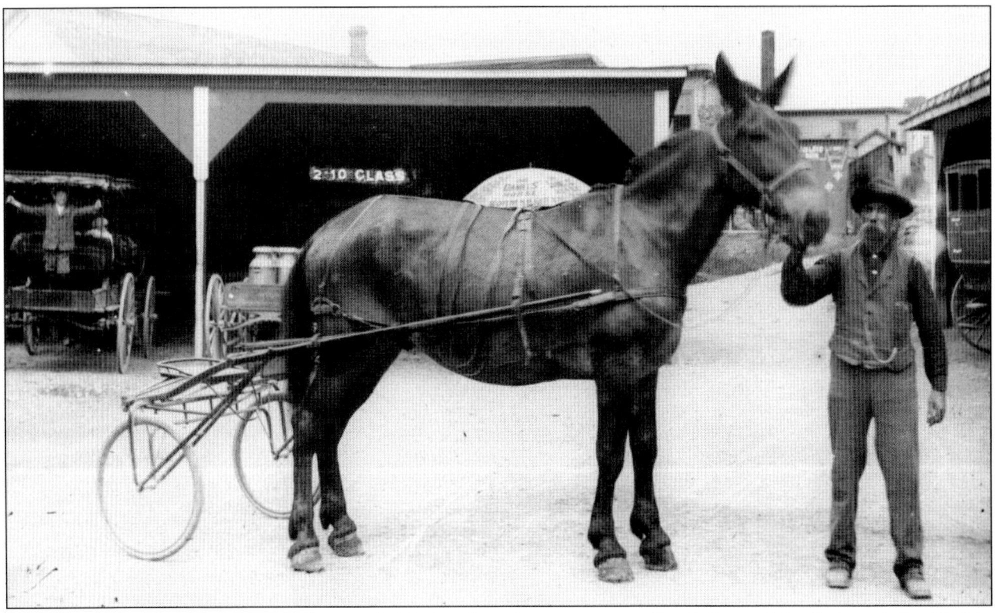

This oversize mare is called "Trotter, 2:10 class" and is seen outside of the stables behind the Goble Inn. The station wagon can be seen to the right in the barn, and a young boy is holding on to a surrey with fringe on top, and the ever-present buckboard with milk cans is located directly behind this "racer."

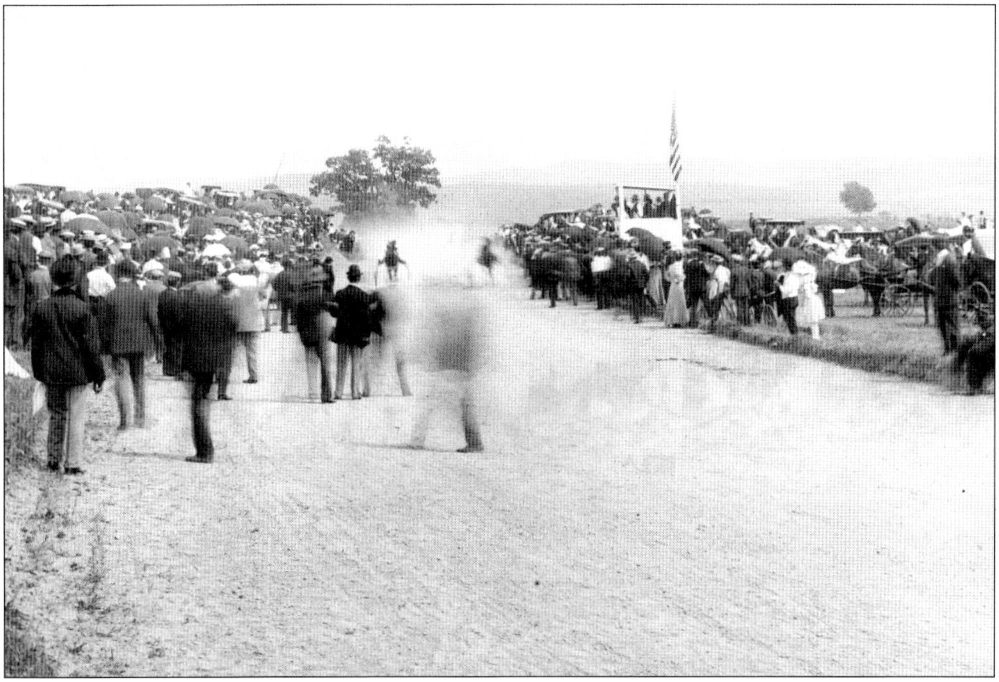

"And, they're coming down to the finish line" at the Wantage Racing Park about 1908. Spectators are walking out onto the track to witness the end of the race. The next photograph shows the winner from the Sussex-Wantage area.

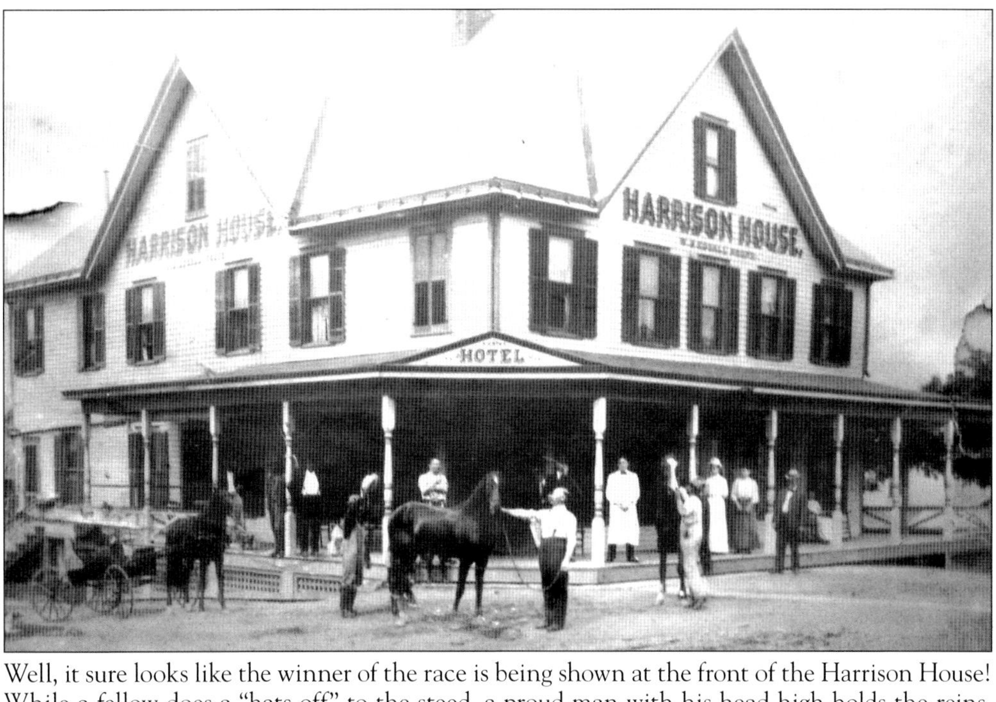

Well, it sure looks like the winner of the race is being shown at the front of the Harrison House! While a fellow does a "hats off" to the steed, a proud man with his head high holds the reins. Looks like a trainer for the runner up is calming the stallion down, with the bartender (probably Harry Harrison) and others looking on from the porch. (Author's collection.)

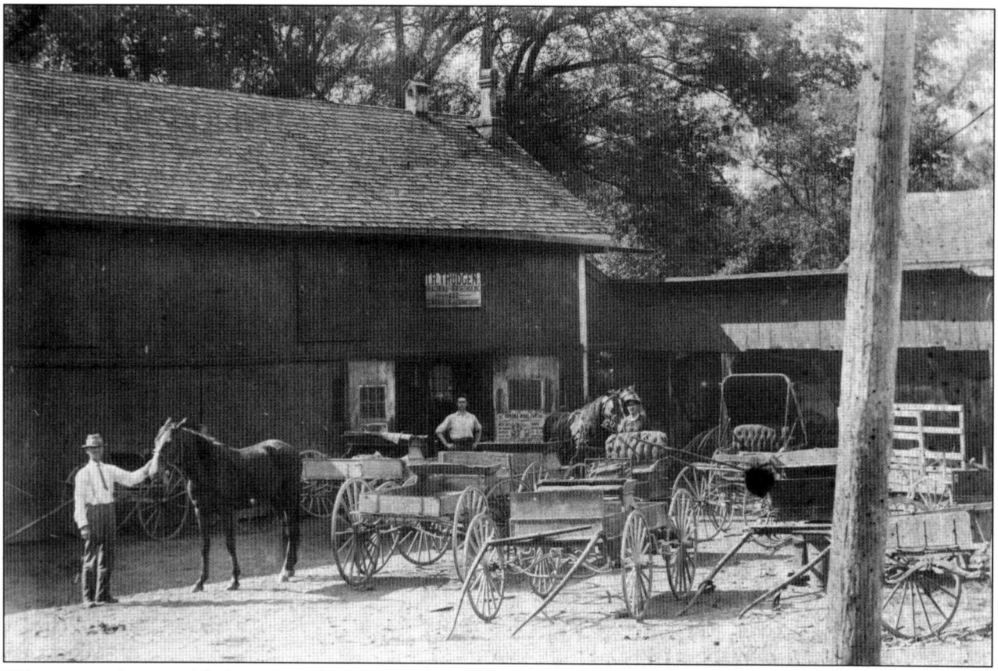

We are at the establishment of T.R. Trudgeon, who provided the town of Sussex with practical horseshoeing and general blacksmithing. A number of rigs are seen outside the shop; it certainly was the horse-powered era.

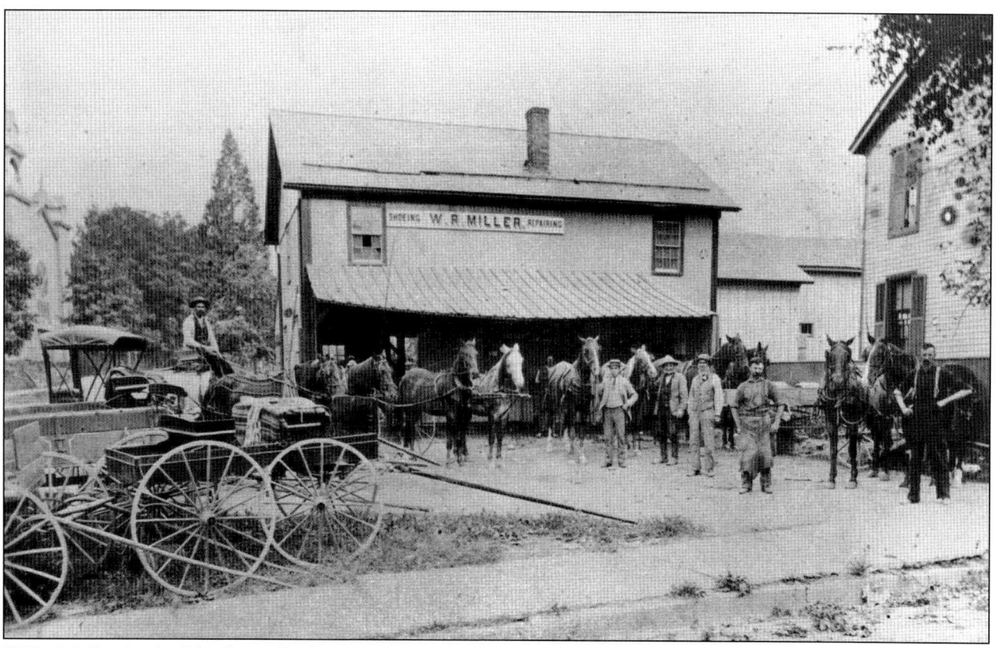

W.R. Miller had a blacksmith shop at the corner of Green and Bank Streets. This site is near where Peter Decker's homestead reputedly stood. Note the Methodist church in the background.

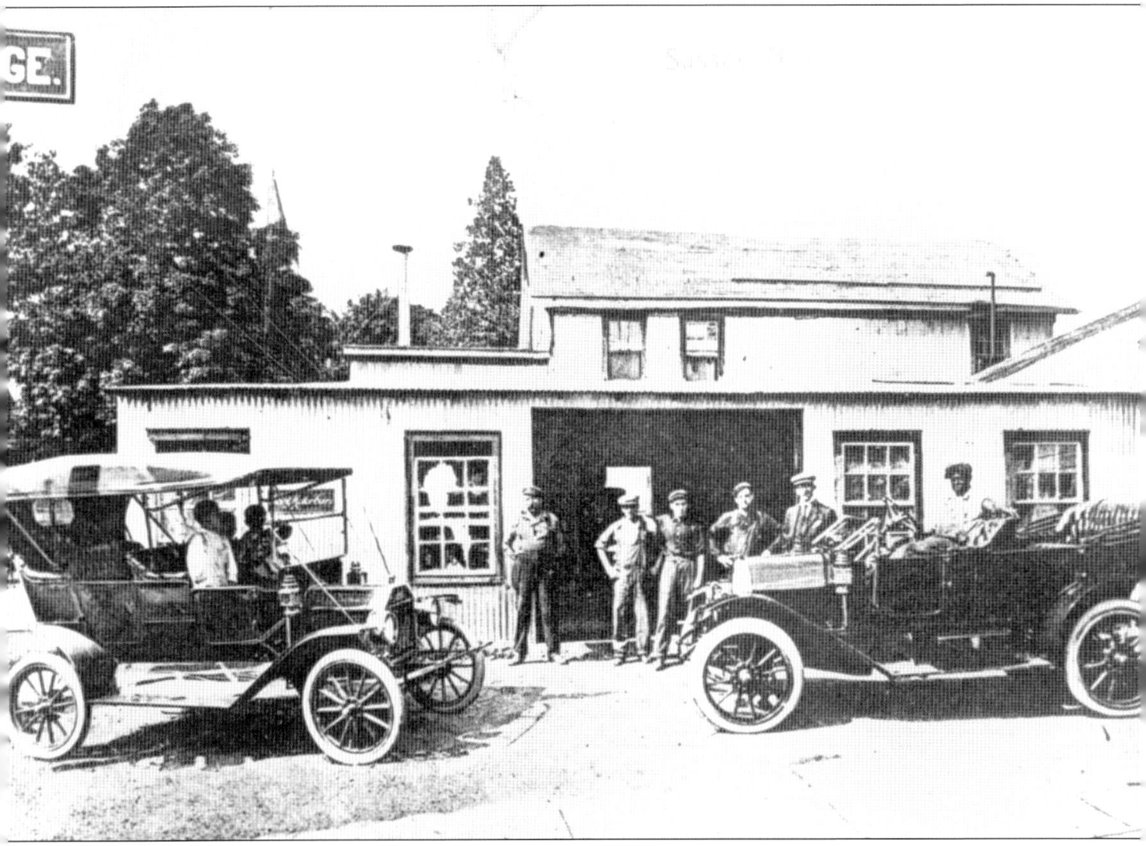

Just a few years after the last photograph, another one was taken at the same location and angle. There is no evidence of a blacksmith or his handicraft to be seen; it is now the age of the automobile.

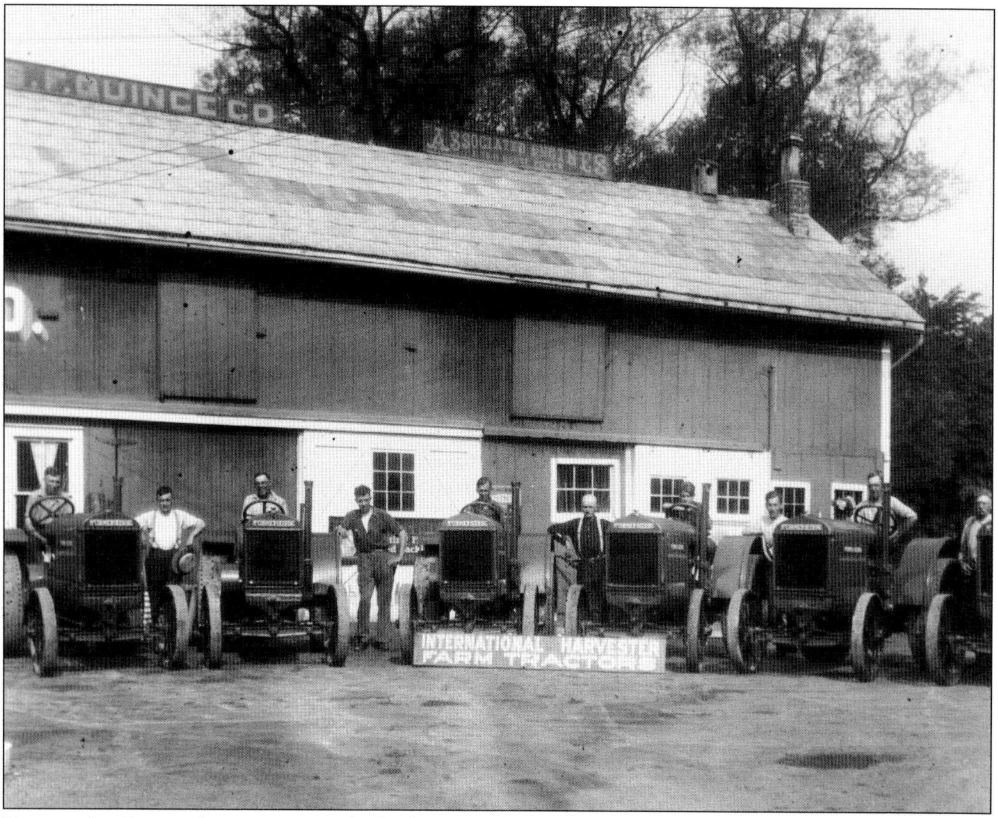

Here is the dawn of a new age, with the horse replaced by the motorized tractor. Commonly seen today in the fields plowing the cornrows are Farmall, John Deere, and International Harvester.

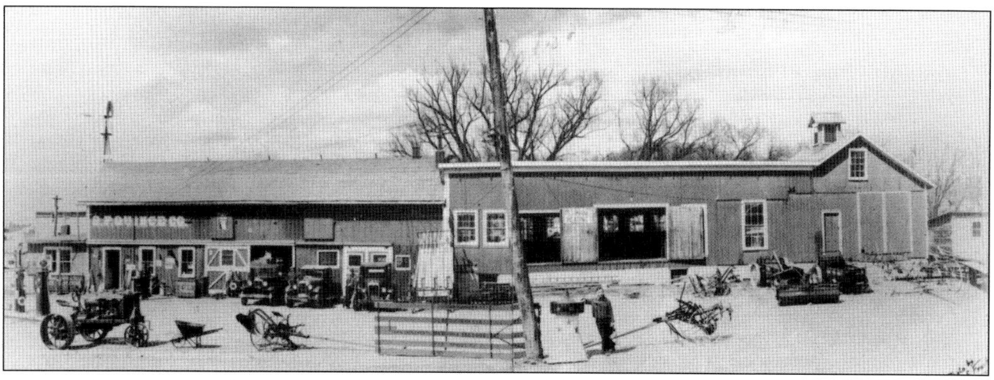

A close look at this photograph shows a number of the modern conveniences for sale for the modern farmer and gardener in the Sussex-Wantage area.

Eight

MILK

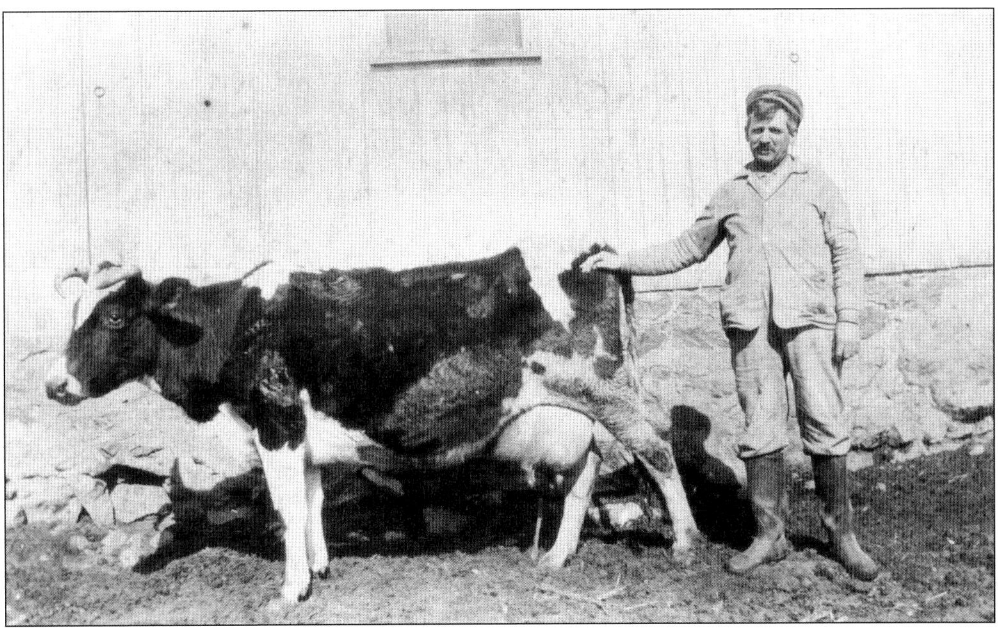

One of the most notable aspects of the Sussex-Wantage area in the last 150 years has been its milk and dairy production. The stock has been mainly Holstein cows (as shown here), the best for milk production; and also Jersey cows, which are better for butter; and Hereford cattle for beef. This photograph was taken on the Havens farm. This chapter is about the dairy industry in the Sussex-Wantage area and is set up to follow a sequence from farm field to factory. (Courtesy of the Havens family.)

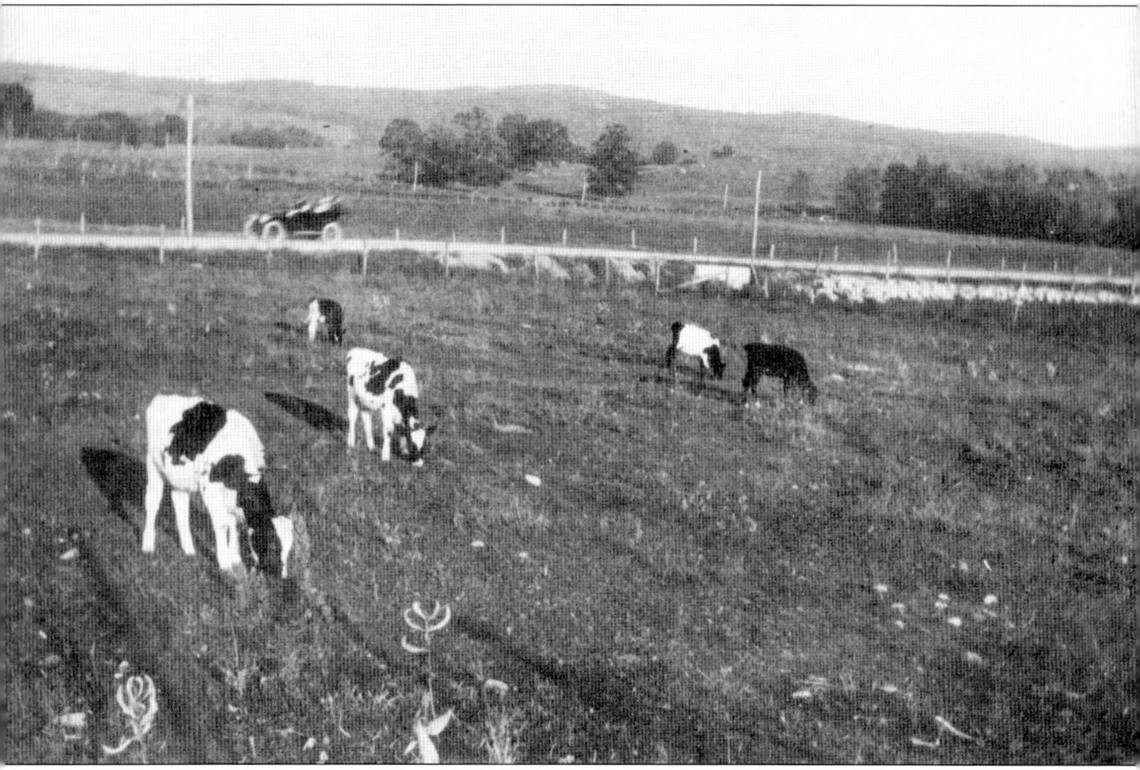

"Cattle-crossing" signs have been common in Sussex County, and until recently, such signs have also been seen outside of Sussex in Wantage Township. Periodically throughout the day, traffic would be halted, and the cattle would lumber across the road, oblivious to the hurried and harried people in the automobiles. The cows would amble along in their routine, natural way following each other from one barbed wire fence with the weathered cedarwood posts to the other side of the busy highway, leaving muddy tracks and perhaps a cow pie or two in their wake. The farmer guiding them, and holding up traffic, would then close the fence and let the motored traffic continue its modern-day race with the clock, while the cows would continue to the rich country pastures of the area. This is the Havens farm around 1915. By the way, it is pretty much the same scene today. (Courtesy of the Havens family.)

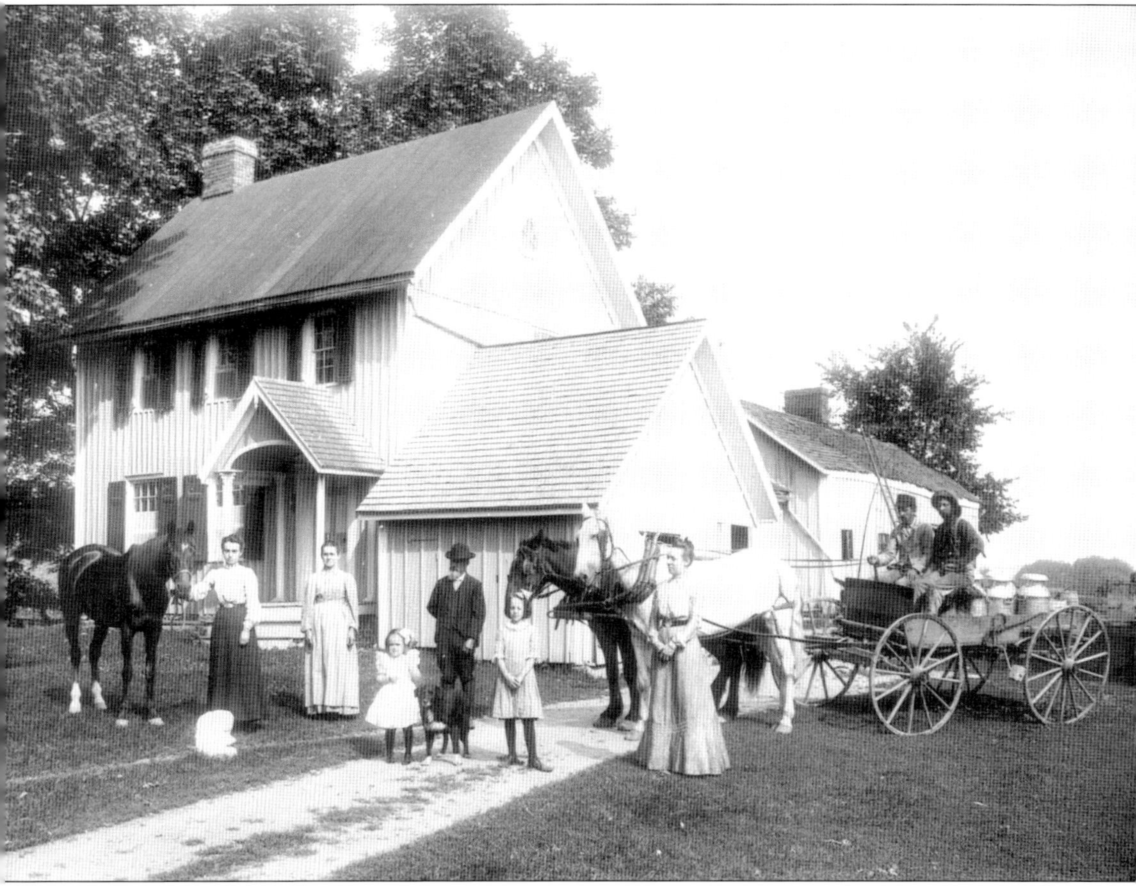

An unidentified local family from the Sussex-Wantage area is proudly standing with prized possessions outside its impeccable homestead. With reference to our sequence of images concerning milk production, at this stage the milk has been taken from the cows and perhaps kept cold in the spring house, and is now being taken from the farm to the milk processing facility to be readied for consumption in the metropolitan areas of the region.

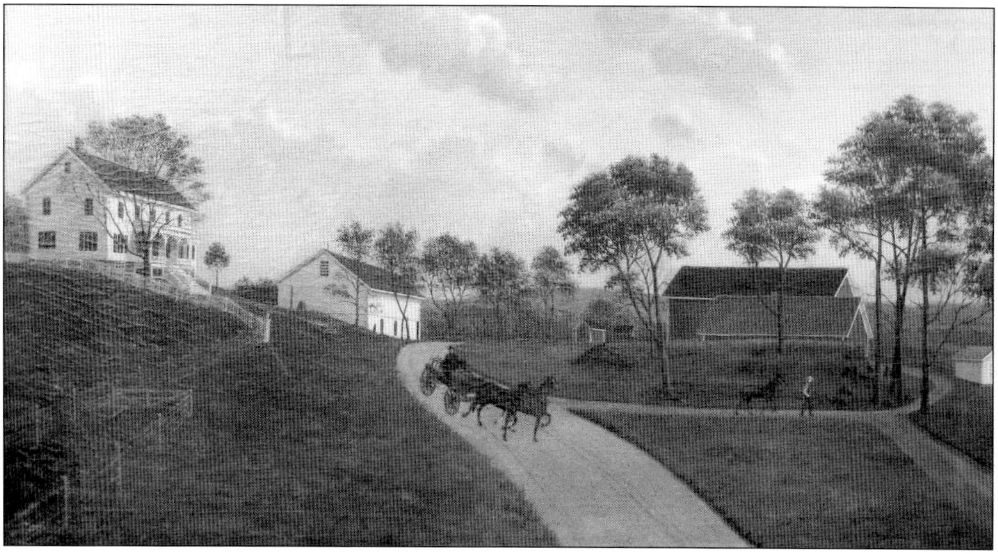

A farmer is depicted on the way to market with the farm's produce. This is a painting from the well-known local artist Louie Larsen. This is the Wantage farm, known as the Layton Homestead, in the year 1915. Peggy Gilman Checkur says that her dad milked the cows before dawn, put the warm fluid into the springhouse for cooling, and then drove to Unionville to the creamery. He then traded butter and eggs for flour and sugar. (Courtesy of Richard Martin.)

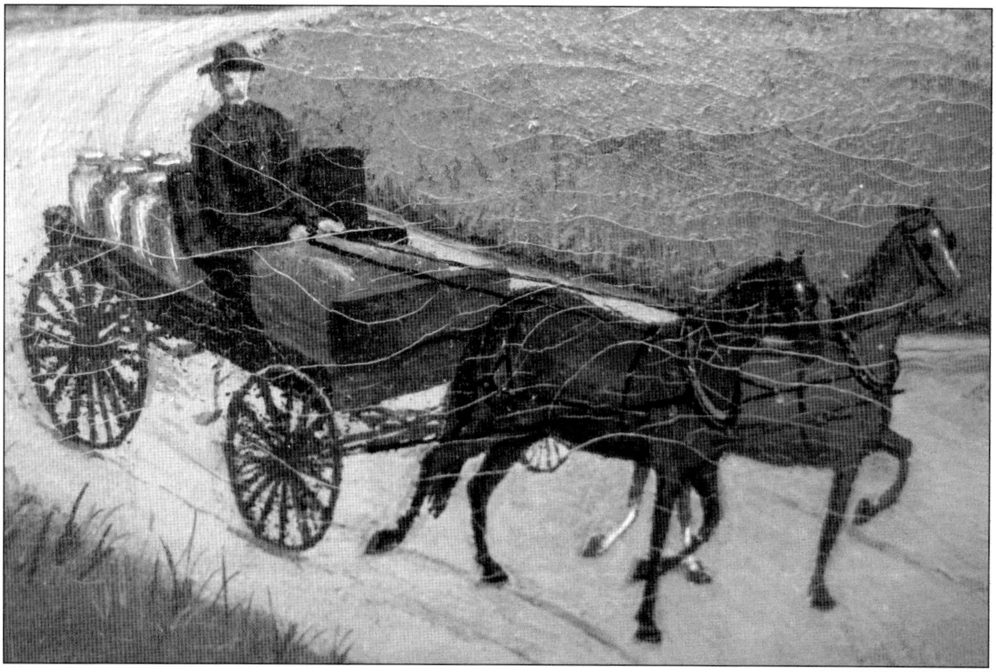

Here is an artist's rendition of taking milk to the creamery. This view from a time before the automobile depicts how important these trips were. The excited horses are stretching the boundary from the farm to the town. There will certainly be the delivery to the creamery and some needed cash to pay the grocer and the dry goods store. There will be time to enjoy perhaps some chewing tobacco and a cigar and the Sussex-Wantage specialty drink with apples, dating from before the Revolutionary War—applejack liquor. (Courtesy of Richard Martin and family.)

Out along the countryside just outside of Beemerville stood the creamery. A creamery is where the thicker cream is separated from the milk. It may also perform pasteurization of milk that has been skimmed, which means it is heated and cooled, minimizing microbes that may contaminate the liquid. The author's great-aunt Mary Coddington Garrity related to him that her family—the Courtrights and Coddingtons—would take the milk to this creamery by horse-drawn wagon or to Pelletown and let the horses go down to the stream for their refreshment.

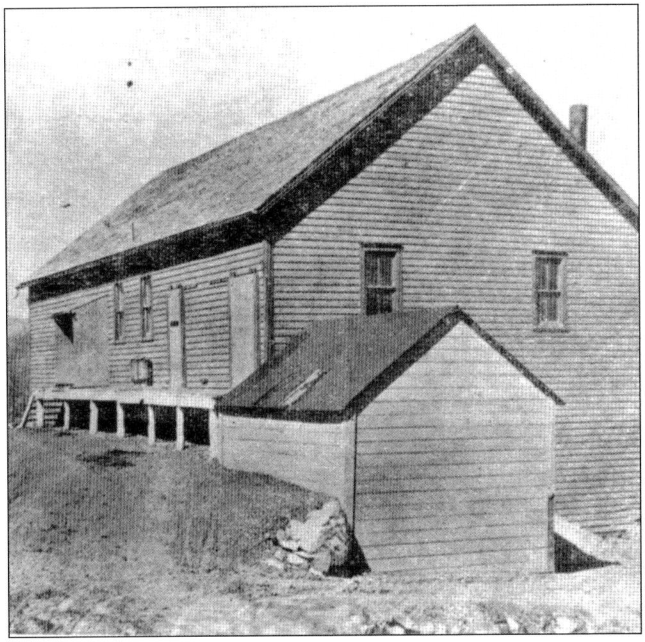

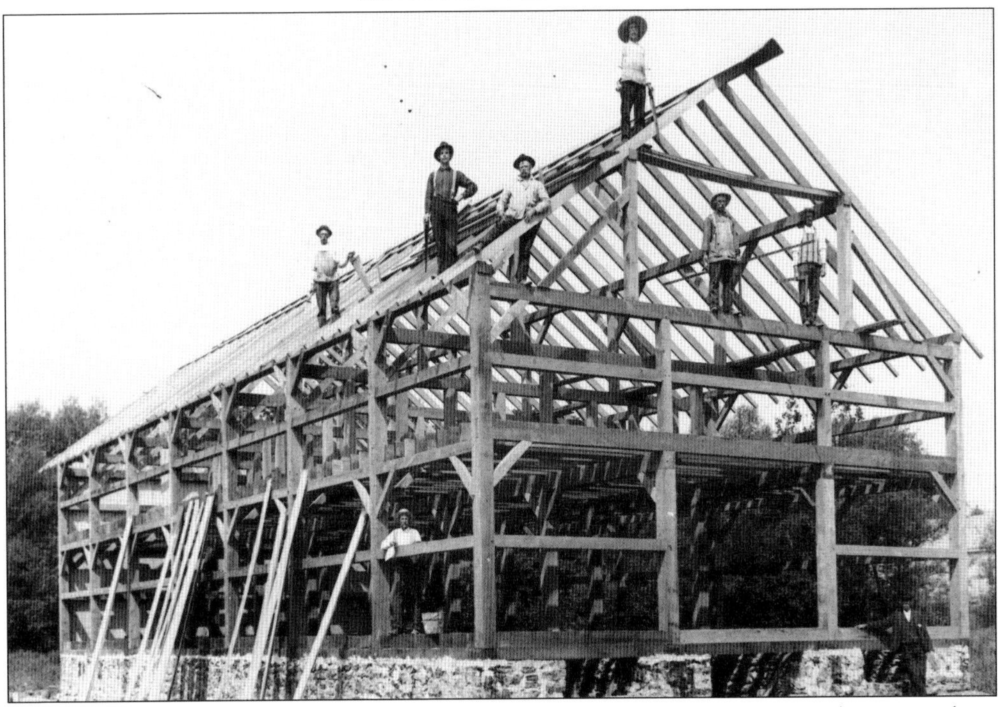

Here, the Walling Creamery is being rebuilt after a fire. In the town of Sussex, there were three milk-related buildings: the creamery near the Lehigh & New England Railroad station down on Walling Avenue, another near the New York, Susquehanna & Western station on Munson Street, and the condensery across from the *Wantage Press*. A condensery is a plant where most of the water that is in milk is evaporated by heating up the milk. Fires unfortunately were a common experience before running water, better safety, fire hydrants, fire pumpers, and trucks and the decreased use of candles, open-flame oil lamps, and fireplaces.

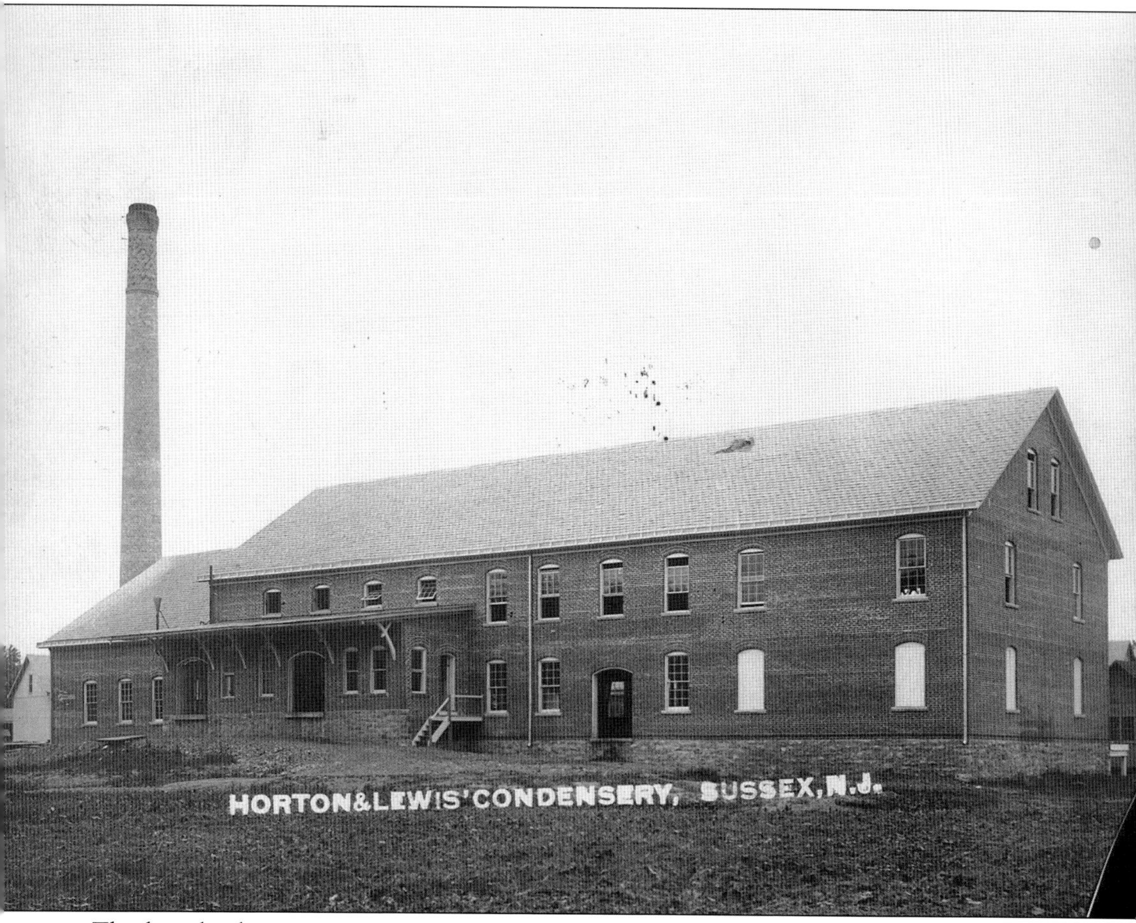

This large brick structure was in a great location. It was along the Clove Brook where water could be obtained easily, along with ice, and, in older days, power. This building was also along the L&NE railroad for receiving coal for energy and for shipping products out. There were several large creameries in the Sussex-Wantage area, along with smaller ones. Two of the larger companies were Bordens and Nestles. (Courtesy of Olga Bazylevich Stefkowich and family of Mike the Jeweler.)

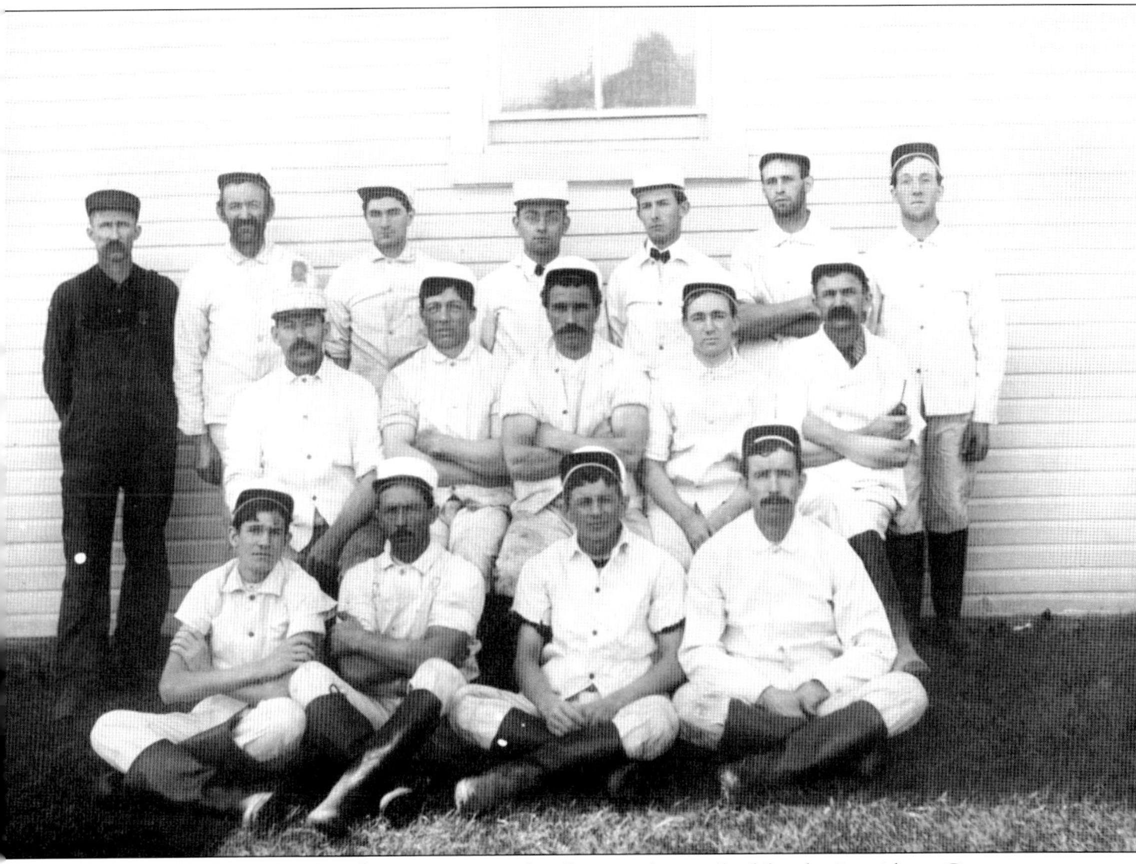

Shown in this photograph is the contingent of milkmen who worked for the Lewisburg Creamery. The milk that had been taken from the cow, delivered by horse and wagon to the creamery and condensery, processed, and then delivered to the local companies to be bottled was now ready for delivery to the customer. While much of the dairy products were shipped by railroad to the cities, the locals here in Sussex County also were eager consumers. Milk would be delivered in the morning and left within the milk box on the front porch. They came in glass bottles with a paper pull cap and later aluminum foil. When the milkman arrived, he took yesterday's empties with him from the box before putting in the fresh bottles. This photograph was taken about the year 1900. (Courtesy of Thomas L. Smith and Clarence Ayers.)

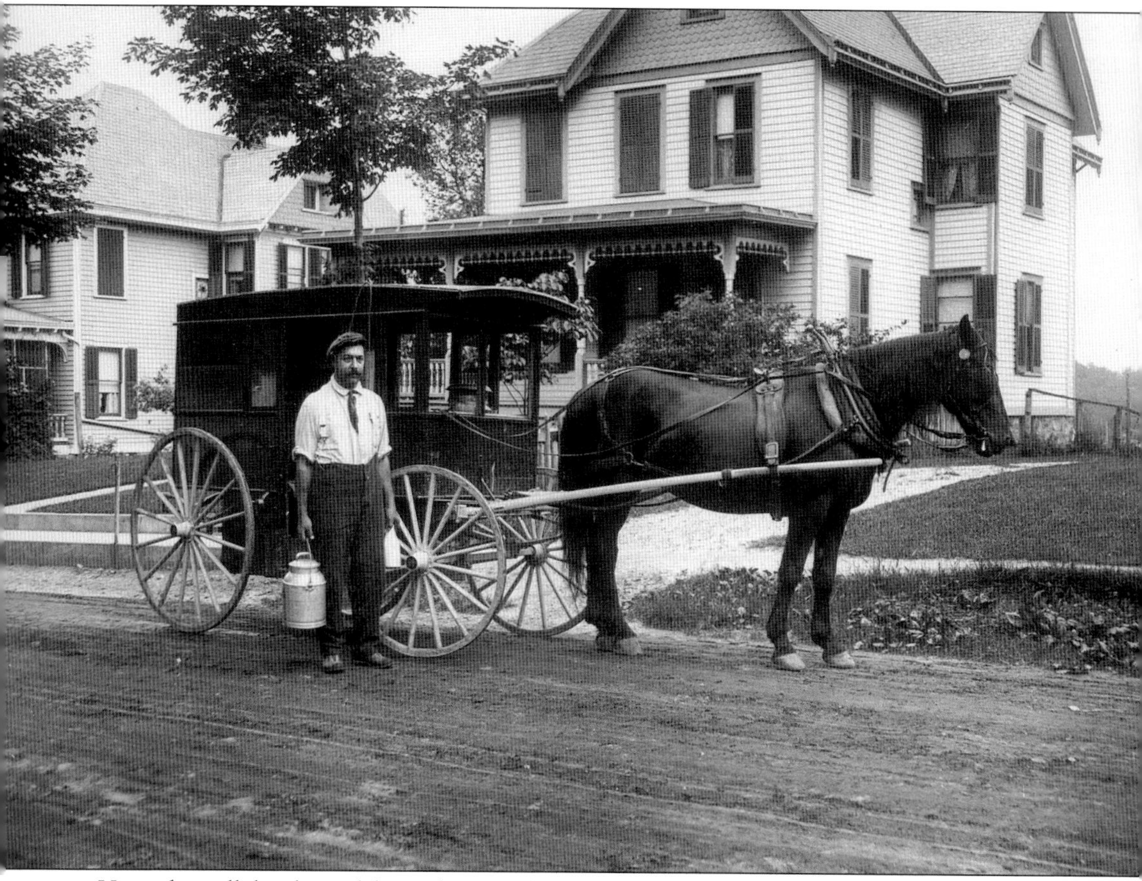

Here, the milk has been delivered to people's front doors in quart bottles. This photograph from around 1900 shows a delivery on Vernon Avenue in Hamburg, as photographed by the prolific A.J. Bloom on a glass-plate negative. Many farmers were members of organizations and cooperatives, such as the New York Dairymen's League. Some local milk companies, with unique bottles still to be found at antique sales or in attics, include: Reeve Harden of Hamburg, Dagmar Dale Farms of Sussex, Joseph Bicsak of Franklin, Fred Moore of Newton, Franklin Lakes Dairy, and others. (Courtesy of Art Jordan & Antique Photographs.)

Nine

TRAINS

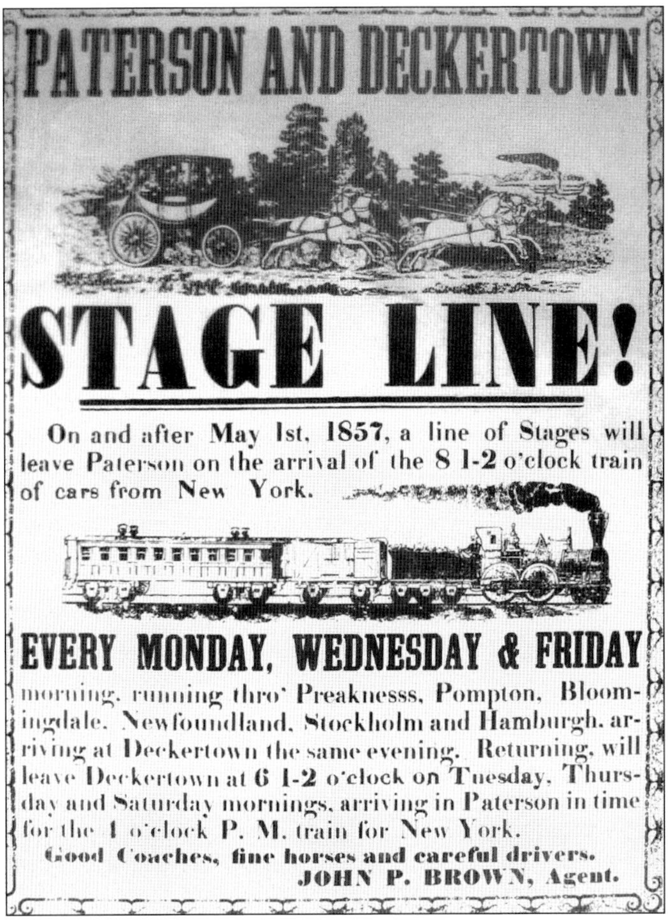

When Peter Decker became the first known person to inhabit the area, travel to the outside world was very limited and was mostly by foot or horse. The trails were of limited size and primitive in condition. Shortly after 1800, as America was opening up to settlement, turnpikes came into being and roadways improved. The stagecoach brought many visitors and people passing through during the period of about 1810 to 1870. The railroads came through the area about this time and quickly supplanted the stagecoach—they went out of business shortly thereafter. Note here the advertisement that depicts the stagecoach and also the train service. Of particular note is that the earliest of passenger train cars looked almost identical to the stagecoach. (Courtesy of Howard Case.)

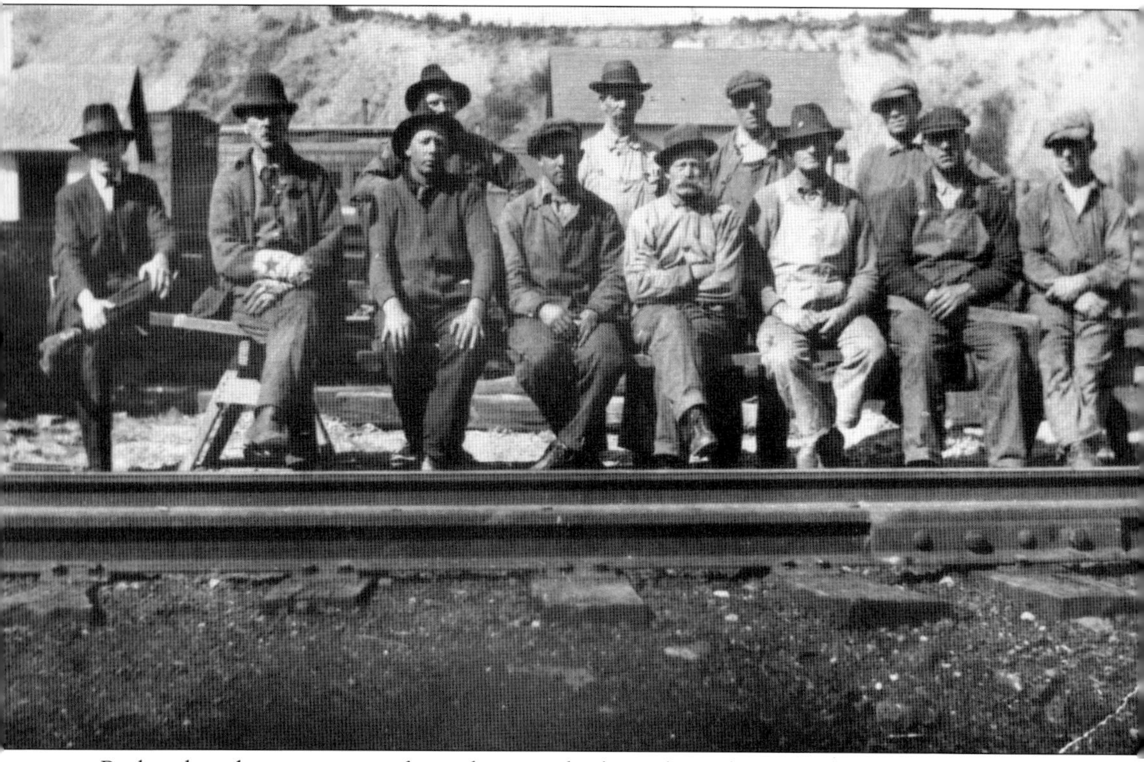

Railroad workers are sitting for a photograph along the railroad tracks. Two rail lines served Sussex, aiding the incoming deliveries of coal, furniture, and lumber. The area produced ice, dairy products, and stone from Fuller's Bluestone Quarry in Quarryville. This was used for stone flagging, curbing, gutter coping, sills, steps, and bridging rock. The stone can be seen in construction throughout the area.

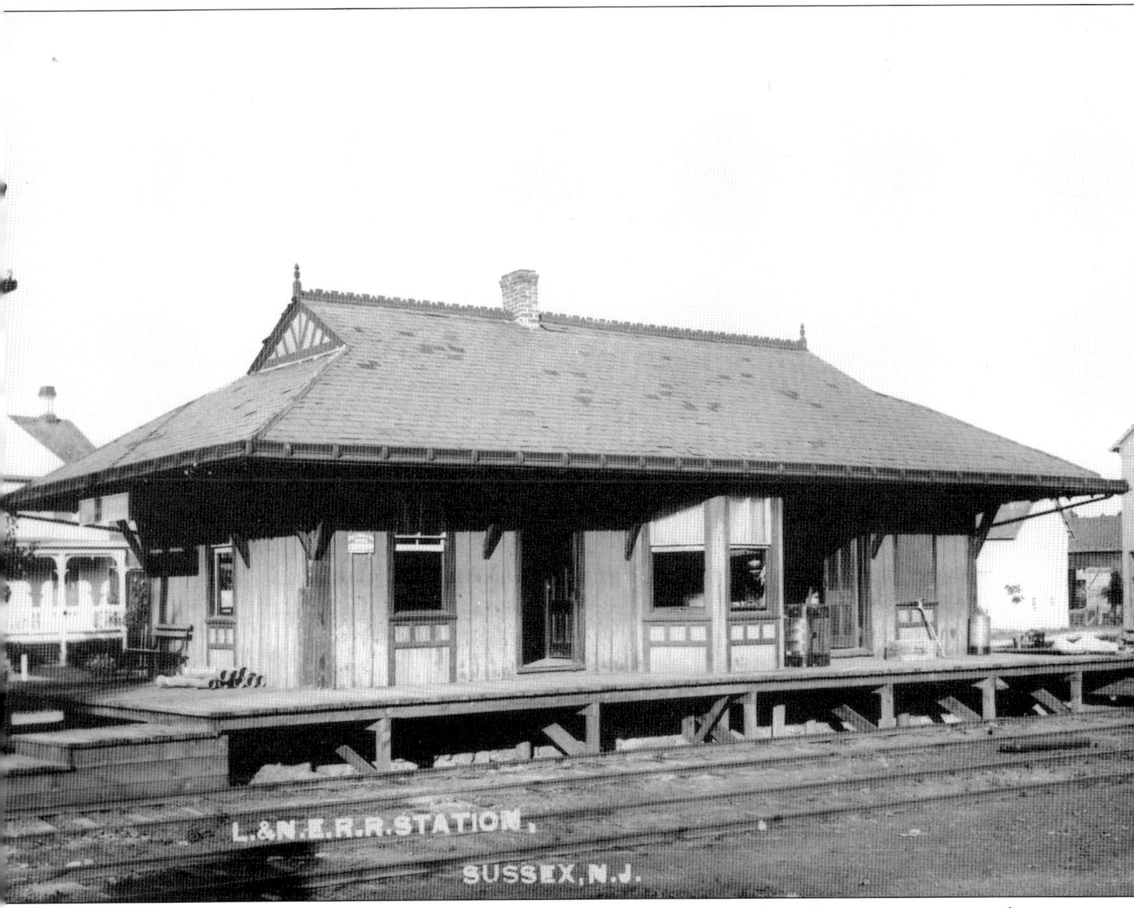

The train station of the Lehigh & New England Railroad is depicted in the sun on a quiet day. The L&NE connected Northeastern Pennsylvania, through New Jersey, and up through New York State to the Poughkeepsie Bridge and on to New England. It also allowed for land access to New York City, as the rails terminated at the river and barging across the water would have been required to reach the city otherwise. After about 1870, great change took place in the countryside of Sussex-Wantage with the emplacement of the rail lines, as well as the sounds of the steam train. Transportation changed from the horse to the mechanical.

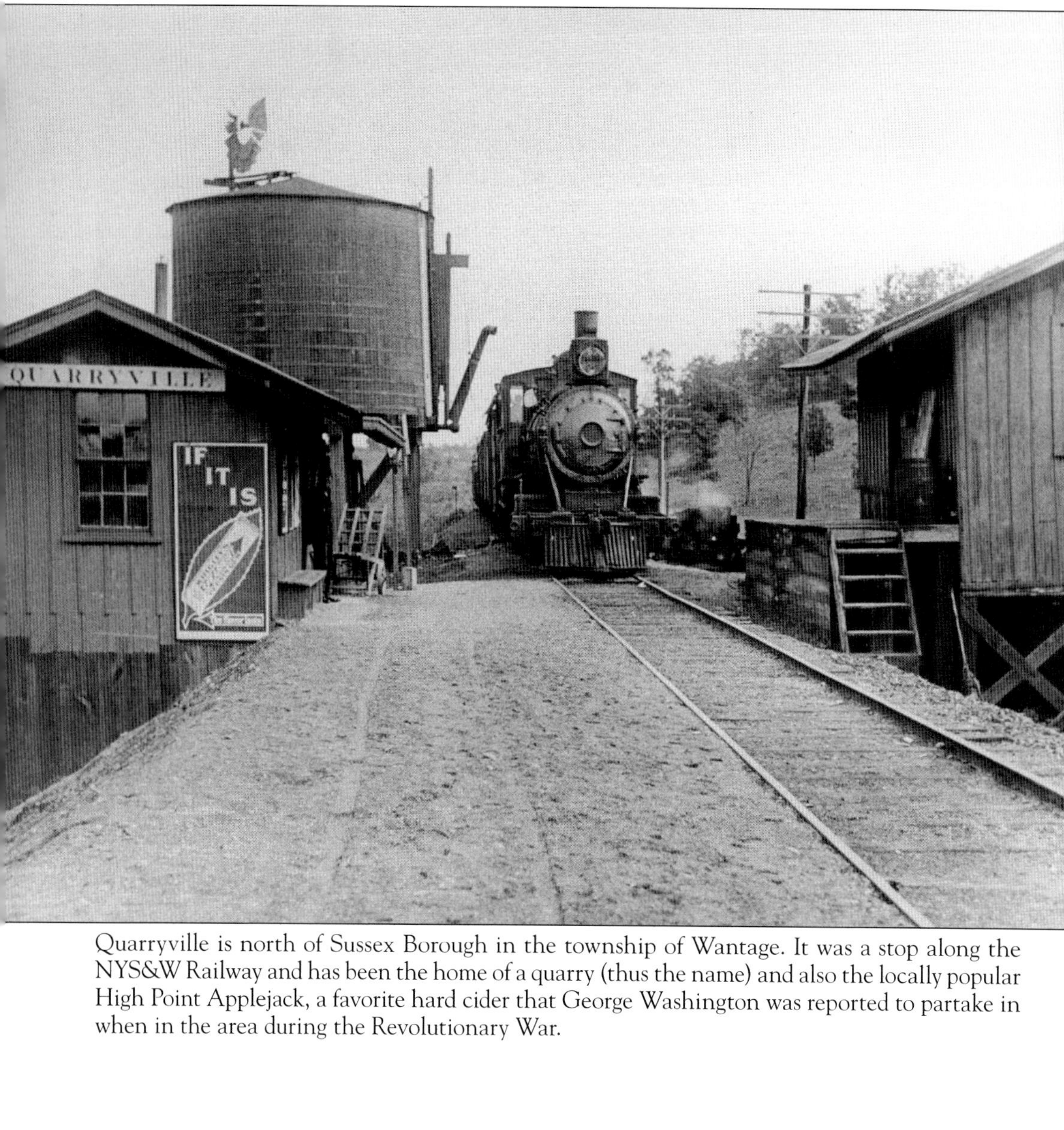

Quarryville is north of Sussex Borough in the township of Wantage. It was a stop along the NYS&W Railway and has been the home of a quarry (thus the name) and also the locally popular High Point Applejack, a favorite hard cider that George Washington was reported to partake in when in the area during the Revolutionary War.

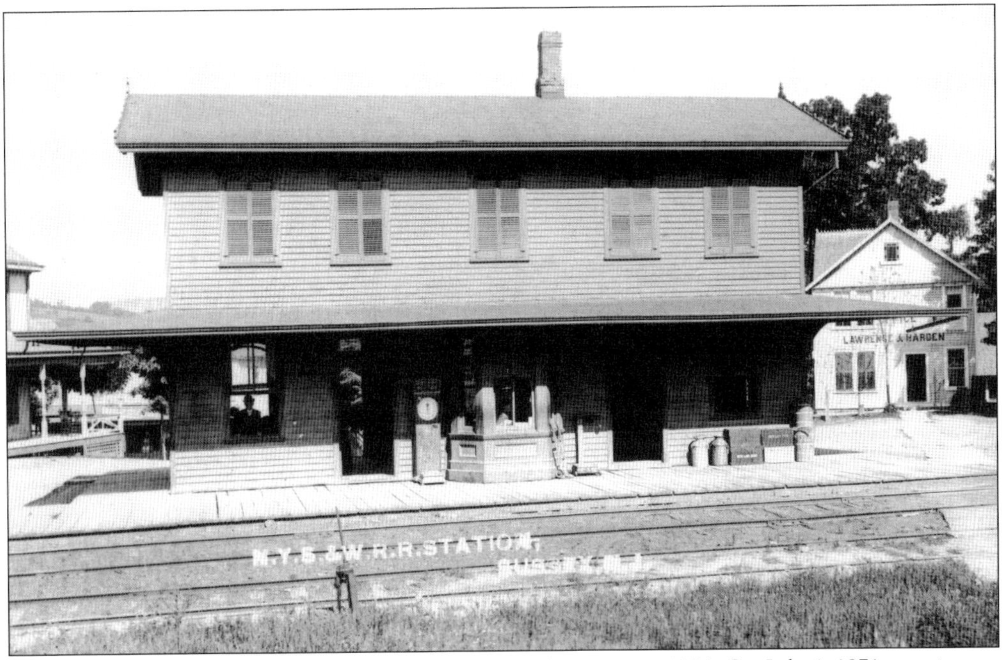

The Midland Railroad began construction near Deckertown in 1870. On July 4, 1871, a train ran from Newton, through Franklin Furnace and Deckertown, to Unionville, New York, over two roads (Sussex Railroad and New Jersey Midland). The Midland became the New York, Susquehanna & Western Railway. Notice the ticket agent inside the window with a bowler hat on.

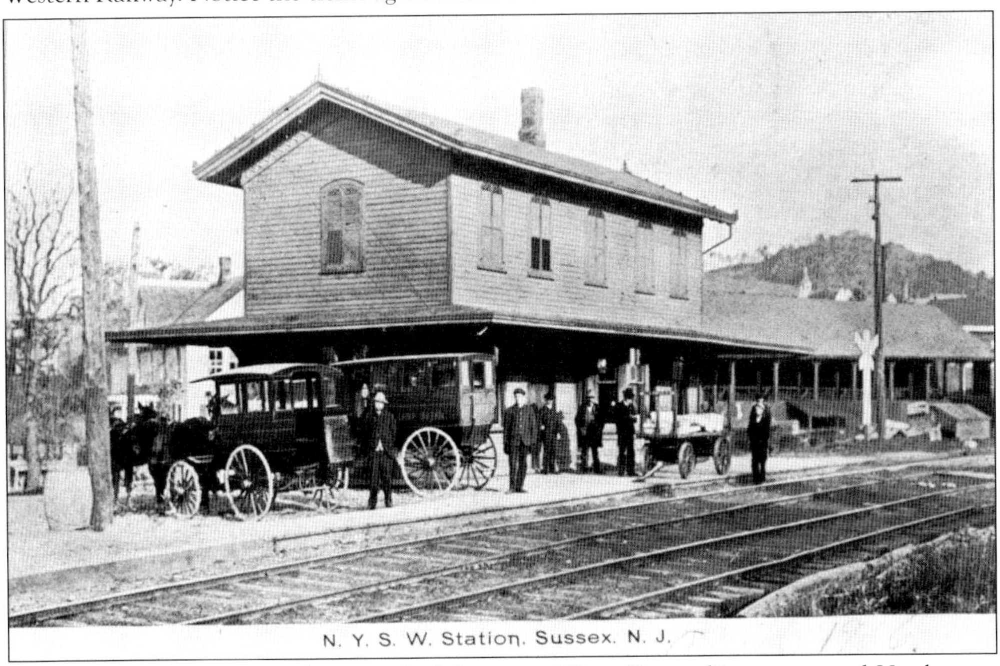

Many people are awaiting the arrival of the train. The offices of Lawrence and Harden are behind the station. Reeve Harden was a prominent man in Hamburg, where he had worked at the railroad station and also provided coal for fuel, milk production and delivery, lumber, and other services.

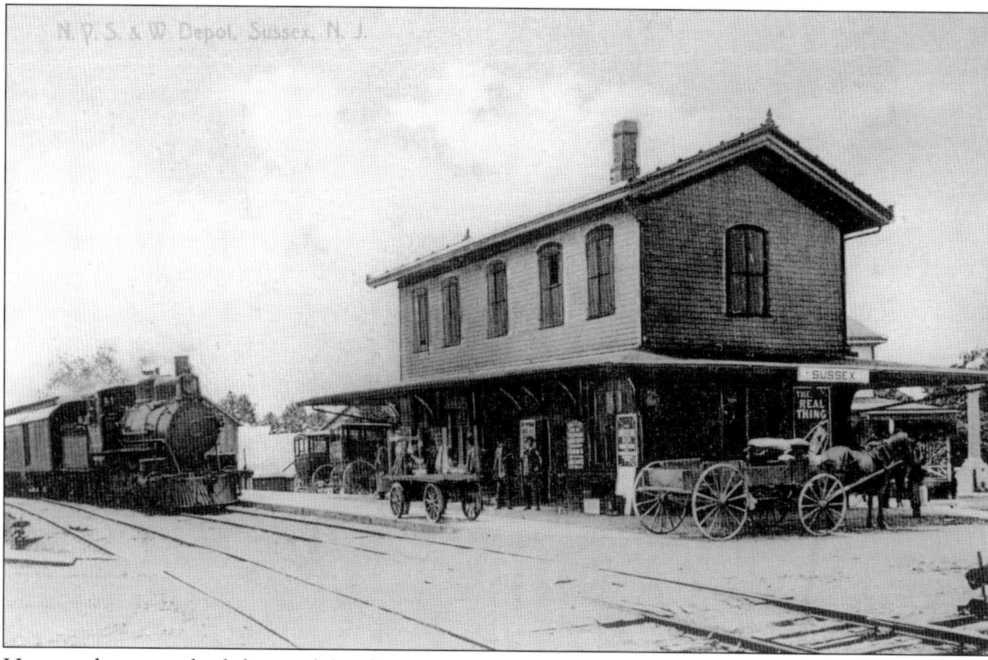

Here is the arrival of the coal-fired steam locomotive with a mail car behind it. This area of Sussex was known as "Gingerville" reportedly because Amos Munson had a horse by that name and was located nearby.

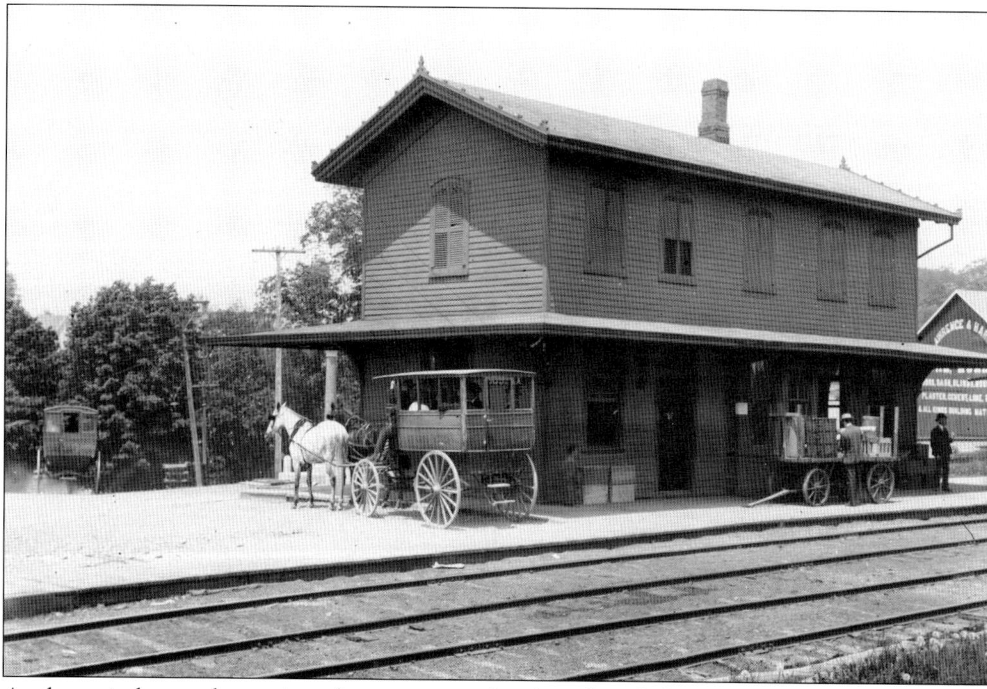

As the train leaves the station, the wagons are heading downhill to the hotels with their newly arrived guests. Perhaps they are on business or are coming to enjoy some country air and relaxation from the bustle of the city. Sussex County was well-known for such rest and relaxation, with many hotels or summer visitors staying over.

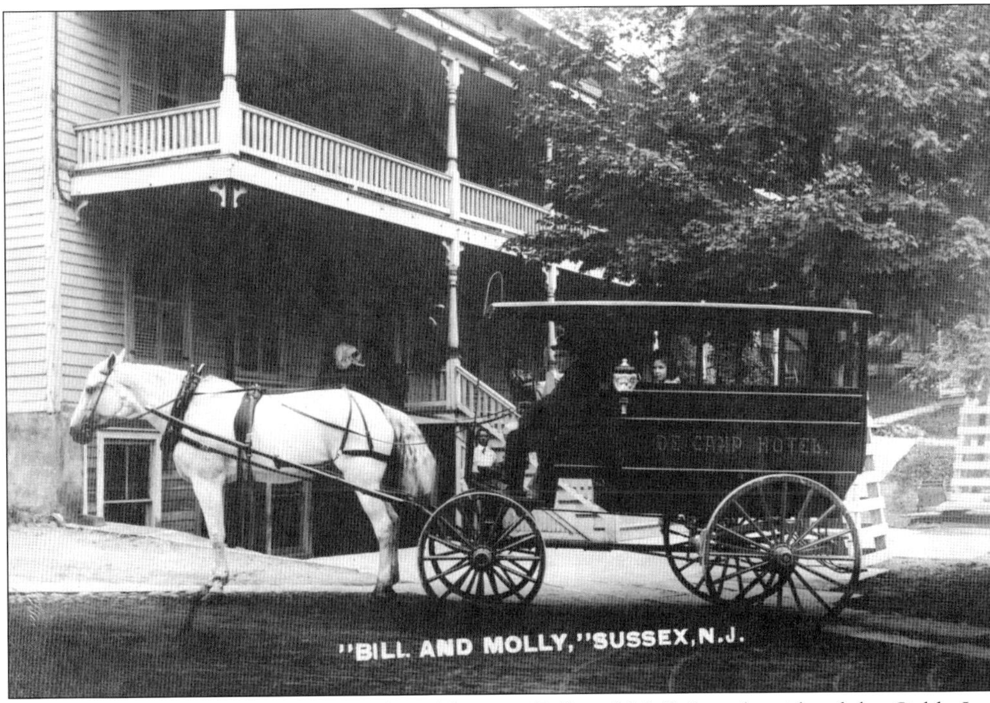

Well, the wagon arrived at the hotel, and here is "Bill and Molly" at the side of the Goble Inn around 1900.

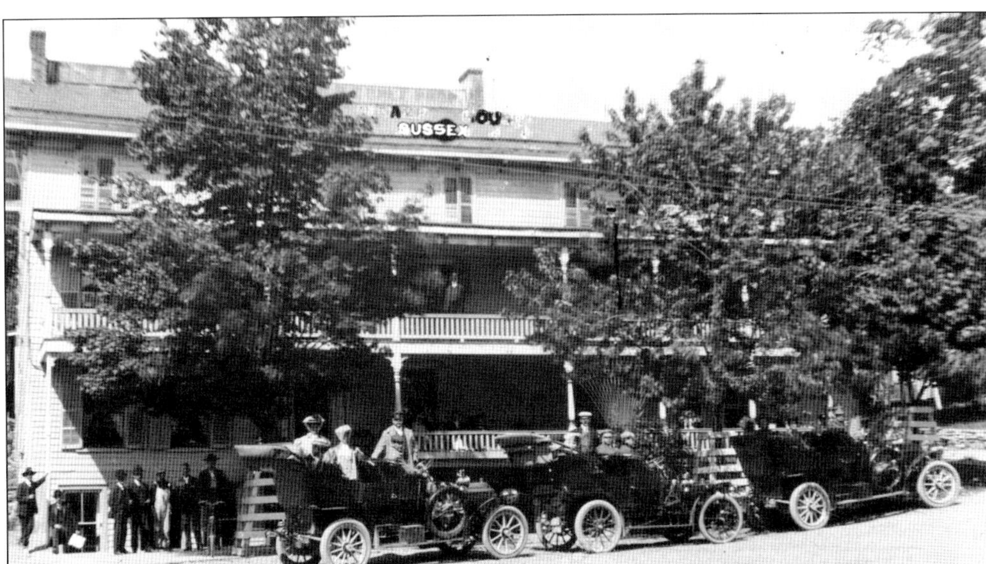

We see transportation changing again in Sussex from the stagecoach to the railroad and now to the automobile. A caravan of cars and their riders pose for a photograph in the early 1900s.

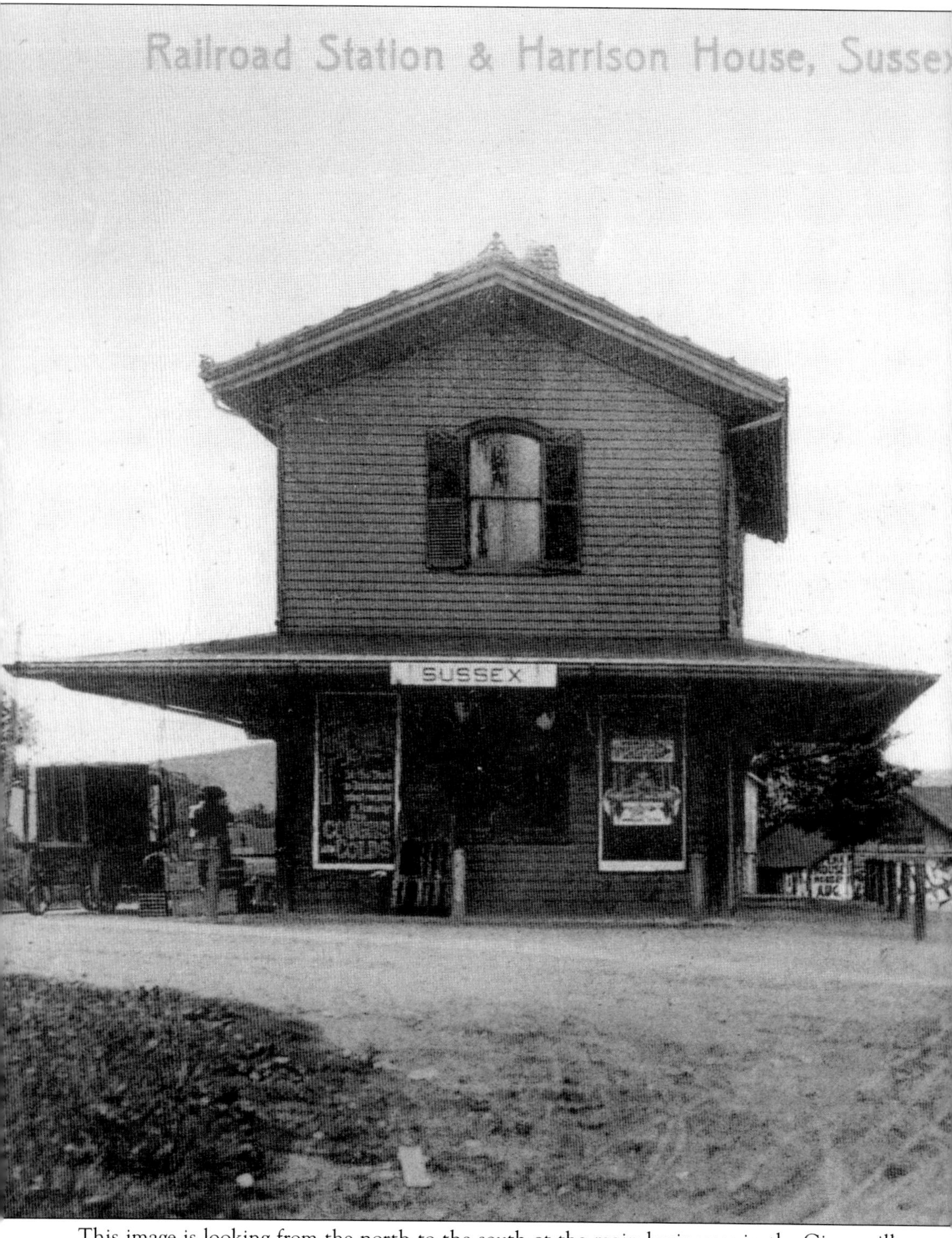

This image is looking from the north to the south at the main businesses in the Gingerville area of Sussex. To the left is the train station for the NYS&W Railway, and in the center is the Harrison House, the location of the celebration of local horse racing. In front of the Harrison

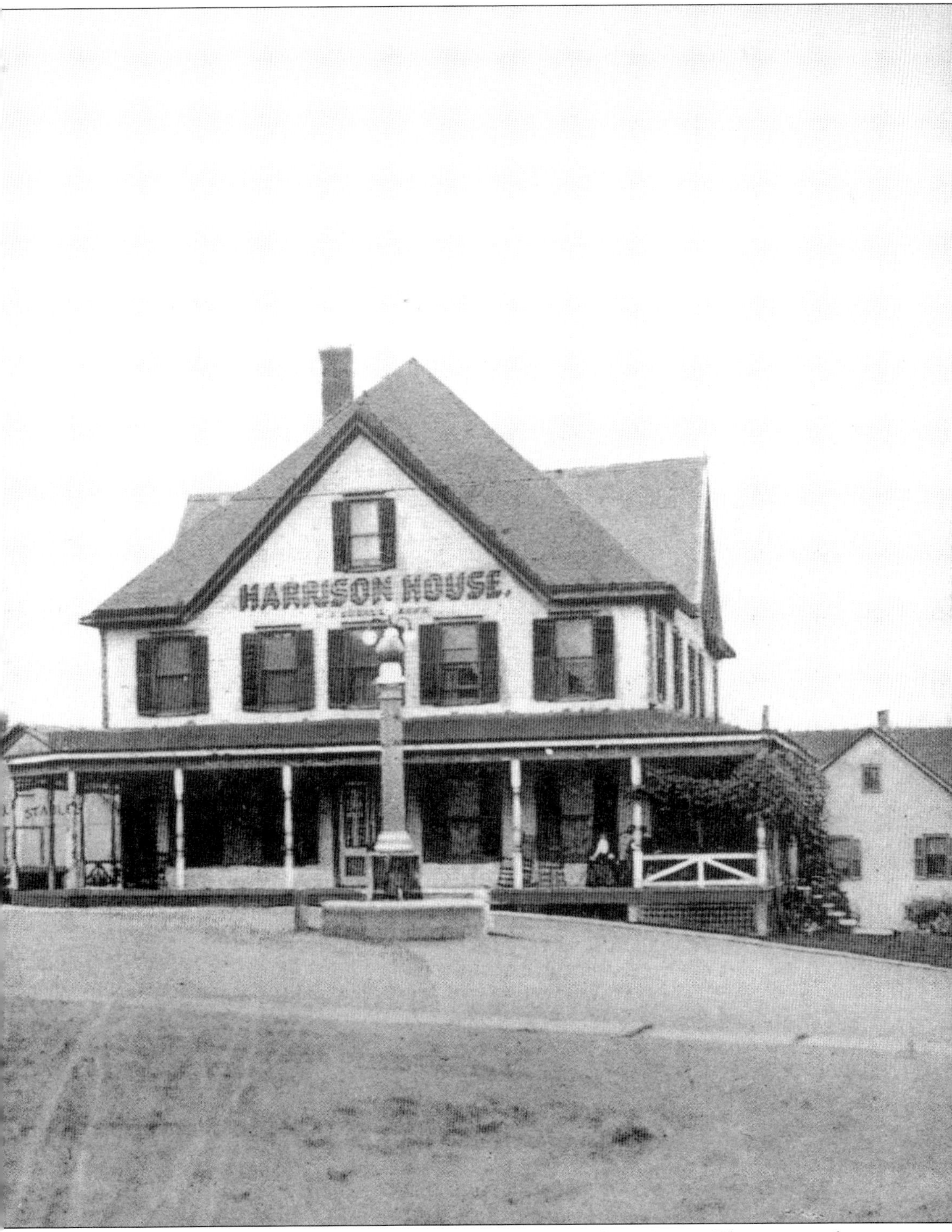

House, one can see the upper of the three fountains that were gifts to Sussex. This one was from Thomas Jefferson Dunn.

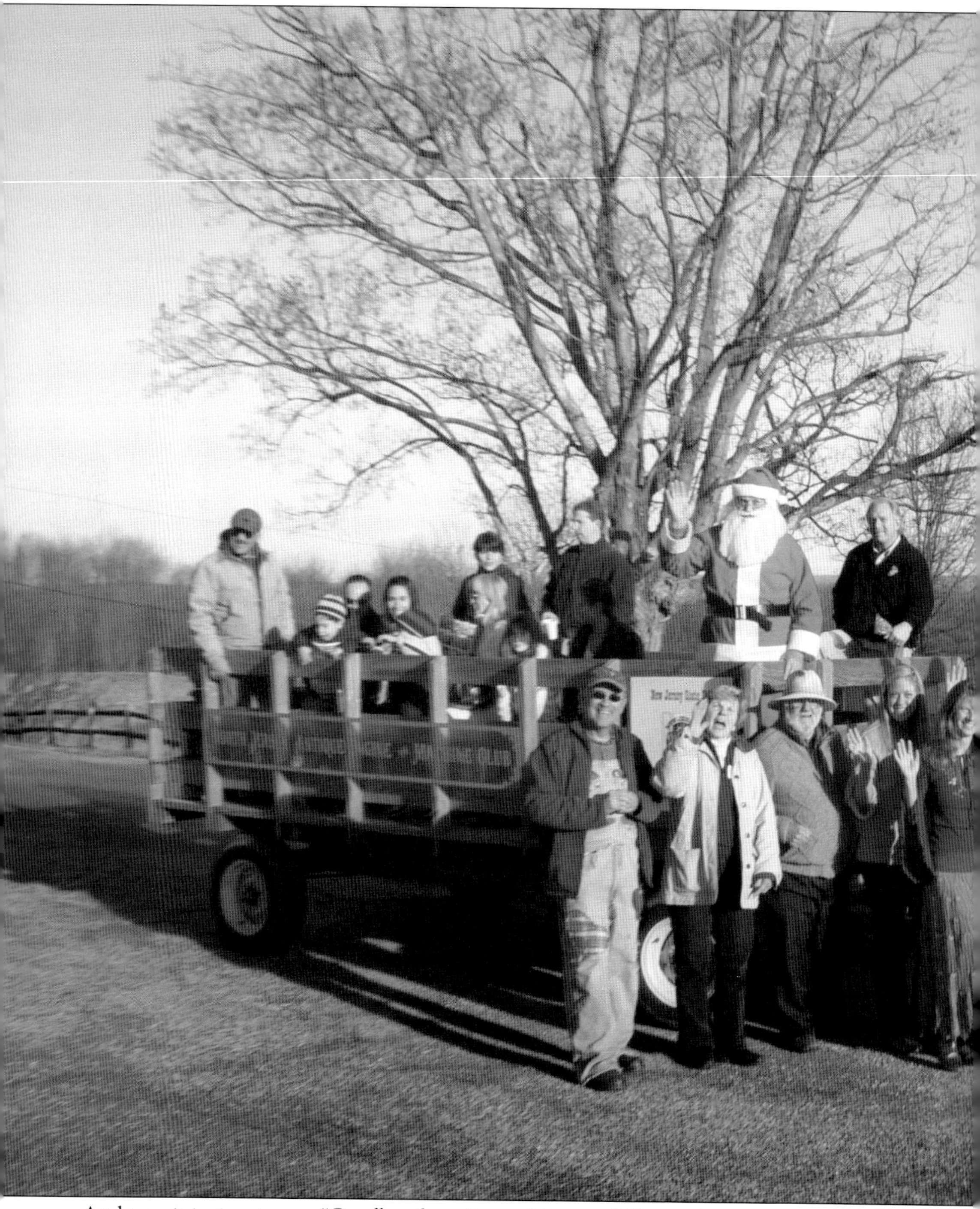

And now it is time to say, "Goodbye from Sussex-Wantage." Shown here is a recent gathering for a holiday event in 2011 at the well-known Lusscroft Farms. This farm was the prototype for research on artificial insemination for cattle with Rutgers University in the 1930s and exists today with volunteers maintaining the plowed fields and crops. With Santa aboard, this was a Christmas hayride, pulled by an antique tractor; the Lusscroft barn is visible in the back.

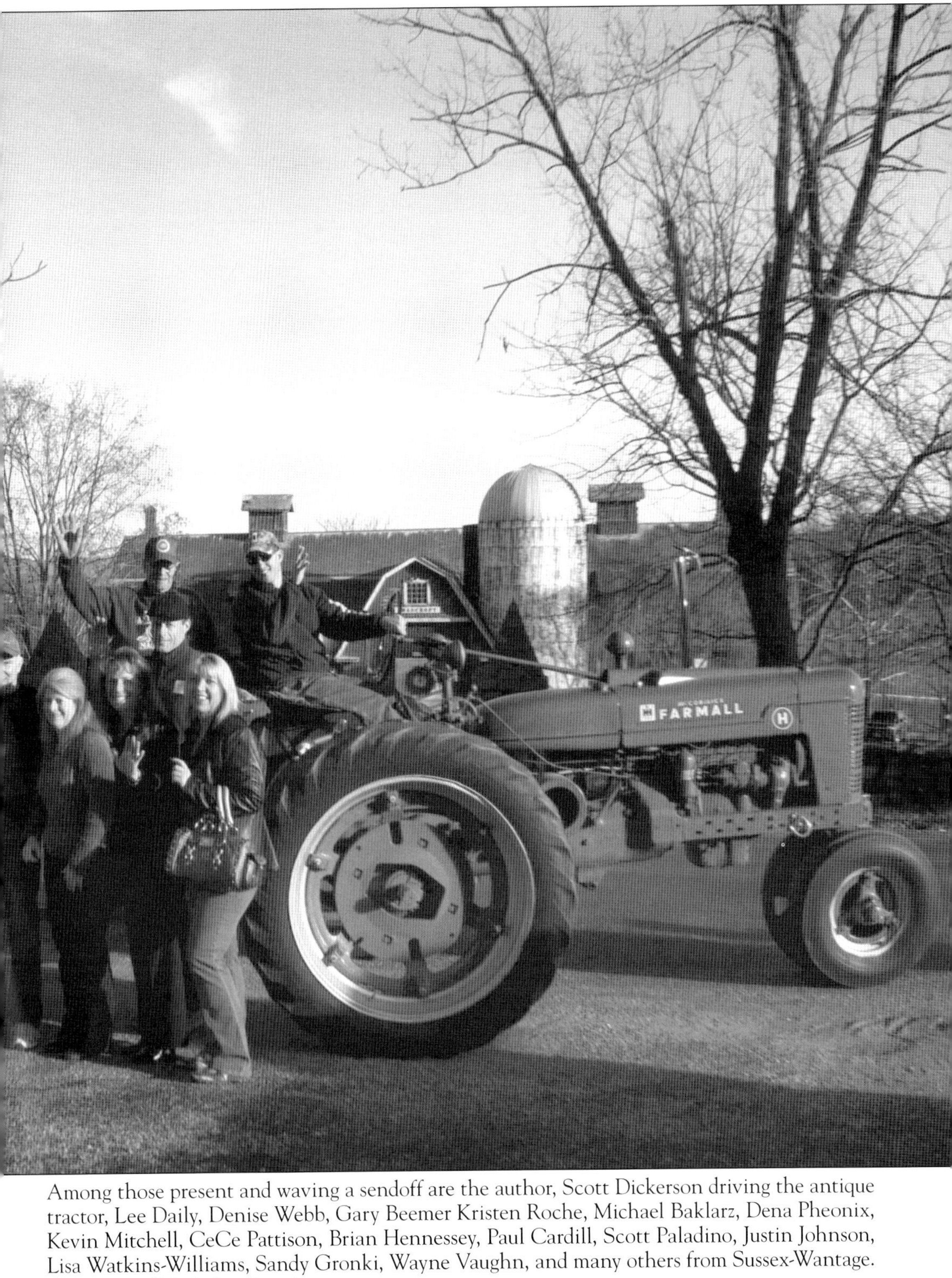

Among those present and waving a sendoff are the author, Scott Dickerson driving the antique tractor, Lee Daily, Denise Webb, Gary Beemer Kristen Roche, Michael Baklarz, Dena Pheonix, Kevin Mitchell, CeCe Pattison, Brian Hennessey, Paul Cardill, Scott Paladino, Justin Johnson, Lisa Watkins-Williams, Sandy Gronki, Wayne Vaughn, and many others from Sussex-Wantage. (Courtesy of Nicholas Ortiz.)